Praise for *The Tender Path of Grief and Loss*

"*The Tender Path of Grief and Loss* tackles the pain of loss and the deep grief that accompanies it with powerful descriptions that will resonate with anyone who is struggling to heal after experiencing loss. The guiding light and the strength of this book lie in the disparate stories of grief that Jackman includes as examples of healing and transcendence.

The 'tender path' to healing embraces three phases: the shockwave, the stretch, and the solace. Each holds insights key to understanding the process and moving along each phase. Jackman's focus on maintaining fluidity and strength . . . outlines the invitations and signposts that point the way to growth and healing. The result is a primer that should be on the reading list of those who have lost and are grieving and any human being who wants to better understand how to find hope in hopeless situations.

Choosing the 'tender path' involves an amazing journey of growth and realization. Its message offers wide-ranging opportunities for reflection, discussion, and insights for both the individual and those in groups, making *The Tender Path of Grief and Loss* a top recommendation for libraries."
— D. Donovan, Senior Reviewer, *Midwest Book Review*

"Readers will be comforted and inspired by Robert Jackman's erudite masterpiece on grief. This rare book ingeniously weaves lovely prose, enlightening aphorisms, brave self-reflections, inspirational case stories, and, as usual, instructions and exercises that are easy to comprehend and perform. This one-of-a-kind guide is a sterling example of self-help literary genius, tapping into the human spirit despite the heart being crushed, aching, and wayward in grief. *The Tender Path of Grief and Loss* will open long-closed doors that invisibly shield people from their own catastrophic grief. Any book that helps readers to courageously recollect, process, and eventually integrate any form of stuck grief is one to cherish."

— Ross Rosenberg, M.Ed., LCPC, CADC, psychotherapist and author of *The Human Magnet Syndrome: From Soulmate to Cellmate*, creator of the Self-Love Recovery Treatment program

"No one is eager to learn the lessons that loss and grief teach us. It is a skilled author who offers these lessons with sensitivity, depth, vulnerability, voices of insight, and pragmatic tools and resources for healing. Robert Jackman covers the topic with such breadth, approachability, and integrity that his book appeals equally as a healing balm to the reader experiencing loss, as a guide to family members and friends, and as an invaluable asset to healthcare workers, clergy, and therapists.

This book provides a memorable structure to the grieving process. Jackman gives wise counsel, teaching professionals how to provide agency, acknowledgment, and grace; that is, how to be a witness, listen with attention, and be a nonjudgmental presence. I was struck by his ability to address grief in contemporary issues, from COVID to reproductive justice, from job loss to gender identity. His use of metaphors enhances the book's healing power.

Each of the nine personal stories illustrates a different facet of loss and grief. Jackman gently invites all of us who will walk the tender path to 'take the time to find a place inside to honor the loss, to create a safe container to hold this sacredness as we continue on with our lives.' I encourage you to read this book and return to it as a rich resource."

— Rev. Linda S. Slabon, M.Div., M.A., MSW, LCSW,
Minister Emerita, Unitarian Universalist Fellowship,
DeKalb, Illinois; Affiliated Community Minister,
Unitarian Church, Rockford, Illinois

"Author and psychotherapist Robert Jackman opens this compelling book with a vivid visualization of an elderly weaver spinning the individual yarns and fabrics of life experiences into a beautiful tapestry of life. This backdrop, underlying the heartfelt stories of those who have experienced a wide variety of losses, creates the foundation for a sacred journey into the three phases of grief. Jackman travels along with the reader as we go deep into these personal stories and discover the power and tenderness of grieving.

I'm excited to share this book with my clients as a powerful tool and reflection of the emotional stages of grief and loss. Jackman's skilled, tender, and wise approach enabled me to explore my own grief cycles and heal myself further."

— DK Foster, Birth and Death Doula, Yachats, Oregon

"With insight, empathy, and compassion, Jackman creatively blends stories of several types of grief and loss experiences with exercises and tools to help the reader navigate through this challenging journey. In *The Tender Path of Grief and Loss*, he describes weaving together the tapestry of life and honoring our losses—each thread representing an important and significant component to our healing journey."

— Sherry O'Brian, LCSW, DCEP, author of *Peaks and Valleys:*
Integrative Approaches for Recovering from Loss

"Another great book by psychotherapist and author Robert Jackman. In *The Tender Path of Grief and Loss*, Jackman presents a difficult subject in a sensitive yet compelling way, incorporating information backed by research with his own clinical discoveries and life stories of his contributors. It is evident he has a deep knowledge of the subject. He not only imparts his expertise, he allows himself to be vulnerable by sharing some of his own journeys of grief. He shows us how to recognize unresolved losses and walks us through helpful tools and effective techniques to hold the grief and weave it into the tapestry of who we are.

The stories are a testament to the compassion and connection Jackman has as a skilled therapist to his clients. This relationship has allowed them to share their most painful and personal journeys. The reader will be left feeling compassion, inspiration, and hope that they can create a fulfilling and meaningful life and find joy again after loss. I will absolutely recommend this extraordinary book."

— Jacqueline Marshall, LCSW

The
Tender Path *of*
Grief &
Loss

The
Tender Path *of*
Grief &
Loss

Compassionate Stories and
Practical Wisdom to Help You Heal

ROBERT JACKMAN
MS, LCPC, NCC

 PRACTICAL WISDOM PRESS

 Published by
PRACTICAL WISDOM PRESS
www.theartofpracticalwisdom.com

paperback: 978-1-7354445-6-7
ebook: 978-1-7354445-7-4

Printed in the United States of America

The author may be reached through his website at
www.theartofpracticalwisdom.com.

Edited by Jessica Vineyard, Red Letter Editing, LLC, www.redletterediting.com
Book Design by Christy Day, Constellation Book Services

Published by Practical Wisdom Press

For my sister, Cindy Van Liere, my late brother, James Thomas Jackman, and those who hold space and sit with the grieving: hospital and nursing staff, hospice workers, death doulas, ministers, and caregivers.

Author's Note

The image on the book cover is of a bowl repaired by the centuries-old Japanese art known as *kintsugi*, also called a golden repair. The artist applies a lacquer called *urushi* to the cracks in the broken pottery, then dusts the lacquer with powdered gold. This technique follows the Japanese aesthetic of *wabi-sabi*, a worldview centered on the acceptance of transience and imperfection, and of appreciating beauty that is imperfect, impermanent, and incomplete in nature.

I chose this image as a metaphor for how we can feel broken and shattered as the result of a loss, but become whole again through honoring our grief on the tender path. Just as the gold makes the repaired vessel more beautiful than before, we can become stronger, wiser, and grander as we repair our hearts. The greatest outcome of the internal process of carefully mending a heart treasure is finding the unfolding gifts in loss, encouraging beauty to blossom from the most unexpected places, instead of discarding and ignoring something of great value.

Taste Your Sorrow
by Robert Jackman

Loss and sorrow spiral us, unwilling, into deep caverns of the soul, uncharted land where even shadows are lost in the dark. Here beyond the veil, naive innocence is without license, crumpled in a discarded heap, no longer fresh-faced. Rawness of an unvarnished truth is brazenly displayed, sitting bold-faced, taunting and tempting us with the invitation to examine this siren song of new pain. We fear that this loss, this missing, will be our undoing.

But fearful sorrow is not the bogeyman. We are, in actuality, in fear of ourselves, seeing ourselves so small and trivial next to this titanic grief. This unwelcome friend is more a part of us than we know, our beginning and ending. Take a pinch of this raw sorrow, so new and unknown. Taste its bitter edges and realize it isn't lethal, but ignoring it just may be. Pain becomes the teacher, the guide, when we realize that ingesting and embracing it is the way through and out. Our ability to feel the contrast of life now depends on it.

Taste your sorrow. Hold your pain and witness its fragile origami unfolding into what will become your tempered strength. Let it flow through your veins until you feel all parts so that you can say, I have eaten that which I feared would kill me, and now I know the taste of freedom from illusion.

Contents

Acknowledgments

Thank you to my partner, Drew Caldwell, for being my number one fan for over thirty-five years. Your encouragement and inspirational support buoyed my heart throughout the process of writing this book. Thank you for your consistent love as you created a soft place for me to land while I explored, examined, and wrote about the grief and loss journey. Your soulful perspectives on life helped inspire me in so many ways with this sacred topic. You are a blessing in my life beyond words. I love you.

Thank you to my sister, Cindy Van Liere, for your uplifting and enthusiastic support and for your wise insights, especially those related to shared stories from our family experiences. You are such a bright light in my life and an inspiration for many. Every day, in so many ways, you make me so proud to be your big brother, and you make my heart sing. You are loved.

Thank you to my late brother, James Thomas Jackman. You left us too soon. I wish we could have experienced a lifetime with you brother. You live on in our hearts.

Thank you to my late parents, Rose Mary and Bob Jackman, for always believing in me and for telling me you loved me and that you were proud of me. Thank you for showing me that love and kindness triumph over pain and fear. Even though there were some hard times growing up, the good, loving times always outweighed the bad. I always felt and knew your love, and this is the greatest treasure I carry in my heart. Your loving energy and kindness lives on within us. Thank you for your encouragement and your love.

A tremendous thanks to all of my story contributors. Through your courage and vulnerability in sharing of some of the more challenging times in your life, you are helping thousands of people around the world to heal. We all heal our heart pain more deeply when we hear another's story and we don't feel so alone, as one person's journey is a reflection of those we all walk. This book is a much richer and deeper work because of your heartfelt stories. You each encourage hope in those you will never meet.

A special thanks goes to many wayshowers for their inspirations: Francis Weller and his beautiful, soulful book *The Wild Edge of Sorrow*, and Sherry O'Brian and her book *Peaks and Valleys*. I am grateful for and found tremendous value in the following books as well: *Grief Day by Day* by Jan Warner; *Healing after Loss* by Martha Hickman; *Broken Open* by Elizabeth Lesser; *The Orphaned Adult* by Alexander Levy; *On Death and Dying* by Dr. Elisabeth Kübler-Ross; *You Can Heal Your Heart* by Louise Hay and David Kessler; and *More Beautiful than Before* by Steve Leder.

A heartfelt thank you to Jessica Vineyard with Red Letter Editing for the careful and thoughtful work she openly gave in her expert editing of this book. Thanks to Christy Day and Maggie McLaughlin, both with Constellation Book Services, for the beautiful cover creation and interior design, and to Martha Bullen with Bullen Publishing Services for her advice and deep knowledge of the publishing industry. All of you helped with the birth of this book and helped me in ways too numerous to mention.

A special thanks goes to all people who hold space and give counsel and care to those who feel the great sorrow and anguish of grief and loss. You are bright lights on this planet.

As with all of my previous works, there are many people who helped me along the way, directly and indirectly, providing support, deep wisdom, and insights. I felt your intentional energy as I wrote this book. Thank you.

Introduction

Grief is like the ocean; it comes on waves ebbing and flowing.
Sometimes the water is calm, and sometimes it is overwhelming.
All we can do is learn to swim.
—VICKI HARRISON

You may have picked up this book because you have just experienced a loss and are trying to make sense of it, or perhaps you're having a hard time moving past a loss that happened some time ago. Wherever you are in the process of understanding your loss, know that where you are now is okay and that you are still the same person you were before. You've just been through one of life's big lessons, so you feel different now. Your relationship to loss is a deeply personal and brave journey that you alone are curating, and as each day passes, you will uncover and learn something new. We can read books and learn how others have gone through their experience of loss, but until we experience loss ourselves, we really don't know what it's going to feel like or how the experience will unfold.

While we can't always be prepared for a loss, we can learn to be kind to ourselves during the process. Grief and loss experiences challenge and mock our status quo, cracking us open and leaving us in a scattered heap of pieces, with the herculean task of finding ourselves again. We think we are broken forever, but the broken part eventually becomes an opening, an invitation for us to discover a new, unseen part of ourselves, a new wisdom that is patiently waiting for us. Grief and loss experiences are the teacher and we are the student. Grief, loss, and sadness are normal; life would not be the same without them.

I am a psychotherapist and have been in private practice for more than two decades. Throughout this book, I curate my experiences of counseling those who have suffered grief and loss as well as my own process. The information I present here may give the impression that I understand the depth and transcendence of loss and have it all figured out; I don't. What I have are my life experiences of loss and my work in helping others to walk the tender path of healing loss in its many forms, both in my clinical practice and earlier in my life as a hospice volunteer. People come to me in their darkest hour wanting to understand their feelings around loss, and from these experiences I have developed some novel perspectives of how to look at loss, approaches to help acknowledge and develop a relationship to loss, and how to integrate and honor these profound experiences over the arc of a lifetime. Here I offer the best of these practical techniques to help the reader better understand and move through loss to enter into a state of wholeness.

Writing this book took me longer than I had anticipated, as I had to go into a deep interior world with the material, which itself mirrored a grief and loss process. The writing took me down quiet, reflective, lonely roads of silence and tears; I had to explore my relationship to my own losses in order to write these words for others. I realize now, after this deeper examination of my grief and loss journey, that I could have been kinder to myself in the past and reached out for help during those hard times instead of trying to do so much on my own. It is in this reflection on the past that wisdom comes through in our healing, informing the future self. Grief work is ongoing in its unfoldment, and we are always growing and softening in our solace as a result. This expansion provides new perspectives that allow us to move forward more fully healed. We don't really learn or understand the gifts of grief and loss until we go through this crucible of sorrow.

If there is ever a time when we need to be gentle with ourselves and others, it is certainly during or following a loss. Throughout the book, I describe practical yet gentle ways of how to approach, move through, and transcend a loss. I didn't set out to write the definitive book on grief and loss—that is beyond the scope of my work—but the information and stories herein will invite you to gently heal your losses so you can move on and live wholly. My goal is to help you begin to consciously recognize and name the losses that have occurred in your life so that you can honor and incorporate them into your life's journey. I want to help you understand the many ways you can learn to hold on to hope for the unknown outcome of the loss journey and transform the energy of grieving, mourning, and loss into a learning and personal growth experience. I also want to normalize the feelings of confusion, anger, and doubt that we have around everyday small losses as well as significant losses such as death.

I believe it is important to also acknowledge our subconscious fear around global losses such as the COVID pandemic, inflation, mass shootings, social unrest, and other existential crises of humanity. The depth and complexities of the effects of some losses, especially those that are traumatic, are limitless in how they can manifest and impact our lives. Each day we are inundated with stories of vicarious trauma losses that are instantly updated to the phones in our pockets, giving us immediate ringside seats to these events. We need tools to deal with the heaviness that comes with the messages that slowly seep into us. Even when we have no direct connection to these events, we are emotional beings and so are impacted at some level. Some of these global losses carry an extra heaviness that is not visible and not consciously known yet is deeply felt subconsciously. Social pressures tell us to move on—nothing to look at here—but the loss and trauma linger in our hearts.

> *Ungrieved grief is what makes us sick*
> *and keeps us from feeling whole.*

Loss isn't something that we just need to get through; it deepens our perspective of ourselves within the context of life. The relationship we develop to the emotions we have around loss greatly influences whether we integrate or dismiss these natural and inevitable experiences. Loss gives us the opportunity to reflect and regroup, to remember that life is poignantly beautiful. Each loss invites us to grow, stretch, and transcend that which we knew before and the space we enter into afterward. As we grow, losses teach us how to hold and embrace the idea of impermanence.

One thing I know for sure is that most people experience many losses throughout their lives that they don't recognize as losses. Chapter one, "Understanding Grief and Loss," introduces the concept of how and why we accumulate losses of all kinds. Unacknowledged losses pile up throughout our lifetimes, filling what I call the loss bucket. Once we have acknowledged a loss, we give ourselves permission to begin the healing process.

Chapter two, "Loss Comes in All Shapes and Sizes," discusses the many kinds of losses we are likely to experience at some point in our lives. Most of us can clearly describe significant losses such as a death, but few people specifically name small losses. Seeing small losses as true losses helps us heal and free up space inside to live more completely. Following chapter two is Brandi's story of loss through the death of her first husband and her second husband's chronic disease.

We move through grief and loss at our own pace and in our own way, whether gentle, quiet, soft behaviors or crying and lashing out in anger. We may become enamored with feeling lost, lonely, and sad until some kind soul reaches out to help us and we receive their compassion. However we move through it, over time we weave the energy of the loss into the tapestries of our lives. Most of us don't like to think about a loss because it's painful to remember, so we push it away, rush through it, or neglect it altogether and hope it goes away. As we heal, we come to understand that loss exists naturally in the ebb and flow of life, with creation and rebirth. Chapter three, "Bravely Facing a Loss," discusses how to acknowledge and face a loss and what to expect along the way through grief. Following chapter three is Diana's story of loss through a catastrophic fire.

The intimate journey of loss generally follows an arc that manifests differently for everyone. As a way to conceptualize how we blend and fold losses into our lives, I have identified three phases that describe how most people experience loss, what I call the tender path: the shockwave, the stretch, and the solace. Each phase has unique characteristics, lessons, and meanings for everyone. There are no timeframes associated with these phases, as they are only signposts to help group our feelings of reality as we move through the grief.

In the first phase of the tender path, we respond to the loss based on the emotional landscape within us at the time of the loss. This emotional state greatly influences our healing progression, sense of hope, and acceptance or denial of the loss. Chapter four, "The Shockwave," discusses the many ways the initial shock or emotional impact is experienced. You will learn the difference between grief and depression and the reasons why some people can't move on. You will also learn how to determine whether you are choosing restorative or indulgent responses to the pain of your loss. Following chapter four is Bonnie's story of loss through the suicide of her teenage daughter.

Chapter five, "The Stretch," discusses the long period that follows the initial shockwave. There is no right or wrong way to process a loss, only the way that works for you in each moment. We cannot force the pain of loss to heal, but many people avoid touching on this pain altogether and can get stuck in their grief. Dealing with loss with the best of yourself is a life skill. Everyone experiences loss, and how we handle it and find grace makes all the difference. The stretch gives us many invitations to heal, and here I give you signposts along the journey to help you find your way. Following chapter five is Nicole's story of loss through the difficult choice of terminating a pregnancy.

Solace is the emotional season we enter to more completely integrate the loss into our lives and begin to hold space for who we are now. Chapter six, "Moving toward Solace," discusses how to incorporate the loss into your new normal and live with it as a part of who you are now. You will learn about the emotional landmines we encounter after a loss and the acts of ceremony that help us to process and honor the loss. Following chapter six is David's story of living with a chronic disease.

Many of us carry unhealed inner childhood wounding into adulthood. This wounding can acutely impact how we respond to loss, causing us to act out, get angry, or hide from reality, all of which interferes with healing. Chapter seven, "Loss and the Inner Child," discusses the strong relationship between our unhealed inner child wounding and how we react to loss as adults. Following chapter seven is my story of the loss of my innocence as a result of taking on adult responsibilities long before I should have.

After a loss, we have all asked, why me? We take the loss personally, and some even consider it a punishment, a validation that they are unworthy of happiness. Of course, losses happen without regard to whether or not we have pleased the fates or been a good person. Chapter eight, "Deepening the Work," explores various circumstances that can arise after a loss, such as how to interact with well-meaning people, ove-ridentifying with a loss, and why you may wonder, why me? Following chapter eight is Kathy's story of her journey with and through her daughter's transition from male to female and how this brought forth a tremendous love for her child.

We celebrate milestones such as births and beginnings, but losses are often pushed aside, silently ignored but deeply felt. Dealing with the milestones of loss are uncomfortable for some, and many ways of acknowledging them are being lost to the march of time. Chapter nine, "Practical Tools for Honoring Loss," offers many ways to honor loss through various practices and exercises, such as symbolic letter writing and loving detachment. All of these suggestions will help you to clear space inside so you can open up to a larger healing landscape. Following chapter nine is Gary's story of his experience after a major job loss.

I believe we are given only what we can handle and that there is always a new perspective waiting for us. When we lose perspective, we feel as though a bleak future and an unending stream of uncertainty stretch in front of us. In reality, new life and rebirth is all around us, every day. Chapter ten, "Helping Others through Loss," addresses one of the most personal ways to live with joy and grace, and that is to extend your heart and hand to others experiencing loss, perhaps even the same loss you are experiencing. When we extend compassion to others, this same compassion returns to us magnified a thousandfold. Following chapter ten is Willow's story of compassion and support through her work with cancer patients.

Chapter eleven, "Growing Hopeful," offers a summary of the information and a review of the tender path of grief and loss. This chapter discusses how you can look back over your grief work equipped with new tools of naming and creating an honoring space for loss, and how to recognize the unseen gifts that are available from your loss journey.

There is no beginning or end to grief, especially for significant losses such as death. As writer and grief psychotherapist Sherry O'Brian states, grieving is an emotion and a process. In a way, we are always working through a loss, turning it over in our hearts, like rocks on a beach. We try to make sense of something that our minds don't understand. As we heal, we learn to simply be with it, to hold it, walk alongside it, befriend it.

Please note that throughout the book I reference people dying, passing away, at peace, at rest, and so on. All of these words are ways we name the loss of someone, and these words have relevance to us. I also reference spiritual or faith-based approaches to dealing with loss, but the tender path is not exclusive to any form of religion or spiritual practice. If I refer to prayer or meditation or intention, think of what that means to you and how you would use this technique. Use my examples as starting points to find tools that work for you to transform the pain of loss into an enlightened recognition. I respect where you are.

Following each chapter, you will read the stories of people who have had extraordinary experiences related to loss. Some of the stories are brutal and raw, but the truths within each are eternal. You will learn how each person went through emotionally intense life situations and the perspectives they now embody after these seminal events. You will read about their pain, struggles, perseverance, and how they found hope in what many would consider hopeless situations. You will discover how they found self-compassion, courage, and re-silience to get through their loss experience. What is similar across all of the stories is that they did not want their lives to be defined by the worst thing that had ever happened to them, so they found ways to reach through this pain and triumph.

The stories are not meant to be one for one with the discussion material in each chapter; rather, they are windows into how others went through and transformed the energy of a specific loss. The intention is that their stories will encourage you to sit and hold your grief and loss instead of pushing it away as an uncomfortable annoyance. You may relate to some of the stories, and some may not have any relevance to your life. I encourage you to read each story, though, as I think you will find some gems of insight within each.

It is through the witnessing of someone else's struggle and triumph that we can learn how to find this courage within ourselves. I am forever grateful to each of the contributors and am truly honored that they entrusted their stories with me to share with you. As a way to honor each contributor's time, courage, and openness to sharing their story, I asked for a charity they would like me to give to in their name. Their chosen charities, along with additional resources, can be found at the end of each story.

This book is not just about stories of loss because that would be really depressing and I wouldn't want to read, much less write, a book like that. The information herein is about how you can shift your perspective away from the pain of loss to find the lesson and the gift in the loss and transcend the experience—in other words, how to not get lost in the sadness and anger. This information will stretch you to discover previously unknown parts of yourself. Prepare within yourself a place to hold these words. Let them sit within you. Keep them safely tucked away for when you need them sometime in the future. Know that you are a beautiful embodiment of your traumas and triumphs.

You are stronger than you think. Trust and know that you will get through this time, that you will get your life back on track. It may not look like it did before, but you're going to go on and create a new reality for yourself with your hard-won wisdom. Be gentle with yourself as you walk this tender path. Your grief is your love in action.

The grief process is not about getting over the loss,
it's about gently incorporating the loss
into life's unique tapestry.

The Tapestry of Life

Ring the bells that still can ring. Forget your perfect offering.
There is a crack—a crack in everything. That's how the light gets in.
—LEONARD COHEN, "ANTHEM"

In my mind's eye, I saw myself walking down a dusty road past small shops selling everything from shining copper pots and exotic, aromatic spices to vibrant fruits and vegetables. Among the clamor and bustle, one shop caught my eye. Tucked away in a corner, almost hidden so that I would have missed it if I had blinked, was the weaver's shop. My feet were volunteering me into the shop before I even consciously decided to go in.

The shop was much larger and deeper than it had appeared from the outside. When I entered, the room kept expanding into what seemed to be infinite space. There were shelves stacked high with woven cloth in neat rows, each more vibrant, more complex than the next, each pattern wildly different. When I looked at the cloth more closely, I saw that the threads were vibrating and coordinating with unique color-energy palettes. One after another other, stacked high to the ceiling, the piles of cloth were inviting me to touch and admire them, as though needing to be felt. Each wanted to be seen, each seemed to have a life force pulsating from within the fibers.

The weaver sat in a back corner, quietly doing her work. As her hands intuitively worked her loom, she raised her head to acknowledge me. She gave a sweet smile, her eyes twinkling like a friend and saying *I love you* without words, then she purposefully went back to her work.

I stood transfixed, watching her hands flow like water through the threads as she guided the shuttle back and forth. When she looked up at me with a knowing glance, I instantly felt that she knew everything about me. But how could she? I had just walked in, yet I felt deeply connected to her, my heart center opening and warming up to her.

As I intently focused on the weaver, everything else in the shop receded from view. As she wove, each strand of thread lined up into a perfect pattern. She hummed as she worked with clear, quiet confidence. The sound was deeply comforting and loving. I saw patterns developing from the colors of thread she chose, as if each thread had a specific purpose and meaning. Some matched those that came before, but others were wildly different colors. I wondered how all of the colors worked so well together even when they didn't look as if they would. I knew nothing about weaving, and as I watched, I felt as if I were being taught how to weave.

Gracefully, the weaver stood up and went to the other side of her loom, where a long stretch of woven cloth hung. Her talented hands gently picked up the cloth and held it out for me to examine. Silently, she pointed to specific portions of the tapestry that stood out from the others. Some sections had fine gold thread running the width of the cloth. Others were purple, red, or dark blue. Each was unique and varied from the others, but all coordinated perfectly.

The weaver stretched out her arms under the cloth to show the range of colors and patterns in the large sections she had completed. As she did so, the colors started vibrating. I had to rub my eyes, as it looked like they were dancing and coming to life. She pointed to specific sections, trying to communicate to me some meaning that a particular section held.

She held a section of rose-colored thread with one hand and placed the open palm of her other hand over my heart chakra. I became electrified by her touch, awakened in a way I hadn't been before. She then guided my hands to hold the cloth, and instantly I realized that this cloth she was weaving represented all the different parts of my life. Each woven strand of thread was a living record of every thought, feeling, and deed, good or bad, that I had experienced in my life up to that point. She was weaving the tapestry of my life.

She guided my hand to a purple section, and I immediately saw and felt the grief over my mother's death. In a green section, I saw the pride and happiness I felt when I graduated from my master's program. Other colors represented other experiences, like when I was unkind to my spouse or was in a place of fear or worry. Many sections were joyful and happy, but others that I touched were not happy memories at all, and it was hard to go there and feel the pain again. The cloth held all of my emotional and energetic memories from my entire life, all of the random gestures large and small, all of the triumphs and tragedies.

I didn't like looking at or feeling the sections of cloth that were "bad" or represented times of struggle in my life. I looked at the weaver, worried that she would judge me for those behavioral choices I made when I was not at my best. But with certainty and calmness, her buttery-soft hands simply smoothed out the cloth so I could see the totality, not just the parts I didn't like. She told me with her piercing deep eyes that she did not judge me or my choices, that I was the one holding judgment. She took the same care to weave, with honor and respect, times of joy as she did with times I didn't want to remember. She was teaching me how to hold these painful memories with the same unconditional love.

I still didn't like what I now realized were the times of loss and suffering that were recorded in my tapestry. A part of me wanted to bargain with her to change those times of struggle, sadness, and pain to different colors, or erase them altogether. I didn't want to remember those times, much less have them recorded in a tapestry. I wanted to see only the events that were good and held pride. Patiently, she pointed out the various sections that represented all the times of my life. As we looked over the larger expanse of the cloth, I began to see all of the colors together. I saw how the tapestry was a beautiful piece when seen as one, even with those sections that I didn't like and wanted her to take out.

The bands of threads and the patterns were magnificent. One section that represented a sad or tragic time was followed by a section representing times of great joy and expansion. Each section supported the parts that came before and after. Each thread needed the others in order to be held in the cloth. Together, all of the threads represented the totality of my life, and all of the parts held value. The tapestry would not be as strong or durable if those sections I didn't like were taken out. It would not have held up if it were just made of the "all-good" parts. What I thought of as losses in my life actually made me—and my tapestry—stronger, wiser, and more vibrant.

The weaver held my hands, then she hugged me. She knew everything about me: my triumphs and losses, my loves and fears. As she held me, I felt her unconditional love for me.

Even with knowing all about me, she accepted and loved all of me. She was teaching me to do the same.

Once you become awake to yourself,
it's harder to fall asleep in the living world.

PART I

The Many Faces of Loss

CHAPTER ONE

Understanding Grief and Loss

In grief, the first person you wish you could talk to is no longer alive.
The second person is another who understands grief
and wants to meet you right where you are.
—DAVID KESSLER

It was 2010, and my mom had just had a devastating stroke. Wanting to feel in control, I went to my familiar coping skills of doing and staying busy: how is she today, is she making progress, what does she need, what can I get her, what are her symptoms, how is she functioning. I was trying to stay in the moment, but by doing these tasks and worrying, I was also avoiding the big, scary feelings inside of me, knowing that my mom was not improving and that her health was sliding. I didn't want to face this uncomfortable truth, I wanted to stay in doing mode so my scared inner child could feel safe during this unpredictable time.

My mom fought hard to regain her strength and abilities, and seeing her that way was hard for me. I had been living in the Chicagoland area for more than thirty years, so the six-hour driving separation from my parents' day-to-day reality and mine was well established. My hurting self could pretend things were okay, that my mom didn't really have that stroke, that my parents were doing the things they always did, going out with friends or being out on their boat. The little boy inside of me desperately wanted this reality to come back, for everything to be like it was before. I didn't like the unknown waters that lay ahead. I didn't like having to make adult decisions with my dad and sister for my mom's care. I wanted my parents to still be my parents and me to be their adult son. I wanted them to be strong and independent, not with my mom in and out of nursing facilities. I didn't want to see my dad tenuously hold on to a reality that was no longer feasible; he was physically exhausted but was stubborn and did not let us help.

My mom's death two years after the stroke was the greatest shock of my life. I moved from innocence and naivete to reluctantly holding a hard reality. I can see now that at some point in my mom's final days, I had checked out mentally and emotionally. I wasn't myself. I could do basic things but couldn't make big decisions, as my mind was preoccupied with new emotions and thoughts that made a traumatic, swirling tornado inside of me. My usual positive outlook on life was dimmed, and everything was shrouded in a heavy cloak of somber gray.

I look back on how I responded to my mom's death in 2010 and realize how lost I was. Intellectually, I knew what I should do, but all that knowledge escaped me. After all, my mom had never died before, and these were new feelings. The inner child part of me was hurting and in deep pain. The adult part of me was numb; I was doing responsible things, but I was definitely walking wounded.

Navigating loss, especially a big loss, is like being in a great body of water. Sometimes the loss is turbulent and tossing, and at other times it is slow-moving or calm. But even when the water appears calm there is movement under the surface; this is what our relationship to loss is like. We are always moving with and within loss, consciously and subconsciously. We are immersed in the process, and it is never still. Each internal movement brings us closer to a greater awareness of the lessons of grief that are held in the depths of our consciousness—if we take the time to be quiet and still inside and listen for the wisdom.

All of us experience loss at some point in our lives, but we interpret loss in our own unique way. Some losses are as small as having had a bad day when nothing goes right, while other losses may cause our entire world to fall apart. Sometimes we recognize and honor our losses, but too often we don't identify or name events as a loss. Most people carry around a random collection of unhealed emotions related to their losses, and those emotions begin to pile up. At some point, all of us will carry an accumulated backlog of emotions—slights and resentments, betrayals and traumas—related to losses large and small.

We all deal with loss in our own way.
We ignore it, push it away, jump into the emotions of it,
or become highly task-oriented to "fix" the loss.

Whether we lose or break a treasured object, someone betrays us, or a loved one dies, we have experienced a loss. Such losses result in a change between what we knew before and what happens in the moment of the loss. I was driving in rush-hour traffic one day, and the driver of the car next to me didn't see that a car in front of him had stopped. I watched in slow motion as the car next to me hit the bumper of the car in front. In that instant, I was witness to a loss. Immediately, the schedules and attitudes of both drivers were altered. It wasn't a devastating loss, but this fender bender meant that what each driver knew about their day before the accident had suddenly changed. This small loss shifted each person's timeline away from how they thought their day was going to unfold. I wonder if either of them took the time to honor their feelings around the accident and name it as a loss.

We have all had experiences of life before and after a loss, when we knew our lives one way and then it was changed in an instant. We often feel naive or ignorant after a loss: *How could I not have seen that coming? I was foolish to believe that my experience of the "before" time would go on forever. I thought that would always be in my life.* But we are not naive or ignorant, we are just going through and experiencing life, which means we know what we know in the moment. We also know that loss is normal, so some part of us isn't surprised.

The dream metaphor of the tapestry weaver illustrates that as much as it pains us to have losses, loss teaches us how to have perspective and to see the contrast between hardship and times that are good and stable. Ultimately, our experience of life comes down to our perspectives. Some people are in a self-limiting trance and see only what is missing, enabling their losses to define their lives. Others see abundance and the good all around them. Throughout our lives, depending on where we are emotionally, we move from one perspective to another, changing the lens we look through to see our triumphs and traumas at a particular moment in time.

The view of our life is shaped by our family of origin, life experiences, and the way we learned to navigate these tragedies and triumphs. Over time, we learn to understand beginnings and endings. We move out of the magical thinking of a child that everything will last forever and eventually integrate the idea that loss is a natural part of living.

SHIFTING PERSPECTIVES

The power of shifting perspectives is the greatest coping skill we have, and it is in our control.

Everything we experience in life runs through our emotional filter, so our interpretation of an event impacts us based on what is healed and unhealed within. When we experience any kind of loss, the loss itself doesn't change; a loss is what it is. What does change are the perspectives and choices we make after the loss, based on the clarity or cloudiness of our filter. How we interpret a loss at any given time in our life matches where we are emotionally at that time. If our emotional filter is already clogged with feelings of hopelessness, depression, or anxiety, for example, the loss will turn up the volume on each of those feelings. We look at the loss through our lens of perception, so if the lens is cloudy and hurting, that is how we will either process or avoid dealing with the loss.

Think of a recent loss in your life. Do you feel this loss in a balanced, reasonable way? That is, it hurts, but do you acknowledge it and are working through your feelings? Or does the loss feel heavy because you were feeling depressed or anxious before it happened and now you have the loss on top of your sad or worried feelings? It's hard to be resilient after a loss when we are already hurting and our battery is low. We just don't have the same capacity to navigate the loss as we would if we had a full charge. It's a hurt on top of a hurt.

One person's loss is seen as an ending,
while another's loss creates an opening, a beginning.

Each loss experience is unique, and until we go through a specific loss, we don't have any idea how we will think, feel, interact with, accept, or reject this particular experience. In other words, we don't always know what is healed and unhealed within us. When I was younger, my fears would cause me to imagine how I would feel when my parents died, even though I didn't want to think about it. It sounds strange to me now, but I think this was my way of dealing with an anxious fear, thinking that I could better prepare myself for what would happen someday. I thought that I could lessen the impact for one of my worst fears. However, when my parents did pass away (my mom was first), I didn't feel any of those things I had imagined. My feelings were much deeper, more complex, and more nuanced than I had expected and prepared for. I felt like I was in a bottomless pit of despair, and I didn't know how I was going to climb out.

I was trying to use my coping tools, but I was also trying to escape my pain by drinking too much, eating poorly, going through the motions on autopilot, and not treating my partner kindly. The two years leading up to her death took a toll on me. I thought I was handling things well, but loving friends would inquire, Are you okay? What do you need? Even with everything I knew to do to help others through their pain, my loss turned my world upside down. I now realize I needed much more help than I wanted to admit. My pain kept me lost, numb, and depressed. A part of me was afraid to feel the gut-wrenching anguish because I thought it would swallow me whole.

I wish I had taken more time off from work and given myself more space to have quiet, still, tender moments instead of trying to do so much. My indulgent response was to try to go back to my life as I remembered it instead of honoring what I was going through and feeling. In time, and after I was exhausted from ignoring the pain, I allowed myself more reflection. Through my men's groups, therapy, and trusted friends and family, I leaned into the pain as I slowly walked through my grief. The support from others helped me find an internal strength. Examining my feelings helped me to better understand myself and other orphaned adults. Even though it was hard, I am grateful for this crucible of healing. Sometimes we learn our grief lessons in brutal ways.

What I learned in my healing journey was that what I knew could take me only so far in recognizing and healing my loss. I had to join with and experience the loss, to swim within the depths of my emotions. My earlier attempts to prepare for this titanic grief seemed so trivial and innocent. I hadn't emotionally gone through losing a parent before, so there was no way I could have prepared myself. I had to give myself permission to surrender, to go within and let my emotions speak to me through this experience. I had to learn to honor my heartache and my heart wisdom. I had to learn how to give this pain a voice, even though I felt like I was stumbling around in the dark looking for a light switch. Loss was my teacher. It is a teacher for all of us.

A New Now Time

Each moment in time is the now. In a magical-thinking world, we believe that whatever we are experiencing in this now time will go on forever. Then, when something changes, we look in the rearview mirror and are shocked, saddened, and surprised. How could that have broken? How could he have betrayed me? How could she have died? Suddenly, we are thrust into a new now time. Some people get stuck in a jaundiced view of anger and resentment over what has happened. Others move on to create new experiences in the new now with their newfound wisdom, weaving into the tapestry of their life.

Grief work is not meant to be sanitized and wrapped in a drive-through experience topped off with platitudes. The more we ignore honoring our grief, the longer we will feel disconnected from life and its revelatory gifts.

When we talk about how to accept, embrace, or acknowledge pain, the instinctive reaction is to reject the idea. We naturally want to avoid pain; few of us lean into pain or welcome it. The depth of the pain we feel after a loss can become so intense that we don't know what to do with it. Being slammed with this much grief and loss all at once, even if we have anticipated the loss, can be frightening. We are suddenly thrown into a new reality, and everything seems to be going in slow motion. We are numb and poignantly aware of the fragility and mortality of life and the situations that we had taken for granted. This tidal wave of grief shocks the system into the harsh reality that we are not immortal and that nothing on earth lasts forever. We know this intellectually, but when a sudden loss happens, our hearts are burdened with heaviness.

This is usually when one of two things happens: we either accept that the loss occurred or deny it. We may only intellectually or reluctantly accept the reality of the loss at first, but this step begins the process of thinking about how we are going to get through it in the best way we know how. When we deny it and pretend that it didn't happen, we distract ourselves away from the uncomfortable reality, perhaps by resorting to unhealthy and indulgent behaviors. As you learned from my story, this avoidance only prolongs the inevitable grief work that awaits.

When we don't acknowledge the loss consciously, this denial creates a temporary relief from the reality. But the harder we work to ignore the pain, the louder it will get. As the volume increases, we have to keep doing more to distract ourselves. Eventually, we become so filled up with grief that it has to go somewhere. It often comes out as anger, depression, or numbing out with substances. On the other hand, when we consciously acknowledge the reality of the loss and the pain we feel, we can make better choices in how we express that pain. We want to find our way back to connection, back to a place of healing. Then we can remember that all of these feelings are normal.

Grieving isn't a thinking exercise,
it's an emotional, immersive experience.

THE LOSS BUCKET

I often see people in my psychotherapy practice who do not acknowledge their losses. When the normal feelings following a loss are ignored, the loss experience gets tossed into what I call a loss bucket. This is where all of our unresolved, unacknowledged losses pile up as we silently disregard them or wish them to magically go away. We want to move on, to not feel sad or in pain anymore, so we just cram our losses into this metaphorical bucket. The pain and sadness of these losses sit in our loss bucket, often contributing to low self-esteem, depression, or anxiety and reinforcing the blanket of sorrow that can suddenly overwhelm us.

Some of us learn how to create a loss bucket from our parents or relatives who ignored or downplayed a loss. Their lack of response or emotional unavailability became energetically imprinted in the children, so there was no model within the family of how anyone is to grieve. All of the heavy emotion and ripples of grief were pushed aside as everyone tiptoed around the elephant in the room, pretending all was well. When the older family members and relatives shut down any expression of sadness, they were saying to the children, This is too much. We don't want to go there. Let's just move on. Nothing to see here. The family put all of their unexpressed sorrow into an intergenerational loss bucket. Then, when we grow into adults, we ignore new loss events and cram them into our already-filling loss bucket. Our mind thinks it has outsmarted our emotional pain, but our subconscious is keeping track of these feelings. They aren't going anywhere, they are just waiting to be processed.

It is true that we may not be ready to look at or hold some losses. A loss that just happened leaves a wound that is fresh, raw, and tender. We try to reconnect with the rhythm of life as we knew it, to go back to that before time. We try to convince ourselves that we've moved on. Our loss bucket may have already been overflowing with past losses, and now, here we are adding new ones. During a significant loss like a death, we may feel like impostors in our own bodies, hoping no one notices that we are shells of our former selves, holding on by a thread. We try hard to pretend; we paste on a half-smile and move forward, even though the loss is omnipresent and we feel its shockwave even when we are standing still. But what else do we do with all of these crumpled-up, unexpressed feelings?

The problem with storing things in our loss bucket is that we aren't designed to hold on to such intense emotion for a long time. This unexpressed emotion will eventually come out as physical illnesses, such as heart attacks, strokes, panic attacks, ulcers, headaches, gastro issues, and shingles. Turned inward, it manifests as depression or panic attacks. Unacknowledged emotion has to go somewhere, so once it builds internally to a toxic level, it has to spill out. The question becomes, do we want to consciously be in charge of our grief process?

When we don't have the time, energy, or desire to process a loss, it gets stored within us at a cellular level, adding to the energetic signature of the unacknowledged grief we hold in our loss bucket.

When we push down feelings, two important processes happen. The first is that the hurt, pain, and intensity of the loss are denied and intellectualized away. We tell ourselves, *It's for the best. It was going to happen anyway. I have to move on, I can't just dwell on this.* This avoidance and intellectualization is a self-protective measure from the part of us that wants to move on so the pain will go away. The second process that happens is that the denial fuels reactive or impulsive behaviors of avoidance, which then reinforces the denial. We think that if we change or control things on the outside, we will feel different on the inside.

It takes a lot of extra energy that we don't usually have to hold the energy of grief and keep piling it into our loss bucket. The longer the losses sit there, the heavier they get, placing more of a burden on the whole system. The weight of grief starts to crush the strongest of spirits if it is not openly held and seen.

The great philosopher and psychologist Carl Jung said, "Until you make the unconscious conscious, it will control your life and you will call it fate." If you can name a loss, honor it, and give it a proper place in your emotional landscape, you can live a more balanced and fulfilling life. The more you sit with and hold your loss, the more you will deepen your understanding of what your work is and the path you need to take. As you keep reading, you will learn how to hold, cherish, and heal what is sitting in your loss bucket.

When people young and old come to me and start talking about a loss, I can usually quickly tell if they have acknowledged and felt the grieving energy around the loss. If they tell me a story that happened years ago and start tearing up, or if it's hard for them to verbalize what happened, chances are they haven't dealt with the loss or have some level of trauma with it. For example, someone whose parents died years ago has difficulty talking about them without sobbing. This type of response is often tied to another preexisting psychological issue, a multiplier that intensifies their reaction. In other words, it's more than a sadness over their parents' death, it's a weighty sorrow, an ungrieved grief. The comfortable denial and avoidance they created within works to a point, but once they get triggered and put words to their feelings, the tears start. Simply put, tears are the ungrieved emotional energy that surrounds the loss. When we name a loss, we can walk with it. We become joined in the journey.

Regrets over something that happened in the past are commonly found languishing in the loss bucket. Many people who come to me have regrets about something they said or did in the past that they just can't shake. They see their action as a lost opportunity or how it damaged a relationship. I tell them that the way I get through a regret cycle is by being clear and gentle with myself, reminding myself that when I made that decision I now regret, I was using all of the knowledge and wisdom I had at the moment. I wasn't trying to purposely make a bad choice, I was trying to do my best. I remind myself that it was the best decision for me at the time based on everything I knew then. I forgive myself, and I move away from regret.

As a gentle practice right now, think of something you feel regret or shame about. Gently hold this experience within, even though you may wince just thinking about it. Now say to yourself that this was the best choice you could make at the time. Hold that idea; let it sink in deeply. See if these words and a new perspective can begin to transform the energy of regret into an acknowledgment that you did your best with what you knew. Be curious about your feelings and let yourself explore your feeling inventory. Your feelings aren't going to kill you. They may feel intense or hard to hold, but you are stronger than you realize. With this, you give yourself the gift of perspective to heal the pain of regret.

You can set the course for how you move through your grief and loss process. You can acknowledge the loss, and you can be in control of your hopefulness. You can imagine a hopeful beacon at the end of a dark, lonely hallway, a promise of better times to come. This may seem unimaginable right now, but see if you can say to yourself, *I'm hopeful that things will get better*. Just this action of declaring your intention will begin to bring this reality to you. You may not be ready to start pulling feelings out of the loss bucket today, and that's okay. There is no time schedule that you have to follow in your grieving. Grieving is the action, the response to the loss.

A Tender Path

The emotional energy of loss says, I'm a part of your life now as you try to peel this deep, heavy pain off your heart. You will go back and forth between rejecting and accepting this inconvenient truth.

When you are willing to face the losses you have experienced or are experiencing now, you will find yourself on the tender path of grief and loss. You embark on this path when you begin to address and hold what happened without resistance. This acknowledgment is the signal that your grief journey has begun. You will bravely and lovingly move through the loss by claiming your own time within each phase of the tender path.

The first phase is the shockwave, the immediate and abrupt disturbance that alters the course of outcomes and lives. It's the hollow thud of incredible pain that we want to quickly pull the covers over and deny. Once the shock has settled, we enter into the second phase, the stretch. Some losses feel so intense that they stretch our ability to cope and do basic tasks. They unapologetically stare us down as we bend and contort ourselves into a highly inconvenient new normal. We stretch beyond what we knew before as the grief slams into our consciousness just when we thought we were doing better. After we have stretched and done all of our groaning and moaning, we slowly drift into the third phase of the path, the solace. Being in solace is a time of great reflection, when we see the long view of our life events and how our losses fit snugly into place. We may not like these losses having a place in the arc of our story, but they're there nonetheless. Solace is a softening of the pain, a velvet pouch that holds this thorny truth.

The tender path is of your own making, and these three phases are simply signposts along the way; you will fill in the journey between them. A loss is simply an event or occurrence; you are given the opportunity to determine its meaning and the place it has in your life. You are curating your journey, incorporating the losses along with the joys into your tapestry.

We all have our own journeys with loss, in moving from shock and disbelief to a resigned sobriety and acceptance that this change has happened. The shape of loss fits uniquely into our lives, eventually becoming a familiar chapter among many in our life stories.

CHAPTER TWO

Loss Comes In All Shapes and Sizes

It is through our experience with loss, sorrow,
and pain that we deepen our connection with
one another and enter the commons of the soul.
—FRANCIS WELLER

Imagine the shock of coming home and discovering that your home, your sacred space, has been violated. Jessica came home to find the contents of her bedroom and closet upended and all her jewelry stolen. Much of this irreplaceable jewelry had been her mother's and grandmother's and had deep sentimental value to her. The shock of the burglary and its aftermath were overwhelming, as she had to go through the detailed process of making an insurance claim even as she mourned her treasures. Sadly, all of this happened when she was ninety years old. When she had experienced a burglary in her thirties, Jessica had been angry and disappointed, but this time, at this age, she was devastated. The trauma of the loss gutted her so much that she buried it in her loss bucket and tried to put it out of her mind.

We all experience loss throughout our lifetimes, and our response to loss changes over time. A loss that was easy to navigate when we were young can be much more difficult to navigate later in life. Our perceptions and how we experience loss, like so many things in life, are uniquely our own. For example, one person who loses a spouse will be absolutely devastated and lost for the rest of their life without the person they loved, while another person will feel sad but will eventually move on and establish a new life. One person who loses a game will accept the loss and move on, while another person throws the game board across the room. A devastating loss for one person is a momentary setback for another.

You may have loss experiences and emotions that you aren't ready to look at, or maybe something happened that you don't think of as a loss but rather as bad luck or fate. As you are learning, after a lifetime of such losses, your loss bucket can get loaded up with so many unacknowledged losses that it leaves you with heavy feelings of sadness, loneliness, or rejection, all of which are related to those unexamined losses.

Loss comes in all shapes and sizes, and understanding various types of loss helps to put a particular loss into a context. In the following sections, I use various descriptors to name different types of loss, but the experience and magnitude of individual losses are personal to each of us.

UNACKNOWLEDGED LOSSES

Unacknowledged losses are those that we don't think of or categorize as losses, leaving them to be tossed into our loss bucket. We overlook or discount experiences that are, in fact, losses, such as missing out on an event, losing track of a friendship, or breaking a favorite treasure. We say, well, that's what happened, that's just my luck, or that's life. We become so caught up in fixing or denying the loss that we don't see it for what it is. We quickly try to get over it, to move on to the next thing and leave this disappointing experience in the past. We want to erase it, like I did in my tapestry dream sequence. We don't honor the loss experience through naming or an act of ceremony, instead denying it the important place it deserves. Jung referred to this aspect of ourselves as the shadow self, explaining that the unacknowledged feelings in the shadow will eventually run our lives. The way toward healing the feelings around these losses is to bring to light what we've thrown into the loss bucket and haven't dealt with for years.

SMALL LOSSES

Small losses are silent losses that no one else knows about, as we often dismiss, disguise, or hide them. They are when we scratch a favorite piece of furniture, make a small mistake, are ghosted, or have a bad day get worse, when people exclaim, Why do bad things keep happening to me?! If we were to tell someone about such losses, they might think we were being petty or ridiculous. Nonetheless, these losses usually end up in our loss bucket by default, adding up over time. When these types of experiences are put into the context of loss, however, we immediately understand that they are in fact losses, something we wish hadn't happened. Individually, they are not life-changing, but if there is a pattern of such losses, then the loss bucket becomes heavier to carry.

Some events are counterintuitive losses, such as giving up smoking. Smokers who give up smoking describe the process as giving up a friend who has been there through thick and thin. We all know smoking isn't good for us, but for many smokers, it's a way to cope with life. If this coping mechanism goes away and is not replaced by anything else, it really is a loss. This is especially true if the smoker is giving it up for someone else; what will they get in return other than satisfying someone else's needs?

Here are some other examples of small losses that, when they happen again and again, build up over time:

> Someone is trying to increase their performance at the gym but is having trouble meeting their goals; when they step on the scale, nothing has changed.

> A parent no longer feels a connection to their teenage child.

> A person always gives a hug and a kiss to their partner before they leave the house, but the partner never does the same for them; they just say bye or ditto or okay—or worse, nothing. Day after day, this lack of response leaves the first partner feeling empty.

On the surface, none of these examples seems like a loss. We just go about our day reluctantly experiencing these micro losses and respond with a heavy, silent, melancholy sigh. But if we connect to how these experiences feel *and* they repeat over time, each event begins to register as a loss or disappointment. It stings a little each time, and eventually, the dull ache begins to hurt.

The person who always kisses their partner goodbye but doesn't receive the same in return begins to feel empty, which leads to disappointment. If they are codependent and don't know how to set healthy boundaries, they accept this lack of reciprocation from their partner as an unfortunate fact, thinking that they somehow deserve it. This aligns with their narrative that they aren't good enough or deserving enough. They don't see these individual events as losses but rather as treatment they should expect. The resulting hurts get piled up in the loss bucket, supporting the false narrative of feeling of less-than.

The need for reciprocity is not the problem; the problem is the lack of perspective and boundary setting by the person not getting their needs met. It may be that their partner is not able to meet this expectation because of their own wounding; not everyone can be emotionally available in that way. Whatever the reason, there is no acknowledgment of what is missing in the relationship, which creates a hidden loss.

Hidden Losses

Old, unacknowledged losses are amplified by new additions to the loss bucket, where they pile up, waiting to be felt and expressed.

Hidden losses are often unmet needs. We all have needs that are meaningful to us, but a need often becomes an expectation, and when the expectation isn't met, we feel disappointed. This is the "expectation gap" between the perception of what we need and what we actually receive. This gap, in turn, feeds into the feelings of disenchantment, and we begin to doubt that our needs are valid or worth fulfilling. We can spin in this confusion and blame ourselves, or project onto others that they are at fault. All of these unmet needs get poured, like a sticky syrup, into the loss bucket. They become hidden losses that linger and fester and greatly affect our mood.

We may also see hidden losses as something else altogether. For example, an ex-spouse remarrying brings up a cluster of feelings that circle the loss of the marriage. It may not register as a loss, but when an ex moves on, some people feel the loss of the relationship again but in a new way. These feelings are hard to explain, but it comes up enough in my sessions with patients that I know it's a real loss to many.

You may feel many micro losses related to unmet needs throughout the day and not even realize it. A good gauge of this is to notice how disappointed you are at the end of each day. If you think you are often disappointed, then you are probably loading up your loss bucket with expectations (needs) that aren't being met. You may not be expressing those needs, which sets you up for a loss bomb. When you go to bed at night, your subconscious spins with the losses of the day, which were, in reality, misplaced expectations you put on others who couldn't fulfill your needs in the first place (or didn't know you had them).

Sometimes we intellectualize away our losses and make up stories so that our logical minds can make sense of the loss. We might think, *That's how it is* or *He doesn't say good night to me because he's tired* or *She doesn't like to hug because of her traumatic past.* These may be true statements, but when our minds explain them away, we disregard, minimize, and push away our feelings and needs. We say to ourselves that we don't matter.

Unmet needs and other small losses add up over time, eventually overfilling the loss bucket. People who have an overfull loss bucket often feel overwhelmed, frustrated, exhausted, and angry but do not understand the root of these feelings.

The following are examples of small losses that add up:

- Missing the physical body you once took for granted

- Not being included in social events

- Being ghosted, ignored, or neglected

- Watching parents lose functionality as they age

- Having to give up a favorite food or drink for health reasons

- Someone not showing up to see you

- Not being able to participate in an event because of an illness

- Something being canceled and feeling at loose ends as a result

Over time, each of these micro losses pile up in our loss bucket. Any one of these losses by itself doesn't feel good, and as they accumulate over time, we begin to feel immune, unfeeling, or worn down. Since we don't acknowledge them as losses or as something missing in our lives, we may feel sad, lost, and disconnected at a deep level.

With a soft gaze, take a moment to gently look inside your loss bucket. What are some small or hidden losses that are weighing you down? How do these unexamined losses come out as feelings of sadness, loneliness, or acting out by, say, overspending or lashing out? See if you can do a mental and emotional inventory of what is in your loss bucket. Connect to what feels heavy inside. What are those losses you don't want to look at or feel? Once you have a sense of some of these losses, pick one and give yourself permission to gently hold it. See if you can forgive yourself for not being perfect and not knowing everything.

Your needs are normal and legitimate, so you don't need to apologize for them. Things are going to happen in life that are disappointing. It's important to honor your feelings of disappointment or sadness instead of paving over them and moving on. When you push away the emotional recognition of loss, you unknowingly shut down the grieving process and keep your focus on a logical fix-it space.

Say this intention to bring in self-forgiveness and love:

I forgive myself for not always knowing the right answer and for sometimes making what turns out to be a bad choice. I know that each day I try to make good decisions. I know that something I regret having done in my past was, at that time, the best choice I could make. I am working toward forgiving others who have hurt me. My needs are real and necessary, and I am learning how to express my needs and boundaries to those closest to me. I love myself, and things are going to work out.

SIGNIFICANT LOSSES

Our reaction to a significant loss instantly reveals how emotionally healed or wounded we are. It's an observation, not a judgment, that tells us the work we've done and the work we still need to do.

When a significant loss occurs, most of us feel thrown off course and find ourselves in a state of disconnection. Everything we knew to be true about life before is now in a state of flux. We often feel hurt, deceived, confused, or that the bottom has been pulled out from under us. When we are in the shockwave stage, we don't know which end is up. We want to trust ourselves and life and feel whole again, but at the moment, our world is turned upside down.

Significant losses are easy to identify. They are the losses that cut much deeper and feel more intense than small losses. They are the billboards along the path of life that cannot be ignored and oftentimes change the course of our lives. Big losses are not always sudden; they may build over time. There is usually a moment of stark recognition, a loud moment when we recognize that this big loss is happening, no matter how much denial we have been in. It's a moment when we are honest with ourselves and say, yes, this is really happening.

If we experience a significant loss and are already sad or depressed, we will feel that feeling much more. We don't have the emotional stamina to withstand the shockwave, much less go through the experience. It's hard to be positive when, for example, we don't feel well or when strong medications are poured into our bodies to keep us alive. For example, a woman who is going through breast cancer treatment whose husband dies suddenly will experience a compounded loss that creates a huge shockwave. Each event alone is a devastating experience for her, and together they are overwhelming. It will take tremendous emotional energy for her to navigate these back-to-back major loss experiences.

If the loss event is a completely new experience, we won't have any resilience or point of reference because the experience is so different from anything we know. For example, someone just diagnosed with cancer feels devastated and shocked, and they don't have a reference point other than someone they know who had cancer. They're in frightening new territory and learning unfamiliar words, procedures, and protocols. They draw on any reference point they have to get a foothold in this new loss landscape. They look to others for help and guidance, and they hang on to others who have been through something similar. These wayshowers know where the potholes are and have tips on how to make the journey gentler. The following are examples of significant loss:

- A loved one dying

- A chronic or terminal diagnosis

- A pet dying

- Loss due to addiction

- A home invasion

- A divorce

- A job loss

- Being unable to conceive a child

- Bankruptcy

Significant losses are life-changing, cracking us wide open. They have potential to throw us off course and into a state of disconnection. When we lose a job or our spouse has died, we often don't know who we are anymore; our identity is wrapped up with that job or that person. When they are gone, where does it leave us? When a parent has lost their only child, are they still a parent? Significant losses throw us into turmoil, leaving us with existential questions about life and our place in it. They stop us in our tracks and demand that we examine them.

What are some significant losses that you are carrying in your loss bucket? Take a moment to check in with your thoughts and feelings about one of these losses. Ask yourself what that feeling of loss needs from you. Does it need acknowledgment?

Forgiveness? Love? How does this loss come out emotionally? Are there feelings of sadness? Do you act out by overeating or shutting down? Do you need to write about it, talk about it, or do something expressive that will help you process and move on from these heavy feelings? You will learn how to process these feelings in chapter nine, "Practical Tools for Honoring Loss." You will learn how to heal the disconnection from your suffering and find your way back to connection.

Ongoing Loss

Ongoing loss occurs when there is no ending to the loss experience, such as caring for a chronically ill child or suffering a financial collapse. When we face uncertainty due to an ongoing significant loss, when crisis after crisis happens, we experience great stress. We don't know if the situation will get better or worse, so we sit on the edge of the chair trying to be hopeful, but we are also filled with fear. This uncertainty adds to the anxiety because the ground is always shifting beneath us. We become stretched way past our comfort zone as we try to cope and survive. For instance, the parents of an adult child who has ongoing loss will often emotionally disconnect out of exhaustion. They have gone through so much, tried so hard to protect them, but their adult child keeps making bad choices and losses keep happening.

Another type of ongoing loss is ambiguous loss, which can be harder to identify. For example, a superior, coworker, friend, or spouse continually disrespects your boundaries and regularly puts you down. You know you feel a sense of loss, you miss feeling safe and trusting, and you feel overwhelmed. Or you know that you are a success in your career, but it's a career that doesn't matter to you and you don't care. This happens when we live out someone else's dream instead of our own. Such success is a hollow victory and doesn't feel whole or fulfilling. Ambiguous losses are hard to name and quantify, but you may find some if you check in with your feelings.

Medical Loss

When we go through a big loss, we may lash out or say prayers or words—including curse words—that we haven't spoken in years. This shows how much the loss scares us. We go back to our primitive responses and early spiritual roots, hoping others hear our pain.

A medical loss begins when someone receives a serious diagnosis or experiences a dramatic change of health. It immediately becomes their number one focus, and everything else takes a back seat. After the diagnosis, accident, or other sudden loss to their physical well-being, they are thrust into a new reality. They may reject it, be in denial, and have all sorts of feelings about it. A sudden change in health becomes highly distracting. Immediately the person is being stretched from a known reality into a new, frightening, and unknown world.

People with a serious medical issue feel like they are in a boat that is drifting in and out from the shoreline, where their family and friends are. Before the event, they were walking with their loved ones on the shore, but after their change in health, they're in this boat out on the water, separate from their loved ones. The boat drifts close to shore, where it's easier to connect, and then drifts farther out again, and they feel alone.

A boat carrying someone with a terminal disease sometimes moves close to shore, but it mostly stays adrift as they float in a place of wonder and fear. It's harder for family and friends to reach them. It takes a lot of energy to be in the boat managing the disease, and they don't have much energy to give to those on the shoreline. Others try to reach them and they want to reach the others, but the boat, the disease, takes them farther away each moment, even though they are all participating in the experience. I believe this is why people in this kind of loss experience sometimes stare off into space, preoccupied by the transition that is approaching. They still want to participate and stay connected, but their minds and hearts are drifting into an existential space, questioning what life is all about and the meaning of everything.

If you are going through a medical loss experience yourself, whether through illness, disease, or accident, you may be lost in a fog and overwhelmed by everything coming at you: the diagnosis, the prognosis, the treatment options and their efficacies. You are learning new words and new treatments, and all sorts of things are unfamiliar; it's overwhelming. You may not realize how lost you are, as the survival part of you has kicked in and you're just going through the motions. The smallest gestures from others may have the greatest poignancy and seem timeless and precious. Someone brings you ice chips or lip balm, someone asks if there's anything you need, a friend stops by with something to eat so you don't have to cook—these all become important gifts. The smallest gestures have the most meaning when we are facing what is overpowering our lives in that moment.

When we are going through any kind of loss cycle, not just a terminal disease or other medical loss, we lose track of time and become absent-minded. We'll pour a glass of water and then walk away, leaving it on the counter. It becomes hard to track schedules and tasks, as we are not ourselves and don't have the same energy as before. Our energy is being sucked dry by the fear of how things are going to work out, how things will be tomorrow.

The loss stretches us physically, mentally, and emotionally. We become preoccupied and distracted with the very idea of the life that we had previously taken for granted. Priorities change, and all the things we thought were important before are no longer important. Small things become important, such as saying I love you and thank you to others. Our world dramatically shrinks. The noise of inconsequential things is silenced. What is important comes into clear focus.

There is a grace that is available at this time, after a diagnosis of cancer, say, where within each moment we can become mindful in determining how we want to experience the moment and discern the energy we have to give to ourselves and others. Once the shockwave has passed and we have worked through the stretch of anger and denial, we become open to a grace of immense perspective and begin to understand that there is a bigger picture here. We can see our part in the unfoldment of our journey—but we have to be quiet and still to receive and hold this grace. The stretch we experience after a loss is an invitation to join rather than resist the process. You will learn more about this phase in chapter four, "The Stretch."

Another blessing of this time is that we can say to others those things that we want to get off our chests, or even a simple I love you. This is especially true for those who haven't done so for many years. Cancer survivors, for instance, have stared death in the face and walk with a sense of enlightened wisdom and bravery. When we are conscious of the loss experience, we can join and work with the energy of this time. We can make intentionally aware choices of how we interact with others. This is one of the gifts of loss.

Inconsolable Loss

Deep pools of sorrow are in the hearts of parents who have lost a child. They feel a hollowness in their hearts as they are pulled into knowing they will never feel the same again.

Some losses are so deep and profound that they go beyond the scope of feelings and words. Those who have been impacted by such loss usually have no prior frame of reference to understand the intense grief that they are going through. I often see this inconsolable grief in parents who have lost a child and in people who feel they could have, should have done something to save another—in many cases, a child—from dying. The parents take on a punishing responsibility for the loss of their child and will go into a deep, sorrowful grief. In soul-crushing pain, they push away any attempts from others to help reconcile this loss. They go through their own process of beating themselves up or being mad at God, themselves, and others. They are completely distraught and inconsolable.

The grieving parents, friends, and relatives wake up every day inside this nightmare of reality. They are faced with reminders of their loss all around them. When they look into the faces of their other children, they mourn the loss of the child who died. Often the parents themselves want to die because the pain and grief are so intense and they don't want to feel them anymore. There is an expression that says a parent who has lost a child cries tears of blood.

We don't have to lose a child to feel this inconsolable grief. Losing someone we are deeply, emotionally attached to—a spouse, a sibling, a parent, a pet—is devastating. In the immediate time after the loss, some feel that they will never move past it, that the future feels bleak and lost. Their life is forever changed. Their loss has hollowed them out, leaving a big, gaping hole inside that feels like it can't be filled.

Such inconsolable grief becomes a loud and defining loss. Often this loud grief becomes their connection to the loss, the narrative they live by—a sort of identity aligned with the fact that the person died. *I am no longer a parent* or *I'm nothing now that my spouse died.* The intensity of the grief is so great that they create a place inside to hold it and then don't want to touch it because it's too deep, too searing hot, too intense, too dark. This level of soul-cracking grief is just too painful, and people in such pain may believe that if they open the door to it, even just a little, they will be swallowed up by the enormous emotions they carry. They often don't have any words to describe what this pain of molten agony inside of them feels like.

Days, months, and years pass. Those who have not acknowledged or faced the loss know the deep sorrow is there but are still not ready to look at it. Locking it away temporarily works for most people, especially in the shockwave and parts of the stretch phase that come later, but those who lock it away for years go about their lives on autopilot, numbing themselves to their worst nightmare. This sorrow is locked away deep inside so they feel in control and safe, providing a contrast to their loved one being taken away. They take care of the absolute bare minimum, not caring about much anymore.

This is often when the inconsolable get lost in the Gordian knot of what is called "grief looping." They are reluctantly and often unknowingly living in their own hall of mirrors, stuck in the grief. They revisit the last days of their loved one, contemplating what could have, should have been done, replaying the funeral service and seeing who was there and not there. Grief looping feels weirdly comfortable, as there is a perverse familiarity to this activity. It brings a short-lived comfort, but only because it's familiar. It's akin to putting on the same dirty clothes day after day; they are dirty and abhorrent, but they're yours.

Their fear is that they don't know what life will be like if they get out of the loop and begin to feel the weight of the loss. Unaware, the inconsolable person walks the grief loop in an inward, ever-tighter, toxic spiral, becoming confused in the maze, instead of gently walking the outward spiral, which leads out of the darkness and into a place of connection and love. If you feel you are in a grief loop experience, reach out for help. There will be someone who can help you out of this tangled tornado of sorrow.

The answer is not in knowing why the loss happened, it's in finding what you can do to gently move on and reclaim your life.

In their own time, the inconsolable may choose to peel back the edges of this deep grief, uncovering small parts that they can hold. This process takes a long time for them. I believe all of the concepts and ideas of how long someone should grieve don't apply here, especially to a grieving parent. What I have seen in my work with this deep grief is that bereaved parents will get to a level of stability around the grief and feel some strength, only to become triggered by something and thrown back into the depths of grief. They are riding a tenuous roller coaster, as there are emotional landmine triggers everywhere.

The loss of a child is indescribable, but it is possible, with care and gentleness, to heal the feelings around this loss. I have seen firsthand parents heal from just such a loss. The best way I can describe healing an inconsolable loss is to imagine the loss as a bottomless pit. We can't fill this hole up, but in time we can plant a garden around the edge and honor this pain. The garden restores life and softens the sharp edges of the hurt and sorrow. The hole is still there, but the garden creates an emotional guardrail so that we don't fall into this pit of despair. It helps to hold us in a safer, gentler place from which to look at the grief. This is the imagery that I used after my mom's death so that I wouldn't keep spiraling into a pit of depression. It took so much work to climb out of the pit that I wanted to find a way to cope so I didn't fall into the chasm again.

If you have lost a child or are experiencing inconsolable grief, know that there is help for you. Please reach out and find someone to talk to who is familiar with this kind of deep grief work and can sit with you and this pain. Connect with other parents who have lost a child. You will find comfort from others in this shared profound grief. Read Bonnie's story following chapter four, as her journey will help you understand the walk of this specific grief and that you can come out the other side whole again. This in itself will help you feel better, even if the pain doesn't go away. Please turn to Resources at the back of the book if you need more assistance.

With any kind of loss, the ego is on a search for understanding and a feeling of control because the loss spins our world faster than we can keep up. What is needed, and what is often missing in this quest, is compassion, where we are as kind to ourselves as we are to others. The goal is to achieve a compassionate balance. In the process of walking the tender path, there is a softening, a place where the bittersweet memory of loss can live. This is how we lift ourselves up as human beings in our shared experience of death and rebirth.

Picking up the pieces after a loss is like looking for something you can't find. Along the way, you unexpectedly find other treasures that you have been searching for.

BRANDI'S STORY: LOVE, LOSS, AND ILLNESS

Brandi is a sweet lady, the type of person whom you feel connected to the minute you meet her. Her story has two parts, one of which is still unfolding. Open, trusting, and authentic, she is a mom and a loving spouse. Brandi is married to the love of her life, David, but before they married she was married to another love of her life, Scott. Three months after they started dating, Scott was diagnosed with a terminal disease. Brandi married Scott knowing this, and they had a daughter together. Scott died before their daughter was four years old, and Brandi became a widow at thirty-three years old. A few years later, she met David. They started dating, moved in together, and began creating their life as a couple. A short while later, David was diagnosed with a chronic disease. Even though Brandi has experienced great loss, she remains a positive person who still loves life and believes in people. Here are Brandi's reflections on the major life events she has faced as an adult.

When you were dating Scott and he was diagnosed with a terminal disease, what was your first thought?

Scott's unofficial diagnosis of Vascular Ehlers-Danlos Syndrome (VEDS) came on Christmas Eve 2002. His mother and sister had already died from VEDS several years before Scott and I met. An astute young doctor in the emergency room spotted the disease's unique characteristics and told us the most gut-wrenching news possible. Immediately, Scott was transferred to a hospital that was better equipped to handle the complexities of the disease. As I climbed into the ambulance that snowy Christmas Eve, just ninety-five days after our first date, I said, "I'm going with my fiancé." We were not engaged, but there was no way I wasn't going to be with him.

Every decision made over the next 3,004 days, we made together with intention, honesty, love, and the courage to believe that we could keep him alive. We knew the stories of his mother and his sister. We knew what this diagnosis meant. As I signed the first of more than ten thousand "experimental surgery" medical forms, each of which said that it would be virtually impossible for him to come through the surgery alive, Scott stopped me, grabbed my hand, and said, "It's okay. You can go. You don't have to stay." I simply took his hand, moved it aside, signed the form, and said, "You don't get it. I can't leave. I don't care if it's one more minute or ninety years, I'm never leaving you." That was the driving force for our all-too-brief time together.

Did the diagnosis scare you?

Was I scared? Terrified. Love is an absolutely terrifying thing. But wasting even one second of my life not loving him was impossible.

What were some of the things that helped you to stay, to fall in love with and marry Scott?

I knew on our first date that he was going to be my entire life. That night he carved a space in my soul with his bad Seinfeld impressions and a dinner neither of us remember even tasting, and he has never left that space. Loving him was the easiest thing I've ever done in my life. So it makes sense that losing him would become the hardest thing.

As you were newly in love and married, what was it like to be excited but also wondering what was going to happen next?

We never really had a "young love" stage, even before his diagnosis. We both just knew immediately. As we drove past the airport on our second date, we joked that we should just hop on a plane to Vegas and elope. Maybe it was the universe ordaining it, or maybe it was influenced by how much loss Scott had already experienced in losing his sister and his mother, but we just kept moving forward. We took each moment, each challenge, every celebration, every win in stride.

One day to the next, never wasting. Never wishing. Go on that trip to Hawaii. Go on that fishing trip. Buy the expensive artwork that feels torn from your soul. Invent a reason to have dinner with your best friends. Breathe as much life into every day as humanly possible. We thought we would have more time, but we never wasted a minute.

Did you ever have the "why me" thought?

During the eight years of fighting VEDS, I didn't have many moments of "why me." It wasn't happening to me; it was happening to him. Later, it was happening to our daughter. They didn't ask for this. They certainly didn't do anything to warrant this heartache, this fight, this battle. I made the choice to go through the process of having our daughter, guaranteeing she would not carry on her father's disease but not protecting her from having to endure the loss. We thought he would be on this side of the universe for far longer than he was, and I certainly never imagined his death so soon into her life, but it's a choice I made. I never felt that pang for "normal."

The best part of Scott was that he wasn't normal. He was extraordinary. I was and still am the single luckiest person on the planet to be the one he chose to share his life with. It was my honor and privilege. Do I wish this hadn't happened, that the stars were somehow fated differently? Yes, I do. But I wish that more for him and for our daughter than for myself. He deserved to be here to see the incredible human being she is. He should be here to bask in the wonders that she brings and the joy she shares.

Were you glad you knew of his terminal disease, or does a part of you wish that you hadn't known so you could have experienced your life in a different way?

I am so glad we knew. So many things are left unsaid in our daily lives. Fears, insecurities, worries for our future, and so on. Moments get squandered because someone didn't take out the trash or didn't run the dishwasher or forgot a special day. Those things don't matter.

Yes, I most certainly got annoyed at those moments during the course of his disease, but it's hard to put too much energy into those things when reality is sitting right there screaming that one day you'll cry yourself to sleep because you no longer have anyone to be annoyed with but yourself.

Did you have your moments of anger and confusion?

I've spent more time being angry that he isn't here than I ever did when he was here. Scott had a grace, a way of being, that reminded others that anger wasn't the best use of our limited time. I simply followed his lead. We loved and laughed, and we did our best to make the most of the days we were given. We were never granted much "normal" time where we could fall into patterns of worry or anger, as he was constantly in some type of medical crisis. He would somehow rally and come home months later. Then there were short windows of at-home care before the next crisis.

Most people can't imagine what it would be like if their partner was given a terminal diagnosis. Was there anything you experienced before that had prepared you for this?

You can't imagine it. It's impossible. Even the most overly dramatic mind play I could dream up wouldn't come close to the unrelenting agony of knowing you're going to lose something that great. I have always been resilient, fiery and strong-willed, with a powerful moral compass, so I had an innate way of being, enduring, and knowing. My instincts got me through the challenges of my youth, made me strong, and taught me how to use my voice, but nothing prepared me to literally stand between the medical staff and my husband, who is in a coma, and say, "I know him best, and you are not touching him. Get out and give me one night to help him." Nothing prepared me for signing an Against Medical Advice form and taking him home, where I knew he needed to be but also where I knew I would be alone with him, his medical needs, and our three-year-old daughter.

*In what ways did you look to Scott for strength, inspiration,
and hope?*

Everyone always thought I was the force of nature in our family
unit, but they were wrong. It was Scott. I was loud and chaotic and
he was quiet and stoic, but he was the force. He was the light, the
standard to which we framed everything. The way he embraced
the world and always saw the beauty, grace, and magic inside
everything he witnessed was what kept us from drowning. Scott
was the person who knew everyone's name, knew what was going
on in their lives, and genuinely cared. He simply saw the best and
wouldn't stand for anyone else not seeing it the same way. He was
the best type of human possible. He wasn't perfect, but damn it, he
was close.

*Did Scott set the pace for how your family went through this,
or did you look for this inspiration from within yourself or
family and friends?*

Long before we married, we set the pace of raising our daughter
together. I often reflect back and think that the Universe knew she
had other plans for us, so we had intense, intentional, direct conversations about how we were going to raise any children we might be
given long before we had any. After it was apparent that any child we
had would be an only child, we discussed how to prevent them from
being spoiled, entitled, bored, or carry any of the typical only-child
traits that can come from a house filled with trauma.

*Your daughter was born a few years before Scott died. Was
knowing she could be born with the same terminal disease
frightening?*

We pursued the cutting edge of medical knowledge at that time to
ensure that I would not be burying my future child as well as my
husband. We talked at great length about what life could look like.

We thought Scott would stay alive until she was in her teens. We never expected him to die a month before her fourth birthday. We knew that I would always be the "wild" parent. The one who played on the floor. The one who did dance parties. The one who would carry the physical toll. The one who got up during the night. The one who cared for them during illnesses. I would be the hands-on parent. Scott would be the calm. He would be the books, the crafts, the movie snuggles, the homework, the stories. He would be the cuddle and I would be the chase. Our daughter was then, and still is today, tied to me and measures her safety off me. If Mom is okay, then the world is okay. As she's getting older, we are working to reframe this so she trusts in herself more than she trusts in me.

When and how did you and Scott introduce the concept that her daddy was going to die?

We never specifically introduced the knowledge. It just simply was. A few days after her first birthday, Scott had a massive medical event, spent four months in the hospital, and almost died numerous times. She only knew that Daddy was sick, that Mommy was helping Daddy, and that she was safe and loved. Scott and I knew it and it guided our decisions, but to her this was just life. Daddy would get sick, and Daddy would come home.

As Scott's disease progressed, did his terminal diagnosis feel like a ticking clock that was always looming over your lives, or were you able to take it one day at a time and celebrate each moment?

A year before his death Scott had what would be his last catastrophic medical event. The year spent after that was all about living in the moment. We knew we had been living on borrowed time, but now the clock was so loud that it would literally wake me up in the middle of the night. He could no longer walk and could manage very little time out of bed. He reserved most of his energy for our daughter.

We couldn't escape it, but we never let it run our lives. Having to keep a normal-feeling life for our three-year-old helped root us in normality, for which I'm grateful. But we supercharged every day, every moment, and made the most of out them whenever possible. We knew it was going to be our last Christmas together, but we didn't want it to feel like our world had already upended. So, we leaned in. Loved harder. Listened deeper. Lingered longer. He was not yet gone, and wasting time on the sadness we would eventually feel anyway served no purpose.

What became super important, and what became trivial?

This happened opposite to what I would have imagined. Everyday details became important. The minutiae of life was suddenly all that was needed. Birthdays and such were important, but it was the daily moments that sustained. Holding hands after our daughter went to bed and his medical needs were tended to, and sharing the moments of our days. Play-Doh playtime and watching her favorite cartoon for the nine-hundredth time every evening. The static of all the medical care whirled on in the background, but we paid no attention. We did what had to be done and then found joy in the simplest of moments.

Well-meaning people will want to give advice or comfort when they see their loved ones struggling. Was there any-one in your life whom you could rely on to give you genuine comfort and not just platitudes?

I had lots of people whom I could rely on for different needs at different times. Scott was such a bright light that people flocked to him and so, by proxy, to our daughter and me. Ann sat with me in the darkest moments at the hospital, feeding me nourishing foods and just breathing with me. Scott L. would text, *I've got dinner covered tonight. Be there around 4:30*, and dinner would be hot and delicious. Our kids would play and he would talk music and hockey with Scott so I could breathe. Dan and Kathy would drive two hours out to our house to restock our freezer with home-cooked meals and take care of Scott's medical needs for a day so I could have a reprieve. My parents would take our daughter for a night so I could have a night to be woken up by only one person instead of two. Or they would come stay at our house so that Scott could have both his girls nearby but I wouldn't be pulled between her and him. Mark would bring the party and tell all the stories from high school so I could learn more about who Scott was in his youth. Mark would also be there to hold my hand as I planned Scott's memorial, leaving all the jokes and parties aside and reminding me to be true to who Scott was. I had many people but also felt so incredibly alone. I was, and still am, entirely alone in this life journey. It belongs to nobody other than me, and that's okay. I am the healing I need. I am the love I need. I am the truth I need. As long as they didn't make things harder, every helper was loved and valued but did nothing to ease my aloneness. Aloneness is not a four-letter word, nor is it a bleak, dark feeling. It is truly all that is needed. I am my own divine power.

Anticipating a loss can help the grieving process because it gives us time to prepare ourselves for what we know is coming. How was it helpful to know that Scott had only a certain amount of time left to live?

As much as we knew the end was coming, there were quite a few things that Scott refused to handle, anything that made time seem final or finite, like wills and letters to our daughter to read after his death. That was his one flaw. He felt that the moment he tended to those tasks, his time would be up. In the end, he created a self-fulfilling prophecy, but I could not convince him of this. He never tired of the things he valued, and gave endlessly. He didn't focus on perceived slights or broken promises. He simply carried on loving boldly for all to see.

Was there a beat-the-clock bucket list that you did together?

I tried to do several trips like this with him—ice fishing for the last time, fishing trips with just the three of us—but Scott resisted. He wanted, needed, to be home. He didn't need adventures or activity. He needed to soak up as much of daily life as possible. So we slowed down. We leaned in. We simply breathed in the everyday. It's the one thing I'm certain we did right. No destination or event or moment means more in the end than the laughter shared at a dinner table on a Tuesday night or the joy in our daughter's voice as she would fling open the garage door and announce, "Daddy, we're home!" and his reply, "Yay! It's my best girls." The calm of knowing there was nothing that could mean more than us just simply holding hands and being there. Inconveniences were ignored. Blizzards that shut down our community were celebrated. We stayed in the part of living life vibrant and full, and stayed well out of the part of dying and being separated.

Did you protect Scott from your feelings, or did you share them with him?

I never hid my feelings from him. We were as raw and real with each other as possible. The last few months of his disease, when we knew the time was coming much sooner than expected, we talked and talked about what we needed the end to look like. He wanted to be home. He wanted to see our daughter and me every day. He knew the burden it placed on me because his medical needs were incredibly complex at that point. I did made him agree that he wouldn't suffer in pain, that he would always be truthful with me about his pain, because seeing him in agony was more than I felt I could withstand

Three days before he died, his pain was so intense. We had plenty of pain meds from hospice at our disposal to keep him comfortable, but Scott didn't want to take them. He didn't want to sleep through his last days. The only time I ever lost my calm was on his last day. I raised my voice and spat out, "You promised me! I can't do this if you don't help me." I wish I hadn't yelled. I wish I could have found a more gentle way to manage that day, but his agony was more than I could carry. The end was so close that it didn't matter. He had a rally day, giving me one final gift of some beautiful family photos, and then he slept and slept, only waking if our daughter was in the room or if I was gone too long from his space.

How were you able to make this a transformative experience rather than a traumatic one for your daughter?

I read bits and pieces of books, but I've never seen anything that can even remotely prepare one for this. There is no *Losing Your Parents as a Toddler for Dummies* book. I watched the world around me. I talked to a few people in the mental health field, but in the end, Scott and I did it like we did everything else: together, in our way, on our terms, only factoring in what we knew to be true. Our daughter learned that every day is a gift and that no day is guaranteed

What were Scott's last days like for you?

It was all of it. Fog and hyperawareness. Managing complex medical things and then sitting and holding his hand. Obsessively chopping fresh fruit into tiny little pieces because it was all he wanted to eat, and then slowing down and laughing as I fed him one small piece at a time. It was managing the friends and family while carving space so it could be just us. I took my lead from him. Because he could do it, I could, too. I could not let him down, so I would breathe, lean in, push away the mad franticness of it, and just be. I feel like I wove in and out of moments and did exactly what was asked of me in those spots. I stopped caring about anyone's feelings except what Scott and our daughter needed.

What did you hold on to as you went through this grief storm?

I protected our space like my life depended on it. I just held on to him, knowing he would never willingly leave us. I knew he would find a way to be with us, even after his body wasn't. He led the way, quiet as a mouse but larger than the universe.

Many people become neglectful of self-care during such a time. They have no appetite and feel numb, as they are preoccupied with the person who is dying. What helped you stay available for Scott, yourself, and your daughter?

Scott always called me back to him and our daughter. When life got numb and loud, he would call me back in the softest of ways. Holding my hand a little longer, resting his forehead on mine until he could feel my breath change. Asking me for things he knew would bring me comfort, like baking or watching a bad disaster movie. He knew I couldn't tell him no, so he made the request for himself, but really, it was for me.

I also had to stay physically strong. I was his only way out of bed. I was the only one who could physically care for him in the end; even nurses and doctors didn't know how. I had to stay well for him and our daughter. I would tell myself I had to do it for them, and then find that I was really doing it for me. I found writing and sharing our story with friends and family helpful. But at the end of the day, it was Scott who guided me through the grief. As always, he led, I followed—which almost everyone who knew us would be shocked to hear.

Can you describe what you felt like when Scott died?

It was a Tuesday afternoon in March 2011. I remember it as cold and bleak, as northern Illinois March days can be. I had taken up residence on Scott's floor; his room was downstairs because he could no longer be moved. Nights had become incredibly difficult for him and for me to keep him breathing and his lungs cleared from fluid. Our daughter had been to the doctor the day before because she had an ear infection and an upper respiratory infection. My parents stayed overnight to help care for her because I simply could not be in two places at one time, and Scott could not be left alone.

A friend stopped by that morning, and Scott politely asked if I could have her leave. He just wanted his girls and could not handle my being out of his room. It was time for our daughter's nap, so I had her come in and give him a kiss before I took her upstairs to rest. When I came back downstairs and sat beside his bed, I turned on her baby monitor, and we listened to her for a minute. I took his hand. As our daughter continued to be restless and chatter, I said I should go get her. He squeezed my hand and said, "Don't leave me." I told him I would never leave him and sat forward in my chair to be nearer to him. He softly whispered, "I love my girls." Those were the last words he spoke.

He was fighting so hard to breathe. I just kept telling him that we loved him and that we would be okay. I told him I would be strong for our daughter and that I would make him proud. I told him it was okay for him to go, that I knew he would always be there with us, and that I would see him soon. I said everything I needed to say, and then I just held his hand and arm and listened to him breathe and our daughter's happy chatter on the baby monitor. I listened until it stopped. Just like that, in an instant, the rattle and hum of his breath stopped, and I was alone.

My mind flashed through thousands of tiny memories filled with love and laughter. I cried and smiled and cried. I was alone. I was empty. If it weren't for the babbling of our girl on that monitor, I would have wanted to go with him. But I took a breath and knew I needed to find my way out of the room. I let go of his hand, pet our cat, Beckie, who was his constant companion, stepped back, and said, "For always," which is what we said to each other constantly and how we signed every card. Then I left the room. I haven't been the same person since that moment. That woman is gone. Pieces of her remain in this new version of me, but she could not sustain alone. I will forever hold "I love my girls" at the very core of my soul. I am who I am because Scott loved me and I loved him.

I got our daughter up from her nap, brought her to his room, and told her the truth. Her daddy was dead. He would not be able to talk to her again, and she would not see his body again. We touched his hand, his face. We said "I love you." We cried softly. That night, we started what would become our most treasured tradition: we talked to Daddy. Every night since that awful day in March 2011, we have talked to Scott. We tell him about our day. We tell him the good parts and the bad parts. We thank him for watching over us, and we ask him to stay nearby on the hard days.

Following Scott's death, what helped to make coming home a more gentle process now that it was just you and your daughter?

My grandmother is one of the most important people in my life, and she was on a train to us when Scott died. Her arrival was a wonderful blessing. She was helpful around the house and gave our daughter someone new to talk to and play with. I was still working full time at a highly flexible job, so I didn't keep regular hours and could come and go as I pleased, and I worked from home almost exclusively. Having that routine to tether me helped keep me from floating away into the darkness those first couple of days. Quickly, though, my daughter and I just needed to be us. We needed our routine, our schedule, our things, our quirks. We just needed us. I kept leaning in and listening when things shifted. I watched our daughter for cues, and I listened to my instincts. I trusted myself. I had gotten this far and was doing pretty okay. I figured I could just keep trying my best and we would be okay. No rush. No timetable. Zero care about what others felt or thought. Just me and my girl and a knowing that we would be okay.

What helped you get through Scott's wake and funeral?

Scott didn't say much about his funeral other than he didn't want it to be sad. He wanted laughter and stories and love. I was the creative mastermind behind our lives, so he left it up to me. I planned a service with no sermon, no prayer, no body. No fake platitudes and false promises. His ashes were in a plain box that most people just walked past. We had posters and pictures everywhere. The funeral home was at capacity and had to start limiting people coming in based on who was leaving. His dearest friends, his "brothers," played music on acoustic guitars and sang his favorite songs. People talked and told stories. We had hot dogs, with mustard as the only condiment available—a story stemming from our second date. Our daughter played with the other kids and colored pictures. She was never too far from me, but she was allowed her autonomy, as always.

We cried, but mostly we laughed. I felt like I was hovering above the space, watching over our daughter and watching through Scott's lens to make sure it was something he would have liked. It was what he wanted, what I needed. It wasn't going to be horribly traumatizing and fake to our daughter, and that was all that mattered.

After some time passed, what helped transform your grief into an open space, where you could consider falling in love again?

I never thought about moving on. I had typical widow fears—money, security—but I was truly okay with being alone. I would find a way to land on my feet again, loving life even if I didn't have a partner. It was Scott who I looked to when I looked ahead at life without him. It was his laughter and how he lived life so completely and with such tremendous love that I knew how to honor him and do the same thing. He had shown me how. Now I needed to find the courage to go do that. Whatever came out of that return to loving loudly, I would somehow know what to do. I knew the only thing that would never feel right was if Scott were erased, so I knew I would never connect with anyone who would try to erase him. It was just that easy. It was only when I made things complex in my mind, with the horror stories of the world, that I would falter. I just had to keep returning to our home, the home I carry for us three in my heart. The home that will be forever unchanged. I was going to be okay. I always had us.

Scott is never not with us. I talk to him at all sorts of moments throughout the day. When I see or hear a cardinal, when I see a deer, when our girl is doing something amazing or just a normal, random thing that I know he would love. Some days I feel him just off my shoulder, and some days I can't find him anywhere. But

I talk anyway. Sometimes out loud, sometimes in my head. But there is always a moment of "I love you" every single day. He's our normal and our constant, even in death.

Brandi and David

After some time had passed, Brandi met a new love. (David's story follows chapter six.)

When you and David started dating, were you optimistic about starting a new relationship, or were you tentative, with a sense of waiting to see what happens?

Since I was so truly okay with where I was, I didn't put pressure on anything. David and I found each other through such random ways that I knew he was there with help; Scott was an integral part of David and I finding each other. I was free to feel and be as I wished, if I wished. Much as with Scott, David took me by storm. I knew almost right away that I could spend my life joined with his life.

Did this feel like young love, or was it different now that you had been in love before?

David has two children from a previous marriage and I had my daughter and other adult responsibilities, so the blazing fire of young, wild-abandon love I experienced with Scott wasn't there, but I had been given a chance at a much deeper, more profound type of love.

David was diagnosed with facioscapulohumeral muscular dystrophy, or FSHD. What emotions poured through you when you learned of this?

We were together about a year and a half when we got David's diagnosis. I immediately felt that pull back into my nurse-wife days. It was surreal and powerful, and I could feel the darkness threaten to drown me where I stood. But then I heard a whisper: *Where there is great love, there are also great miracles.* The quote was on a magnet I found while on a trip with a girlfriend before my wedding to Scott. I believed then that Scott and I could find our miracle. When I bought it, it meant cure or management for Scott's disease, but in the end, I could see that the miracle was the love. I wasn't being freed from the heartbreak, I was being given the gift of true love. I had weathered a storm before, and I knew I could do it again.

This time I would show up differently. I would take my lessons from the first experience and apply them here. It would be ugly and messy, but love is exactly that. I was grateful to have two great loves, and I wasn't going to back away now. I knew David was a fighter and that this diagnosis didn't have to end like the other had. The two were not equal, and I had to stay where I was instead of going back to where I had been. I was once again rooted in love.

Having had a spouse with a terminal disease and now a spouse with a chronic disease, did you feel like you had done something wrong or that you were fated in some way? How did you make sense of the "why me" part of this?

I've had more than one therapy session with the "what have I done" and "why me" theme. I have had moments where I've absolutely felt like I was bad or wrong or somehow paying a price for a past mistake. Those moments don't linger long, though, because their diseases aren't my story. Their diseases are their story. My story is a result of my actions. I'm writing my story. I choose how to show up. So when the dark days come, I remind myself that while I have to bear witness to this moment, I can choose to do it with love and that I am fortunate enough to be tasked by the Universe to love two of the most incredible humans on this planet. I am lucky. I am grateful.

*How did going through Scott's terminal disease prepare you
for your experience with David's disease?*

I've had enough time to reflect on where I misstepped and where
I did right as I moved through Scott's disease and death. Taking
on his disease like it was something I could beat was a young
woman's rookie move. The disease doesn't care how strong or
brave or badass you are, it will knock you around like a leaf in
a tornado. Don't exact more control than you actually have. It
wastes energy and time, and distracts you from the joy and love in
the daily life. I've had to remind myself repeatedly that David is not
Scott and that this is a different story. I don't have to do everything
for David as I did for Scott. David is capable, and the longer we
can keep him doing for himself, the better we all will be. He's
got autonomy, just as I do. I also realize that we are both aging,
and accommodations are part of the process. We may hit some
accommodations sooner than our peers, but that doesn't matter;
it's just a date on the calendar.

*What are some of Scott's legacies that have helped you in
your marriage with David?*

Scott taught me to love deeply every single day. Through dark days,
challenges, heartache, and despair, just keep loving. The sun will
rise again, the light will come, and all will be well. Just keep loving.

*What conversations have you and David had that helped
you navigate his chronic disease?*

David is the world's greatest listener. He makes it impossible to not
share. After the initial shock of things subsided, I frankly told him that
I felt that pull to go back to nurse-wife and that I needed help resisting
it. He's kept me fighting that ever since, reminding me that he can do
things but will accept help when things are safer for me to do instead.

Can you lean into David, or do you feel you can't burden him with your feelings?

There is a very deep place in my soul that will just be mine, a place I never speak of, a place where I still can't make sense of anything. But that's mine, and it's as it should be. I could place that with David, but I choose not to. It's not for him. It's only for me. Not everything needs space outside ourselves. David understands that about me and leaves me to my work.

How did you explain David's disease to your daughter, who had lost her father and now had a father figure with a chronic disease?

We explained it exactly as I've explained everything else to her for her entire life: clearly, boldly, and with as much clarity as possible. We knew David's disease wasn't terminal, so we shared that. We told her that he may end up in a wheelchair at some point, and maybe not. I reminded her that she already knew life with a dad in a wheelchair and that some of her happiest moments came while he was sitting in it. We just kept loving boldly. I reminded her that love isn't about someone's physical well-being but about who they are on the inside, because that transcends time. Now that she's a teenager, she's got a strong grasp on it all.

How would you describe the arc of your emotions from learning of David's diagnosis to today? Did you ever just want to run away from it all?

I went from *Dear god, not again!* to *Wait, I don't have to do this the same as last time* to *This is an entirely different story.* David's disease has never made me want to run away. Not once. It's never been something I felt I couldn't handle. I've had days where I didn't want to handle it, but never days where I couldn't handle it. You just don't find a love like this, and I've managed it twice. I'll climb Everest backward in socks if I have to, to keep this. It's my absolute privilege.

When you have gone into a "poor me" or victim space because of your experiences with the diseases of the two men you've given your heart to, how did you move through these feelings?

I've hit moments like this only briefly. I attribute that to therapy and having a growth mindset. I'm here on this planet, experiencing life this way, to grow, learn, evolve, and love. I choose how to show up. There are days to choose to opt out and fall into the blankets and rest, and days to conquer the beasts. I just listen and feel. Validate every emotion, and let it rest without guilt or shame. Some of this way is just my nature, some is easy access to wonderful mental health care, some is a gift from the heavens. Feel that feeling. It's valid. It's real. Let it be. Then let it go when it's ready. Let another feeling come. Let that feeling be real. Let it be. Just keep loving.

Where or from whom do you get your strength to face your unique life challenges?

I was truly just born resilient and with a belly full of fire. Whether that is the Universe, Mother Earth, or the stars above, I don't know. I know what I feel. I know what I see. I know what I've learned and experienced. I put my faith in myself and my ability to do hard things. I put faith in goodness and love, and I know that if I act from those places, I will be okay even when I'm shattered beyond measure. I will still have goodness and love, so all will be well.

I have no idea why this is happening this way. I don't even give it much thought for myself. I give it much deeper thought for my daughter and how this impacts her, and my role in those choices that put her on this path with me. I give it much deeper thought for Scott and how it's possible that he's missed so much from the one joy he ever wanted, his precious baby girl. For him, I will never be able to make sense of the life I've had and the life he didn't get to have. But for me, I just am, and I will continue to move forward rooted in love.

What core strengths did you gain from going through this experience with both men?

I am a warrior. I can do the hardest of things and make them look incredibly easy. But just because I can do this doesn't mean these things don't hurt, and it doesn't mean that I should carry them alone. I don't have to attend every fight I'm called to. I can and do opt out. The biggest lesson is to remember to come back to joy and love, and let that be louder than the fear and heartbreak. I prefer life beside the two men I've been blessed to love, but I'm okay alone, too.

Completion is not an end, it is only the end of a chapter. In a few words, what wisdom do you carry from this experience, just for yourself, that has made you a better person?

Scott often said to our daughter, "There is nothing you cannot do. There are things you may choose not to do, but there is nothing you cannot do." While he said that to her, and wrote it as a reminder in all the cards and letters he left for her, I feel he was saying it to me and to the rest of the world. He was wrong that there are things we cannot do—if this were true, he would be here with us—but the point of the story is true. We are innately powerful, resilient, capable beings, and when we are guided by love, kindness, and grace, with our eyes focused on growth and guiding, we are capable of anything. I carry this always. I've proven time and time again that I will rise from the darkest of days and the light will come again. You just need to take another step, another breath, and remind yourself that all you need is inside you. It might need coaxing or nurturing, but it's there.

∽

Brandi wrote the following note to me after she sent in her answers to my questions. I wanted to include it in the book because it has its own importance and encapsulates the wisdom, vulnerability, and strength that Brandi embodies.

Thank you for allowing me to dive into this project. This is a mere fraction of our story, a fleeting glimpse as seen from a passing train, but I'm glad to have shared it. Your questions called me back to times and places I had not visited in some time, and while the tears were plentiful and the work was hard, it reminded me of where I am, how far I've come, and what truly rests at the core of my soul. I'm forever deeply grateful.

I have to share that this last question was a struggle for me to answer. I was gutted, raw, and so tired. I went to bed knowing that I didn't like my first answer. At around three o'clock this morning, I heard Scott's voice whisper those words I wrote. He often visits me around that time, so it wasn't unusual. I knew immediately those were the words I needed to share, and I smiled and thanked him.

Right after, in true Scott fashion, he shared one of his favorite jokes, and I wanted to share it with you.

How does a frog save money?

Riiibates . . . Riiibates

If I could ask one thing of you, please don't make my journey look easy. It wasn't. It isn't. I don't want another widow to ever read the small highlight sheets contained here and use them as a measuring stick with which to compare herself. There is no direct path to grief. There is no end and no real beginning, either. I will forever remain in grief. Learning to ebb and flow with the grief instead of fighting upstream is one of the things I feel I've done right in this life. There is no cure because grief is not a disease that needs to be cured. I trust that your work and your words and your way of teaching will convey that in your book.

In gratitude, Brandi

Reflections on Brandi's Story

Brandi's journey has the deep and profound wisdom of someone who has had to look her worst fears in the face and make choices for how she wanted to experience and move through and grow from them. Her story is beyond perseverance, beyond just changing perspective. As she says, she is changed but not broken, and her energy and drive exceed being merely strong. She had to keep on being a mom and find the courage to figure out how she was going to move her life forward. Her message is simple: Believe in yourself, and know that you are stronger than you can ever consciously know; that nothing is impossible, it's just a matter of going within and finding that wise voice to set the course; that loving boldly isn't hard work, it's being in the flow with intention, focus, and inspiration.

Brandi went through her stretch with great resolve. I appreciate how she listened patiently to Scott, then David, and most importantly, to herself. Instead of projecting her agenda onto the situation, she developed a response for what the person and the situation required. That is mastery of emotion and wisdom. This contextual action, I believe, is the result of Brandi's search within herself, her ability to hold the pain in the shadows, and then decide how she wanted to go through these experiences. She was able to enter into a place of solace even as her first husband was dying. She was able to boldly accept that this was happening while simultaneously holding a sense of peace about the reality. This reflects her synergy and self-honesty through and with her grieving.

I am amazed at how she went through these experiences as a young woman and new mother. Her words are poignant and raw, and the wisdom that flows through her is freely inspirational. Those who, like Brandi, have faced such life-altering circumstances carry a tremendous love and light within. Inspirationally, at each turn, Brandi kept readjusting to her situation with patience and pacing. She continually would not let herself go down a path of feeling sorry for herself or her circumstance. Some people have a hard time finding this courage and strength. Brandi did not consciously prepare for these challenges when she was a young girl, but she probably had experiences that strengthened her sense of self. When faced with these situations as an adult, she pulled from all of her resolve and belief in herself to do the best she could with what she was given. The message is to believe in yourself and to never give up. Brandi says life is about loving boldly, and I think that applies to loving ourselves as well as others.

- What are some of Brandi's messages that have relevance to your life?
- How does Brandi's attitude and perspective inspire you?
- Do you see yourself in how Brandi responded to life's unexpected circumstances?
- What did you take away from Brandi's story that you can apply today?
- Is there someone in your life who would benefit from reading Brandi's story?

⌒

Brandi's charity of choice for her story contribution is Everytown for Gun Safety. Their motto is "We have a plan to end gun violence." Learn more at www.everytown.org.

⌒

Additional Resources

Healing after Loss: Daily Meditations for Working through Grief, Martha Whitmore Hickman, New York, NY: Avon Books, 1994.

I Wasn't Ready to Say Goodbye: Surviving, Coping and Healing after the Sudden Death of a Loved One, Brook Noel and Pamela Blair, Naperville, IL: 2008.

Your Grief, Your Way: A Year of Practical Guidance and Comfort after Loss, Shelby Forsythia, New York, NY: Zeitgeist, 2020.

CHAPTER THREE

Bravely Facing a Loss

When we cross the threshold, we have a new worldview because we faced our fears and difficulties. This is all you can do now: Serenity in the storm. Keep calm, pray everyday. Make a habit of meeting the sacred everyday. Show resistance through art, joy, trust and love.
—HOPI INDIAN CHIEF WHITE EAGLE

You may have heard of Dr. Elizabeth Kübler-Ross, the Swiss-American psychiatrist and author of the internationally best-selling book *On Death and Dying*. Dr. Kübler-Ross's research and work with dying patients found that the patients' experiences and their emotional process of dying was not being acknowledged or named. A social worker friend of mine told me a story about going to a lecture in the mid-1970s, where Dr. Kübler-Ross brought onstage a very young cancer patient in a wheelchair. Dr. Ross asked the child directly if anyone at the hospital had ever talked to her before about the fact that she was dying. The child said no. She said she saw her parents and the hospital staff tip-toeing around and trying to be positive and cheerful. Yet she also observed sadness, and saw that her parents were upset when they thought she could not see or hear them. The girl would observe that her mother had been crying and wondered why her brother and other loved ones and friends were not allowed to visit her.

This young cancer patient felt like she had done something bad and that it was her fault she kept getting sick and returning to the hospital. This very sick child was left dealing with not only the physical pain of having cancer and its treatment but also the emotional pain of being isolated and blaming herself.

No one told her what was happening to her body. Dr. Kübler-Ross had been the only person who told the child that she was dying of cancer. When she asked the child what her reaction had been when the doctor told her that her disease could not be fixed and that she was dying, the child said she was sad but that things finally made sense. She now knew why her parents were upset and tearful, why she kept returning to the hospital, and why she continued to be in so much pain. The child wasn't happy she was dying, but she was relieved to know what was happening to her and that it was not her fault.

The audience was shocked not only that Dr. Kübler-Ross had brought an extremely sick child on the stage but also that she had told the child she was dying. Up until that point, talking about cancer or any other type of terminal disease or illness was off limits and discouraged. The prevailing approach at the time was to not talk about death, to pretend and sanitize this normal part of life, to keep it away from the patient and society. Just the word "cancer" was forbidden, and people usually talked about it in hushed tones, as if saying the word would awaken a monster.

By naming and claiming what was happening, this child was able to step into her reality instead of being in the dark.

The acknowledgment of loss answered something within her. It connected her to her situation, whereas before, she had been living in a smokescreen of avoidance because her parents were in so much grief that they couldn't bear to tell her. They thought they were protecting her, and most likely themselves, from the sad reality of their child's impending death.

LOSSES ARE NORMAL

One of the most effective ways to move through loss is to normalize it.

Loss and the accompanying aftermath are natural and normal processes that happen all the time. We are taught to look at these events as aberrations, as going against what should happen. We think, if this loss hadn't happened, then I would be happy. The loss becomes the villain in the story, the stain that won't go away. When the stain won't go away—when we can't bring someone back from the dead, when we can't control an outcome—then we feel hopeless, lost, confused, and that things will never be the same. When we think losses should never happen, we ask, why me?

Why Me?

We only know the reality that we have experienced, and when that reality is altered in some way, our worldview shifts.

Many of us believe that we are doomed to have losses in our lives because of a loss or losses we've had before. We feel that we deserve it for some unknown reason, and the "why me" expression looms large in our hearts. If we weren't feeling great about ourselves to begin with, then everything that happens to us is run through a "why me" filter, and we experience life through this victimhood narrative. The false belief becomes the negative-slanting lens through which we see the world. *Of course this happened to me. These things always happen to me.*

Some of us are taught the false narrative that when something bad happens to us, it means that we are bad, we are at fault, we should have known better, or we could have done something to help make the outcome better. We blame ourselves, thinking that we should have known the company board was deciding on a layoff or that the idea of divorce was floating out there. We believe we should have anticipated the event and protected ourselves from the loss. We internalize and intellectualize the loss experience as a moral failing, with an insecure, guilty conscience informing this skewed narrative. Alternatively, we may lash out and blame others for the loss.

For some, this sense of internal shame and sadness becomes a harsh judge and jury. We think about how or what we could have done differently. This shame and sadness become linked with the loss event. We feel bad, we want it to go away, we don't want anyone to know about it. If it's really bad, we just want the earth to swallow us up. A present-day loss event can also trigger an unresolved inner child wounding. All of this piles on top of the festering, unaddressed feelings in our loss bucket, generating confusion and emotions that come out sideways.

We can't control everything that happens to us or others, and unfortunately, we sometimes make choices that, directly or indirectly, lead to a loss. Life happens, and we respond based on everything we know at that moment. We can shut down and ignore the loss, or we can choose to respond with forgiveness, gentleness, and kindness to ourselves.

Once we've gone through a loss and experienced a shift in our known reality, the task before us is to determine what we make of our time remaining in this world now that we are wiser.

When people who are in a lot of pain come to see me, one of the kindest things that I tell them is that they are not alone. This simple expression, letting them know they are not alone in their pain, is comforting for them to hear; it is comforting for all of us to hear. Realizing that others have gone through or feel the same way we do is incredibly validating and reassuring. Of course, we don't want people to be in pain, but knowing that others have experienced a similar pain and gotten through it can be deeply comforting. We each feel and interpret pain differently. If someone doesn't understand, or they think you shouldn't be feeling pain over a loss, they are projecting and implying that they wouldn't feel pain in this circumstance. The pain you feel over your loss is your pain, and it deserves respect even if it doesn't make sense to others.

We can't change history, but we can change how we experience the now.

The message here is to learn to put the loss into a context that protects us from getting so lost in grief that we can't live our lives. When the pain of loss is normalized, we begin to have a sense that whatever happened was normal. It's normal for things to break, it's normal for people to make choices we disagree with, it's normal for people to die, and it's normal to have the feelings we have. We may not like it, but our minds can put loss in this context, and then we can give our hearts permission to follow. Our minds set the intention and structure for how we comprehend and flow through and with loss. Our self-compassionate hearts do the heavy lifting of the weightier emotions.

EMOTIONAL REACTIONS TO LOSS

Despair is the absence of hope.

Emotional reactions to loss often show up as betrayal, anguish, guilt, despair, disbelief, anger, denial, numbness, hurt, bewilderment, freedom, or deserving, among others. You may read this list of common emotional reactions to loss and connect with the word "betrayal," immediately remembering a loss experience with this feeling. Or maybe you read the word "guilt" and can't imagine how someone would feel guilty from a loss. But all of these reactions happen and are normal. Sometimes we know what we feel when a loss happens, and sometimes it takes a while to figure it out. We may feel one way at the beginning of a loss cycle and completely different at the end of the cycle.

Many people tell me of losses that happened like they are rattling off a grocery list: *In the past year my father died, I lost my job, and my kid dropped out of college.* They robotically recite the inventory of their losses; they aren't connected to the immensity and depth of the emotional experience and haven't named the feelings associated with the losses. They often feel beat up by these significant losses, but they learned at some point to push down and push through, disconnecting from the event and the feelings associated with it. They can recall this inventory of loss, but there are layers of cotton between themselves and their emotions, as if acknowledging the loss would destroy them or throw them off course, that they would be crushed under the weight of their grief and sadness. They will often say they don't want to go there yet. They can feel the heaviness of the loss, however, it becomes harder to ignore.

When we acknowledge a loss,
a part of us feels vindicated and seen.
From here, we can begin our healing work.

We get caught up in the distracted doing, fixing, or dealing with the fallout but avoid the tough part of acknowledging what's in our loss bucket. Referring to the earlier example of people with multiple losses, I will say to them, "Wow, you've had a number of losses this last year." They will often reply, "You're right, I guess a lot has happened." They obviously know that, but they are so caught up in the shockwave that they immediately try to get things back on course; they don't take the time to honor the losses and name what they are feeling. In the same vein, I will ask someone who is depressed why they think they are depressed, but they don't have any conscious knowledge of how or why. This is usually the symptom of a constellation of unacknowledged losses.

Most people do not consciously try to avoid looking at the loss so much as they just don't want to feel bad anymore because the shockwave was so hard to go through. We have family obligations or have to get back to work or can't take any more time off. The daily grind of a busy life puts a hold on addressing everything in our loss bucket. This manifests as denial, avoidance, and silent fear. We fear looking at our losses, so we pave over them and make the excuses: *I don't have time to be sad. I have a business to run and kids to raise.* Grieving doesn't fit into the expected routines of being a parent, spouse, or employee. Losses are supremely inconvenient.

Naming a Loss

When we acknowledge our feelings, we are in the flow of life. Our feelings are messengers. When we shut ourselves off from feelings, we restrict the flow.

When we bravely name a loss, it becomes real. We can't play games with it and deny that it happened anymore. Loss is disappointing and disorienting. We don't want to look at it or feel it, we just want to be over the shock, trauma, anger, and sadness. However, once we pull a loss out of the loss bucket and name the feelings around it, then we can claim and control the process that we are moving through. Sometimes our feelings are overwhelming and we feel consumed by them, but we are not our feelings. When we face how we feel, we become in charge of the process and can decide how we want to express the feeling.

The following are some examples of what naming a loss looks like:

I am so sad the car got dented up today.

I feel so gutted and alone because my brother died.

I feel frustrated that no matter what I try, nothing seems to be working.

I'm disgusted and hurt that they lied to me again.

I feel lost and abandoned because they left me.

When we put our feelings into words, we honor ourselves. When we take the time to truly understand our feelings, the words we choose to describe them may be different from words we've used in the past. Taking the time to understand ourselves brings a sense of internal clarity. We may begin to relate to ourselves in a new way as a result of the internal work we do as we find our wisdom. When we give some thought to what we are going through, we become more intentional with our words because we understand at a deep level that words have power. We are more cognizant of the words that reflect our feelings.

Joining with Loss

The joy of life and everyday living has to be part of the healing process. –Olivia Newton-John

At the moment of loss, we can choose how we move through it, even though everything feels like it's spinning out of control. By centering ourselves and being conscious of our perspective, we can bring a sense of control, establish a sense of safety, and eventually, design a plan for our recovery. If we are given a scary prognosis for a disease, for example, we can either shut down and retreat from life or live each day to its fullest. We can be engaged in the process and consciously choose hope in how we move through the experience, holding a space for loss and life at the same time.

Healthy Expressions along the Path

There are many healthy ways to express our experience of loss. The following are examples of healthy choices you can make to be in control of your plan of hope and your level of engagement. If you are going through a tough situation right now, see how you can apply these concepts, and remember this list when something comes up in the future and you need some guideposts to help you along the way. Read these suggestions from a place of gentle awareness of your current situation.

Be aware of and acknowledge that the loss has happened, even though it's painful. Check in with yourself each day as to what you need, then fill that need or ask for it to be filled.

Give yourself permission to honor the feelings you have each day; cry when you feel like crying, be alone when you feel like being alone, and so on. Express to others how you feel; name and claim what happens with you each day.

Honor the place of importance the loss has in your life at this moment; consider the thoughts, prayers, or intentions you need to demonstrate to honor the loss. Acknowledge that there is a valid reason you feel sad and don't have any motivation.

Understand that old habits of coping may come up; see if you can gently guide yourself to make a better choice than acting out with destructive behaviors that don't help. If you have acted out, see it for what it is so you can make better choices the next time you are tempted.

Understand that as you move through loss, each day will look and feel different; be gentle with and nonjudgmental of yourself when you feel like you're being inconsistent and all over the place. Feel the weight and depth of the loss ease up and lift from you as time goes on. Over time, realize that the loss has a place and perhaps a purpose in the tapestry of your life.

Wounded Expressions along the Path

If the loss is too painful and confusing to hold, you may ignore the hope and move through the loss unconsciously, becoming disengaged from the process. The following are some wounded examples of what you might do when you disengage, avoid hope, and fall into despair.

Denying, pushing down, or ignoring the loss. Disregarding emotional signals that you are in pain: crying unexpectedly, having fits of rage or anger, shutting down or isolating, looking for a target to attack.

Disregarding physical signs that you are in pain: frequent headaches, nightmares, or interrupted sleep patterns; stress or pain in your shoulders, lower back, or neck; clenching your jaws or grinding your teeth.

Minimizing or dismissing when others see the loss for what it is; for example, you quickly reassure others so you and they can move on from the loss, you tell yourself that you have to move on or get over it, or you have the false belief that pushing the feelings down will make them go away.

Ignoring tasks that need to be done, such as filing for death benefits, dealing with papers from lawyers or insurance companies, and opening condolence cards. Acting out emotions with go-to coping skills such as overeating, overdrinking, overspending, or sleeping too much.

Adopting the narrative of "poor me" so you don't have to go any deeper in looking at, feeling, or working through your loss. Feeding off the sympathy of others and letting them hold and feel your pain instead of working through your grief yourself. Making big or rash decisions as a way to jump out of a feeling or a reality that you don't want to hold, feel, or experience.

When we engage in these avoidance behaviors, whatever was not healed before will be magnified. For example, if your marriage was in trouble before the loss, all of the cracks are going to get even bigger afterward. If you were struggling with depression before, you're probably going to feel extremely sad. If you had family drama before, everything that was buried will come back loud and unfiltered. Remember that you are in control of how you choose to bravely face your loss as you learn what wounded and healthy expressions looks like. Be gentle with yourself if you recognize a wounded response coming forward. This is a part of you that's hurting and looking for a voice.

(To read more about functional and wounded expressions, see my book *Healing Your Lost Inner Child: How to Stop Impulsive Reactions, Set Healthy Boundaries and Embrace an Authentic Life*, available at your local library or bookstore.)

ANTICIPATING A LOSS

Emotional hurts don't always go away just because time marches on. They sit languishing in the dark as we tell ourselves stories about how "it's not that bad."

Anticipating a loss is when we feel or know an event is approaching that will lead to a life change. We have a hunch or an intuition that a loss may happen, or we see clearly that a loved one is in decline. We begin to make note of things that are happening that are different from before. Anticipation of a loss leads us into the grieving cycle.

When my mother fell and had a traumatic brain injury more than a decade ago, she recovered beautifully with the help of dedicated staff at a trauma hospital. I was so proud of her as she fought hard to regain her speech and motor functioning. Miraculously, she was released after five weeks with many of her faculties restored, and she began to live her life again. However, shortly after returning home, she had a massive stroke that affected her right side. As with her valiant effort to get her motor and cognitive functioning back after her traumatic brain injury, she was diligent with her therapies. My dad tirelessly assisted her with the activities of daily living.

It was hard for me to see my mom struggle, but it was also inspiring to see her fight so hard to regain functioning. During this time, I hadn't realized how painful it was for me to see her this way. I also didn't realize that I was unconsciously anticipating her death. Selfishly, I wanted my mother back as she was so we could communicate and do things that we had always done together. When I wasn't with her, I pretended that she was getting better, that what had happened as a result of the stroke wasn't that bad. But when I visited her, I saw her struggle to do even basic things. These visits began to wear down my denial but also helped me to accept the loss of my mom as I had previously known her. After two years of fighting to regain her functioning, my mom died from other complications. To say I was beyond grief would not adequately describe my sorrow and anguish.

The shockwave of her death threw me into a tailspin of anger and sorrow. I desperately missed her and felt sorry for myself. For the two years leading up to her death, I was unconsciously integrating this idea of loss. I was thinking, she may never be the same, she looks different now, and she can't do any of these things again. Although her death was a shock, it wasn't necessarily unexpected, but inside I was kicking and screaming and saying, no, this can't be. She had gently begun to prepare herself, and certainly the family, for the unwanted. I believe that, even though watching her decline was painful, this anticipatory grief helped me start the grief process more so than if she had died suddenly.

In many ways, anticipating a loss is a gift in disguise, as it allows us to subconsciously join with the grieving process even as we are in a state of suspended animation. We want to move on with our lives, yet we don't know what to do when this loss is on the horizon. We know something is coming, just not when, where, or how.

Many people I talk to are going through an anticipatory grief experience, but they don't see it as such. They are lost in what is happening and caught up in what they need to do. A part of them is fearful to recognize that what is happening is a version of loss, a portent of things to come. They try to stay positive and hopeful, to not get sidetracked in what they perceive as a negative. Not until things start to get really bad do they give themselves permission to accept that this is really happening and that they're scared. In a way, anticipatory grieving is a long stretch. We try to stay hopeful and, at the same time, wake up, pay attention, and release the daydream of denial.

Anticipating a loss and starting the grieving process can also show up when we feel at a deep level that a relationship is failing, that we and our partner, or maybe a friend, are no longer in the same place we used to be, that the relationship is shifting. We are preparing ourselves for a transition, such as whether to stay together or move apart. There's lump in the throat that we wish wasn't there, but we understand all the things that brought us to this point. In a flash, we see where we were and where we are in the present.

When we anticipate a loss, many internal processes are happening that we may be unaware of. We try to gain control over the situation because we can feel change coming. We futurecast or project what will happen by making up stories. We begin to worry about choices we've made, and start to have regrets. We clearly see others entering into a period of loss and wonder where it will lead for them. We want to run away because we know something bad is coming, but we are caught on a nonstop merry-go-round. We don't have the same energy or drive as before because we know something is off. We pick up on the idea that there will a layoff at work. All of these are made-up stories based on a small fact we cling to as we try desperately to feel in control.

Many normal feelings arise when we anticipate a loss, such as having a sinking feeling; feeling frozen as we watch events unfold; feeling shocked, worried, or alone; pretending things are okay when they are not; feeling uncertain of the future; feeling out of control; being distracted; not knowing what or whom to trust; and second-guessing ourselves and others, especially medical professionals. When this happens, we can remember to trust our instincts and what we sense, as this part is wiser than the conscious mind. This is the higher self that holds our wisdom, a patient and knowing guide who watches the play unfold. To get it right, we can separate this wisdom from our fears and hold it with a sense of balance.

Brave Acceptance

> *Losing your first parent is a comma;*
> *losing your second parent is a period.*
> *—Melissa Rivers*

After my mom died, my dad slowly began to pick up the pieces and construct a new life as a widower. He had a great friend group, and he eventually began dating a wonderful lady who was a family friend, a widow herself, whom both my parents knew in their social circles. He was living his best life and always approached each day with a sense of optimism, wanting to have fun and be around people. Sadly, various health issues that he had ignored came to the forefront and necessitated immediate attention. This quickly led to his admission to the hospital for stabilization and evaluation. His decline advanced rapidly, and my dad went from being independent to being incapacitated.

A couple of weeks before he died, he was in the intensive care unit and began having multiple organ failures. My sister and I were able to clearly communicate with him what was happening and what his choices were. One morning, when the doctors were talking about feeding tubes and dialysis and some other procedures that he would have to endure, my dad motioned for a piece of paper. He wrote *No Tubes*. It was a clear directive of what he wanted. I didn't want to admit to myself that this was the beginning of his end, but a big part of me already knew what was about to happen.

In retrospect, my dad gave my sister and me such a gift by letting us know of his wishes. I knew he didn't want to die, but when I explained that he couldn't go back to the life he had had just a week before, he made clear that he didn't want a life of dependence, either. My dad was so brave in that moment, facing a decision that none of us can imagine. He showed me how to honor myself even when I am faced with death. He showed me how strong he was, and I respect him so much for his courage. My sister and I reassured him that we believed we would see him again in heaven, and he held on to our every word. Our dad died peacefully in his sleep in the hospital just as my sister and I returned from a short respite. Now I see that being with him in this decision-making process has helped me greatly with the grief and healing process. In many ways, he guided us through the grief journey.

My dad didn't want his friends or most of the family to know that he was in such decline. My sister and I honored his wishes, and we told only a few family members about his status. After he died, many of his friends were mad that my sister and I had not told them he was close to death, as they hadn't had a chance to say goodbye. They took their anger out on us because they weren't able to anticipate the loss. To his friends, my dad died suddenly; many of them had been out to breakfast with him just a month prior.

My sister and I were overwhelmed by all of the questions coming at us, as it was too much to repeat the story multiple times a day. We let everyone know that we would give the timeline of what happened with our dad's health when we were at the funeral home. We also explained that we were honoring what our dad had wanted and that he left this earth on his terms. Thank God for my sister, as she helped me to not feel alone in the process. My heart goes out to any adult child who doesn't have a sibling to be with them when a parent dies.

> *When we acknowledge loss, we give it the respect it deserves and a place in the arc of our lives.*

The message from my story is to be patient with yourself and others when you are anticipating a loss. Use this time to prepare yourself as best you can for what you know or feel is coming. If someone in your life has a terminal disease or illness, then begin to spend more time with them and tell them those things you've wanted to say. Ask them direct questions, and don't shy away from the tough decisions regarding their wishes for ceremonies or burial. Be proactive and simplify your life so you can be present with them during the time they have left. Determine what is important in the moment, and practice being in the now. And if someone is very private, like my dad, respect their wishes.

THE FIVE STAGES OF GRIEF

> *Weeping is perhaps the most human and universal of all relief measures. –Dr. Karl Menninger*

As you read at the beginning of the chapter, Dr. Elizabeth Kübler-Ross published her seminal work on grief in her book

On Death and Dying. Dr. Kübler-Ross developed her theory on the five stages of grief and loss primarily for the dying patient. As she gave lectures to healthcare professionals, however, many began to see how they could also use these five stages to support those who are caring for the dying person or grieving after a loss.

The original five stages Dr. Kübler-Ross developed are not to be thought of as a linear path but as a five-pointed star. The stages are denial, anger, bargaining, depression, and acceptance. These stages can apply to any type of grief or loss that occurs at any point in our lives. The stages are not linear; you may go through only two stages, for example, or you may not feel any of them at all. Use this concept simply as a reference point. Your grief process is your own.

Each stage has its own meaning within the process of grief, and one is not more important than another. They each play a vital role by identifying or giving a name to what the person going through the loss is experiencing in a given moment. A grieving person can experience one, some, or all of the stages on any given day. They can bounce from one stage to another, feeling calm and accepting in the morning and consumed with anger and resentment in the afternoon. They can even feel like they are in two stages at once.

The following is a hybrid description of each stage of grief, based on my modifications of Dr. Kübler-Ross's theory. If you are in a process of grief and loss, see if you can identify the stages that stand out for you and where you are now.

Denial—Denial is the incredible ability we have of not recognizing a loss because it scares us so much. It is when we push away the reality that a loss is about to happen, is happening, or just happened. We can get stuck in denial for a long time, but in my experience, even those who hold tightly to denial begin to experience cracks in this illusion as time goes on. In other words, logically denying that the loss happened becomes harder to do, and the reality is self-evident. Kübler-Ross writes in *On Death and Dying*, "Denial functions as a buffer after unexpected shocking news, allows the patient to collect himself, and, with time, mobilize other, less radical defenses." It is our desperate attempt to abandon and discard an unfortunate and uncomfortable truth about ourselves or someone else. We taste the bitter edges of the truth, turn away, and then wait to take another bite. Denial gives us some space to gradually acknowledge that something bad has happened or may happen.

Anger—Anger is fear under great pressure. It is a primal emotion that mobilizes defensive feelings we can't consciously name because our grief is so loud and overwhelming. Our expression of anger means that we are engaged with our emotions, getting them out instead of stuffing them down. Being angry isn't the goal, but for many, it's better than not expressing any emotion at all. The goal is to understand, in time, what is underneath the anger expression, whether hurt, sadness, fear, or some other painful feeling. Anger is a gift as we go through loss because it gives us an outlet for the emotions we feel but do not fully understand.

Grabbing the emotion of anger is easy because it allows us to feel more in control, but this emotion is a false front that protects a much more tender feeling. One day we're angry, the next, we're in a puddle of tears. But when we get stuck in anger, we also get stuck in the fear of facing deeper feelings. We do in fact feel anger, but since we just had a loss, we think we should feel sadness instead. Anger can be a protective armor, but when we hold on to and overuse it, we become burdened with it. What once shielded and protected us becomes a bulky, false illusion of safety.

The message here is to get the emotion out no matter you're feeling, and then assess what your feelings are. Anger repeatedly pushed down turns into a dull, numbing, unexpressive, lingering pain that doesn't have a voice and can manifest as depression. You will read more about how to process your feelings of loss in chapter nine, "Practical Tools for Honoring Loss."

Bargaining—I should have . . . If only . . . Why didn't I . . .? These are the words we say over and over as we try to rescue, resuscitate, re-do, or repair the loss, or save ourselves from death or some other undesired outcome. Bargaining happens in real time during a loss when you are the one who is dying. You start negotiating with God, the fates, or some other power to help you. Bargaining is the exchange the soul makes with fated destiny, crying out: If only . . . Just one more chance . . . What if . . .

Bargaining can also happen after a loss, when those who are left scramble to pick up a thousand pieces. Often fueled by guilt, the process of bargaining engages our minds so that we think we are doing something about the loss. Our minds rummage through the bargaining questions, leading us to think we are in control. We tumble, over and over, all of the choices that could have created a different outcome. This grief-looping illusion is a temporary negotiation, a way to calm ourselves down and avoid facing the loss. It is part of the wall of cotton that separates us from feeling the pain of loss. This barrier stubbornly remains in our heads so we don't feel the heart's searing pain. This stage is a close cousin to denial, as both are stages where we flirt with the truthful reality of a situation. We struggle to find meaning for the loss.

Depression—The depression stage is when we begin to deeply feel our great, mournful sadness over the loss. Depression can feel like surrender or resignation. We fall into this heap of sadness after we are exhausted from the denial, bargaining, and anger. We may put off this stage because of the intensity we sense around this sadness.

When we are ready to feel, embrace, and honor our sadness, then the real work of reconnecting with ourselves begins. The gift we give ourselves over a loss is the permission to feel sorrowful and sad. When we can hold this sadness and feel it, we allow ourselves to experience what is natural and normal. But then we have to admit the unwanted conceit that if we feel sad, then it's real. Feeling sad and crying are how we finally acknowledge to ourselves that the loss occurred. At this point, we are no longer in our heads or playing games with reality; rather, we are in the sorrowful pit, feeling the pain and honoring this part of our emotional experience.

It's easy to get lost or stuck in this stage. If you feel you are stuck in the depression stage, please talk with someone who can help you sort through these complex feelings. Sadness has a place on our journey, but it's not the destination.

Acceptance—Acceptance is often seen as the goal in the healing process, but I think that in doing so, we discount the other beautiful parts of the grieving process. I see acceptance as the outcome of moving through some or all of the other steps multiple times. Taking time to honor all of our feelings in creative and open ways is what allows us to get to acceptance; it is the acknowledgment of the work we put in, but the value is in the work itself. Acceptance is the hard-won new-reality outcome of the grief and loss journey. It doesn't come easily, and there isn't some grand moment of fanfare when we suddenly feel it. Rather, it is the slow turning of time as we work through all the other stages and feelings that allows us to finally relinquish the struggle of accepting the loss and begin to embrace it. Someone once said to me in regard to his mother's dementia that he was not yet to acceptance, but he was no longer in denial. I thought it was a brilliant way of describing this in-between state in the grieving process.

Dr. Kübler-Ross explains acceptance in this way: "For someone who is dying, acceptance should not be mistaken for a happy stage. It is almost void of feelings. It is as if the pain had gone, the struggle is over . . . This is also the time during which the family needs usually more help, understanding, and support than the patient himself." Clients often ask me how they will know they no longer need therapy, and my response is, when you are no longer triggered by your wounding. This is what acceptance is, when you are no longer deeply triggered and upset by the experience or memory of your loss. You gently hold it, like a bird, in your hand, and the loss is what it is.

Feeling Stuck

> *Don't be afraid of your tears.*
> *They are the acknowledgment that*
> *something big has happened.*

We can get stuck in a grief loop during any one or all of these stages. I have a theory that we hold on to a particular moment that occurred during the loss because it is one of our last connections to the situation or person. We keep them "alive" by not moving on. Accepting that the situation is really bad, or that the person is dead, feels too final, so we keep going back into the process and rehashing it. I've known people to replay their loved one's last day over and over in their minds; it was the last time their loved was alive, so they jealously guard that last memory. But no one wants to be remembered with machines and tubes keeping them alive. Replaying these kinds of scenes is being stuck in denial, bargaining, anger, and sadness all at once. We go around and around on this five-pointed star as if we are in a tug-of-war with our pain. We wrestle with the sad reality as we try to regain control, comfort, and confidence. This is grief looping within the context of the five stages.

Take some time now to consider a loss experience that you have recently experienced. Using the five stages of denial, anger, bargaining, depression, and acceptance, what stage of grief do you think you are in? How long do you feel you have been in this stage? What is your intuition about what you need to move out of this emotional place? Do you feel you have acknowledged this loss, or are you pushing it down and ignoring it? Are you honoring the loss or discounting it? Remember that you can be in more than one stage at a time.

In later chapters, I will give you some tools to honor the loss and help you move on from this experience so it doesn't continue to impact your life. As you read, begin to look at your life in terms of things that are going well for you and things that you perceive as a loss. What can you do to begin acknowledging the unacknowledged losses? If you are stuck, reach out for help. You don't have to punish yourself through your grieving just because you miss your loved one so much.

The journey of significant loss is like floating in a stream. The energy of the current takes us along as it ebbs and flows to places unknown.

DIANA'S STORY:
TRANSCENDING A FIRE THROUGH WISDOM

Diana embodies living quietly in nature, respecting others, and walking lightly on the earth. She has lived a rich life as a pottery artist and permaculture wayshower, sharing beautiful flowers from her garden with those close to her heart. Her life journey has many chapters that include seminal events: she narrowly escaped assault in Tunis, North Africa; spent a tumultuous time in Central America; lost her husband; and lived through a massive fire, all of which asked that a deep and fiercely wise part of her respond in the now.

As you read Diana's story, you will get a sense of the rhythm and flow of this remarkable woman. True to her core, she is fully immersed in life with all of its highs and lows. To outsiders, she may appear to make the long view of her experiences look effortless and elegant, but on the inside, she survives and thrives by connecting to her unique inner wisdom.

Diana traveled extensively as a young woman, then lived with indigenous people of Central America, helping them sell handcrafted goods to tourists. It was during this time that she had to find an inner courage in ways that most of us cannot imagine, such as fending off revolutionaries and saving herself and others from assassination. For the last forty-some years, she has lived in a cabin discretely tucked inside a quiet, wooded valley, in close union with the earth. It was on this farm that a massive fire occurred, and once again Diana had to call on an internal strength and knowing to keep steady during this fire.

What follows is a conversation with Diana about many parts of her life, demonstrating how she experienced and responded to loss. First she details her time traveling and how these formative experiences impacted her worldview and her view of herself. Then she gives us a window into the fire that swept through her tranquil space, opening up a new landscape inside her heart in parallel with her healing burns and the renewal of the forest. Along the way, you will learn of some other loss events that she internally reframed and transformed with perspective and grace.

You have lived a well-traveled and interesting life. Can you please tell us a little about your background and the internal strengths you have called on to help you stay centered during times of loss?

I lived in Guatemala from 1978 to the end of 1981. I deeply bonded with native people there, more than I was able to bond with some friends in the United States. The social interaction with the indigenous people was my first real experience of community. All of the women were like the mother I'd never had. Their hearts, their beauty, and their relationship to the natural world were inspirations and confirmation of my beliefs. It was a thrilling experience. I built my own little hut and created a co-op to help the weavers get better pay for their work.

My experience in Guatemala taught me the preciousness of the land and its people. I learned the essential skills of living with the natural world: rhythm, patience, and heart. The Mayans demonstrated to me the ability to radiate kindness while standing ferociously for their truth and the dignity of their culture. I have been able to live so softly on the land here in the States only because I was taught by masters who live in a world of love, not fear.

There I was in my paradise when the Guatemalan army came in and began burning down people's houses. This was during the country's civil war, which devastated the indigenous Mayan communities; during the course of the war, 440 Mayan villages were destroyed. I had to hide men in my hut at night because the army was shooting men and dumping them into mass graves.

I looked in my mirror one day and I realized it was time for me to leave. I realized I couldn't do anything more for these people and that I was putting myself in grave danger. It was unbearable to witness and to feel so powerless. I couldn't help these people I loved with their weaving anymore, and everything was being locked down. I left Guatemala as a refugee in rivers of fire, blood, and water. There were fires behind me as I crept out of the country. A friend of mine invited me to Hawai'i, and that's where I went next.

The loss of my place in Guatemala is one of my life's greatest losses. When I returned to Oregon, I created a slide show that I presented in many places along the coast, educating people about what was happening to the beauty of this special land and culture.

How did you stay in the moment, keep focused and purposeful, and not become overwhelmed during your shocking and surprising life experiences?

I survived all of the losses through my commitment to live according to the teachings I had received in Guatemala. I shared these teachings through my work with permaculture in Tasmania and India, and my work on several farms in Hawai'i. Now I practice these principles on my own land. The Mayan people opened my heart and taught me my responsibility to choose love, even, and especially, in moments of crisis.

Another experience that stands out reinforced my trust in my intuition. My husband and I were in the northwest corner of Guatemala, in a town called Nebaj, which is near where the revolution started. There is a lot of beautiful weaving in Nebaj, and we were visiting the native artists, having a wonderful time enjoying the art and the natural beauty.

We were staying at a placed called the Pension de Las Tres Hermanas, the place of the three sisters. A lot of gringos stay there. One morning, while my husband was out, a dozen men in black outfits broke into the place in a surprise attack. They had automatic rifles with bayonets. They split up into pairs, and I remember them using the bayonets to break open the doors. They were yelling for all the gringos to get out and line up against a wall. I was shocked that everyone was just doing what they were told. I couldn't believe it.

You know what I did instead? I listened to my intuition and dove under the bed in our room. I hid there for forty-five minutes while the men with the guns yelled at everyone and told all the White people what assholes they were. Twenty people just stood there throughout the whole ordeal, terrified out of their minds. Nobody got shot, but it was a near thing. It was an experience that made clear to me the trustworthiness of my intuition and being smart enough to listen to it. My intuition kept me safe.

Another experience of completely trusting my intuition happened when I returned to Guatemala years later. I hadn't been to the country for a while, but I was so happy to be back and walking around, enjoying the natural beauty. I was walking to town along one of the many well-trodden paths that one can take. There was a pathway up to the left, and I had a feeling that I didn't want to take it. I could see that it went up to a house a few hundred yards off. I was walking along the other branch of the path when, all of a sudden, three dogs came barreling down at me, barking, snarling, and drooling. I calmly turned around and walked away. I realized the dogs were catching up to me, so I bent my knees a little, like you do in a tai chi stance. I put my arms out in front of me, whirled toward those dogs with all the energy I had, and *YELLED*. I don't know what I yelled, but those dogs stopped in their tracks. When I got home, my friend's son said those dogs can kill people.

That's the closest to death or severe injury that I've ever been. That event made clear to me to stay present in the moment and listen to my intuition. If I had gone into a space of fear and had run, it would have ended very differently. By staying in the moment and listening to my intuition, I was able to avoid a pretty awful outcome.

Fire Energy

A couple of years ago, an electrical short in the large equipment barn sparked a massive fire on Diana's property. Diana was alone at the farm when the fire started and was deeply concerned about the old-growth woods and her beloved valley. The raging flames quickly engulfed the barn and parts of the garden, eventually burning more than three acres of forest before it was extinguished.

Diana received second-degree burns on her face while fighting the blaze before the firetrucks arrived. Eventually, twenty-five fire engines arrived, and dozens of firefighters worked to get the fire under control. Old-growth tree roots can smolder underground and rekindle a wildfire, so Forest Service personnel remained on the property for a full five days to make sure the fire was completely out. The process of making everything safe after getting the main blaze under control was both exhausting and nerve-racking for everyone involved.

After the fire, Diana's once-quiet valley was filled with dense smoke, ash, and soot. Some of the trees, property, and outbuildings were total losses. The soothing forest now looked like a charred war zone.

As she began to process the trauma of the experience, Diana expressed her profound gratitude to the firefighters and others who came from the Forest Service; their efforts helped keep the surrounding old-growth forest she loves from being lost to the blaze.

Most people have no idea what to do when an experience like a fire begins because they're in shock. What were your feelings when you realized the fire had started?

There was no time for feelings! I just had to focus. I had been away from the barn area, eating lunch and taking a swim in the stream. When I came back in view of the barn, it was in flames up to the sky. I immediately called my nephew to alert all help. The roaring, crackling fire was instantly threatening everything on our land. I began commanding in my loudest voice, "Angels, angels, help me, help me!" I repeated this mantra as I dragged a hose, with ever-decreasing water pressure, back and forth, trying to save our orchard, until help arrived forty-five minutes later. Dragging the hose did little good, yet I believe the chanting helped save the orchard.

We instinctively go into a crisis response mode when our survival is at stake. Was there a part of you that stayed calm and focused, or was every part of you activated?

I received second-degree burns while dragging the dribbling water hose, which was literally melting as I worked, but chanting my command to the angels and doing what I could with the hose helped me hold on to a calmness and focus.

During the fire, did you ever stop to think about how devastating it could be?

I never considered the power of the heat. The most terrifying aspect of the experience was when the fire jumped the road. The fire began burning in three places in the forest on the hill sweeping up out of the valley. All I could think of was the vast, magnificent forest that I didn't want destroyed. During the five days that the fire burned and smoldered, only three acres burned. If the surrounding forest had caught on fire, my strength and courage would have been lost.

What or who did you call on within yourself to help you stay centered and focused?

My essential survival tool is a faith in a power greater than myself. The fire was so intense and unbelievable, and we were lucky that it didn't burn down the forest. The major losses with the barn could be replaced, but if the forest had burned down, that could have taken me over the edge. I could only see the fire as transformational, as I've seen all of life's crises.

You worked hard to save parts of your property, and the fire service later commented that it was through much of your

effort that more was not lost. How did their presence and
work help you navigate this experience?

The fire happened in August, so the major fire season hadn't yet started. With the vast timberland above the farm, all available resources were directed to combat the blaze. I will never forget seeing twenty-five fire trucks in the farm's pasture for five days.

What were your feelings and thoughts toward the fire service
as you watched them work so hard to put out the fire?

I was, and am, overwhelmingly grateful. One detail I will always remember is when my nephew put together water lines so all the responders could get showers as they worked tirelessly to save the forest.

You experienced physical challenges after the fire, and your
face suffered second-degree burns. What was it like to wear
this physical reminder of the fire?

All I felt, and feel, is gratitude. My nephew's wife is a nurse. She came out every evening to change the dressings on my burns and apply healing balm to my face. Kindness in all its forms is its own gentle miracle. I'm sure there was also some form of shock that tempered the experience because I did not have any physical pain. I came out the other side without any scars from the burns. I did get some damage to my vocal chords, as I was yelling over the incredibly loud roar and crackle of the fire.

What were your feelings as you looked out over the farm
after the fire and saw the smoldering ruins?

I slept the whole night. It wasn't my first rodeo. What I had created myself—the cabin, the studio, the orchard, the view of my garden—those remained in beauty. I saw the whole area of the burn as an opportunity for my nephew to later create his own expressions, as he will one day have this farm.

Were there items that were important to you before the fire and then became trivial or insignificant afterward?

I had many irreplaceable treasures stored in the barn, all lost. Being a traveler teaches one to let go. Letting go is always expensive.

The fire happened after you turned seventy years old. Did you ever think, why now or why me?

I learned long ago not to take the victim stance. Transform what happened and change the memory into an ally to walk the road beside you. There was a time in my forties when I had a lot of temper tantrums; consider the challenges of living alone, off the grid, with much to maintain. But the tantrums never seemed to help, so I'm over that. Transformation works better.

What was it like to experience this kind of loss at a mature age?

My husband had drowned ten years before the fire, when I was sixty. He was fishing at a place on the ocean where he had fished for forty years. With him was Dave, his twenty-three-year-old friend from work. Dave was a state wrestling champion and nationally ranked wrestler. It was noon on a beautiful day that later became quite stormy. They had expected to be back with their catch some-time in the afternoon.

At nine-thirty that night I called Dave's girlfriend; we had already talked earlier that day. There was still no news, so I went out in that stormy night and found my husband's Subaru, right where he always parked it when he went fishing. I knew instantly that they were both gone forever because one of those powerhouses would have clawed his way up the bank and gotten help if he could.

A small search party went out in the storm that night, then a major one went out early the next morning, once the weather at sea had cleared. I just sat quietly on the sidelines because I already *knew*. I took a month off, and visitors came from the compassionate community almost every day. That event was as shocking as any of the losses I've been through in my life, but I choose joy, love, and beauty as my truth.

What wisdom did you carry into this loss experience that you would not have had when you were younger?

There are many wisdom traditions. My husband was from a family of cowboys, and I relied on cowboy wisdom: Ya gotta play the cards yer dealt. In some ways, the focus on easing the passing of my still-living mother shortly after his death helped me stay busy and move through the aftermath; reaching within to find the energy to be kind as my spirit dealt with the shock was, and is, transformational.

How was your self-care after the fire? Were you in a state of shock, or were you able to do some basic things for yourself?

I received much compassion and help, including financial, from family and friends. The generosity was inspirational. I received it all and could rest for a week. Choosing to find gratitude and stay positive magnetizes the help one needs.

Did you ever feel depressed, depleted, or exhausted, feeling that you couldn't carry on and rebuild?

Always forward, never back. My nephew and I are committed to holding the positive for ourselves and this farm. One always has a choice.

You've lived on this land for more than four decades and know it so well. Now, a couple of years after the fire, how do you look at your land, your garden, and your farm?

This land is in trust for my nephew. The fire opened an opportunity for him to create his own expression, which made things easier to accept. My view of the land remains pristine.

Did the fire experience help you to eliminate unhelpful processes such as negative self-talk and limiting beliefs?

These last couple of years have brought me some long moments of introspection. I have been able to identify abundant negative self-talk and limiting beliefs. Moving through challenging experiences can reveal great inner strength, which then illuminates hidden negatives. My confidence is far more solid. I didn't feel like the fire was some sort of totality of my accumulated life experience; I was already aware, and that helped me through both the fire and the reflections it left in me afterward.

What did the fire experience teach you?

As I write this, I realize I've faced many challenges and frightening situations. I can be vulnerable to anxiety, but I don't back down in a true emergency. I will find a way through. The ability to let go is essential. When we are in a crisis, we have no idea what the outcome will be; all we can know for sure and carry on forever is the knowledge that we gave 100 percent of what we had to give at the time. Fear of danger will never keep us safe. We need to accept the danger of fear. Choose love and stay alert.

Was there a wayshower or an inspirational person in your life whom you looked to for help in getting you through this experience?

I looked to my nephew. There was an excavator in the barn that burned down. An excavator is a large piece of ground-moving and clearing equipment, a cousin of a tractor. The one that was in the barn at the time of the fire was a blackened pile of melted slag. The second day after the fire, my nephew bought a larger one and began clearing up the debris. That was an inspiration to me. He just kept rolling on, even though this was costing him money, time, and energy. It was the affirmation that this is how we are going to work together to move forward. It strengthened my confidence in myself and my higher power. I also have a deeper confidence that my family can weather any storm here.

What would you say was the message from the fire energy that swept through your land?

The message from the fire energy is part of a lifetime chorus of, "Stay in love. Stay positive." By staying positive, I was connecting to what I had learned over and over throughout my life: to choose love. When I saw those fires burning, I called on whatever energies were available to help me, including my higher power and my creative vision. I wasn't going to lose my center. I was tired. I don't have time to do that anymore. Always forward, never back. I've been building my bedrock my whole life.

It sounds like you've always been on a spiritual quest. How did you develop this deep spiritual core that has sustained you for your entire adult life?

I was born into a family with a skeptical worldview, as my father was an attorney and was so skeptical. When I was quite young, he would try to explain things to me, protect me from illusion. I was told that I was an outsider and that I looked at things differently from the way my friends and siblings saw them, but I just wanted to fit in. I knew I couldn't figure it out by staying where I grew up. I knew that I needed to leave and go to college, as this represented freedom for me. College meant I could learn to be who I truly was.

I first went to Occidental College in Pasadena, California, then transferred to the University of California, Berkeley. While in Berkeley I discovered a bookstore that carried Shambhala publications, books on such topics as spiritualism and personal growth. I would stay there all day and read those books filled with knowledge, all the spiritual treasures. Shambhala books were the greatest affirmation of who I was, my beliefs, and what my path was. This was the spiritual teaching I had been searching for, and it confirmed my life path. Carlos Castaneda writes in one of his Don Juan books about how allies will appear as enemies, but if you face them, then they become your allies, they come behind you in support. This is exactly what I told myself when I got cancer. This was my life's path. In *The Teachings of Don Juan: A Yaqui Way of Knowledge*, Castaneda writes: "Fear is the first natural enemy a man must overcome on his path to knowledge. Besides, you are curious. That evens up the score. And you will learn in spite of yourself; that's the rule. . . . Never abandon yourself to fear."

Most people feel transformed after they go through a crisis. Fire energy destroys, transmutes, and creates the opportunity for rebirth. How did the fire transform your relationship to impermanence?

When I was twenty-one I was diagnosed with malignant melanoma. I went to the doctor one day, he discovered the cancer, and at nine o'clock the next morning I was on the operating table. Even at that age, I was determined that the experience would be a transformational force, and it was. I've studied health and healing my whole life. The experience at twenty-one was a benchmark of the beginning of my resilience, and I've cultivated it ever since.

What other experiences have you had where you had to dig deep to find your survivor self, your resilient self?

After I graduated but before the melanoma was discovered, I took a bicycle trip with my husband in North Africa. We were at the train station in Tunis. We needed to go farther to connect with a ferry and had a wait of four hours at the train station. Some nice guys met us there. They invited us back to their house and made us lunch.

I don't know how this happened, but somehow they got my husband in one room and me in a separate room. Each of them came in with an intention toward me. I decided that I needed to become really happy, to tell them jokes and laugh. I kept up this routine until the first man left. Then the second man came in, and I went through the same routine. My reaction of happiness and joking worked. The men then took us back to the train station. If I had been afraid, they would have gone for me. I instinctively allowed faith and happiness and love to dominate the fear. This was my first tangible experience of deflecting an assault. I stayed clear-headed in the face of danger. I guess I'm some kind of survivor.

Completion is not an end, it is only the end of a chapter. In a few words, what wisdom do you carry from this fire experience?

My feeling of completion. It's another experience, another challenge. It was (and is) very challenging to lose the treasures I did to the fire. But I think of the experience as old, as something in the past that happened. I'm looking to the future and the new shop my nephew is going to build and the creative experiences he will have in the space cleared away by the fire. I look to the joy his family will share in their life on the farm.

~

Reflections on Diana's Story

Wisdom effortlessly glides through Diana's rich and adventurous life story, nourishing those who are quiet enough to listen. Her varied and deep life experiences have taught her that there is value in the smallest of experiences.

There is a lot to unpack in her stories, as each one is the beginning of an epic novel. What is remarkable, and what flows through each story, is how Diana was able to stay consistently calm in the midst of the various storms she encountered throughout her life. Her clear presence of mind and conscious choice in the moment are rare responses in a crisis and certainly helped her to literally survive some of her life experiences.

In some cases, she had what's called a "fawn" response to the crisis situation, where she joked around and laughed with her captors, for example, instead of reacting with another impulsive amygdala reaction, such as fighting or fleeing. In her experience in Tunis, she was able to instinctively and adroitly employ this survival skill to keep her aggressors off guard. None of her responses to crises were planned. She relied on her innate ability to sense what was happening at the time and then determine her next steps. This decision-making reflects the clarity she embodies and how she approaches everyday life. Her lifetime of meditative practices trained her to have a focused mind and center herself in the moment.

There is a lot of great wisdom in Diana's writing. The quote that stands out for me is, "Being a traveler teaches one to let go. Letting go is always expensive." This reminds me of the writings of the great sages who teach us about the impermanence of life and the folly we engage holding on to and identifying with "things." This philosophy points to one of her main messages, which is to be in the flow. Any resistance we have to that which challenges us only emboldens the aggressor, as in, a fear begets fear, evil begets evil. The message is not about rolling over and being abused. It is about being clear and centered within yourself when you are going through any challenging situation, and most of all, trusting yourself and your abilities.

I'd like to think I could stay calm in these sorts of experiences, but I don't think that I would have had the presence of mind to stay as calm and centered as Diana did. She is a remarkable lady. I greatly appreciate how she sees the experiences for what they are instead of making them a commentary about herself. As she says, "Change the memory into an ally to walk the road beside you." In other words, learn from life and walk with purpose in the now. This elevated sense of place and purpose allows Diana to rise above the fray and witness the kaleidoscope of life, then hold its complexity and simplicity all at once.

- What are your reactions to Diana's stories?
- What perspectives will you take away from her life experiences?
- How can you begin to have conscious choice when faced with a trauma?
- Can you apply any of her philosophies to your life today?

Diana's charity of choice for her story contribution is her local fire service.

Additional Resources

Becoming Supernatural: How Common People are Doing the Uncommon, Dr. Joe Dispenza, London: Hay House UK, 2019.

The Game of Life and How To Play It, Florence Scovel Shinn and Joel Fotinos, New York, NY: St. Martin's Essentials, 2020.

Mataora: The Living Face: Contemporary Maori Art, Witi, Sandy Adsett, and Cliff Whiting (eds.), New Zealand: D. Bateman Publishing, 1996.

PART II

The Three Phases of the Tender Path

CHAPTER FOUR

The Shockwave

Should his heart break and the grief pour out, it would flow over the
whole earth, it seems, and yet, no one sees it.
—ANTON CHEKHOV

We all experience the time that follows a loss in our own
unique way. Immediately after a significant loss—the death
of a loved one, the betrayal of an affair, the loss of a job, the
tragedy of an accident—we are immediately jolted into the
first tender phase of loss, the shockwave. Time moves slowly,
and we feel like we are watching a movie, detached from everything, instead of being fully present. This is usually when
we launch into one of the categories of grief described by Dr.
Kübler-Ross—denial, anger, bargaining, depression, acceptance—but grief is not a checklist to be completed; it is an
emotional journey, the tender path of grief and loss.

The process I have developed involves broad phases that
describe the emotional experience during and after a loss: the
shockwave, the stretch, and the solace. Understanding these

three phases will help you to better connect to the emotional experience you will have over the arc of any loss journey. The phases are not linear, as one blends into another in its own time. It's possible to feel flooded by feelings and worn down by the experience in each of the phases. They blur together, so it can be hard to identify what particular phase you are in. It's often only after you have gone through a phase that you can clearly see, oh, that's where I was a few months ago. The phases are also not associated with a timeframe. They serve only as touchpoints to better understand your feelings as you move through and with your grief.

THE SHOCK

Experiencing a great shock disconnects us from the reality we knew before, throwing us into a no-man's-land where we don't know the rules. In chapter one, you read the story of my reaction to my mom's rapidly declining health. When her condition worsened and she went back into the hospital, the doctors said there was nothing else they could do. Talk about shock! I wasn't ready for this news; surely there was more that could be done. I asked a nurse if there were any other options; she looked at me kindly, but firmly and gently said no. The bottom dropped out below me as I heard and felt this truth. I didn't know it yet, and a part of me didn't want to acknowledge it, but the shockwave had just begun.

My mom was stable and resting. Her care team said she could still have days or weeks left, so my partner and I decided to drive the six hours back to the Chicago suburbs to resume work. A part of me wanted to stay, to be there in case something happened, but the emotionally exhausted, hurting, and sad part of me wanted to leave, to run away and not see this scene anymore. I wanted to retreat to my pretend world, where my mom would come out of the hospital and be okay and go back to being my mom, as she had done many times before.

When we were only an hour out from the hospital, I got a call from my sister saying that our mom's breathing had changed and that we should come back. My partner had to drive, as I knew something had shifted in me and I wasn't there any more. I remember looking at the crystal-blue sky and the tall clouds of mid-September, staring out through my tears at a fuzzy landscape, and knowing that my life was changing in those moments. When we got back to my mom's room, she was there in the bed, but I could tell *she* was not there. In my mind's eye I saw that she was in the room with us in spirit. I felt her gentle love but in a different way. I kept a vigil at her bedside overnight, holding her hand, talking to her, praying, crying. The next day, she gently took her last breath as the family surrounded her with love.

> *Being present in the moments after death is an incredible gift to yourself, it's a gift to the people you're with, and it's a gift to the person who's just died. They're just a hair's breadth away. They're just starting their new journey in the world without a body. If you keep a calm space around their body, and in the room, they're launched in a more beautiful way. It's a service to both sides of the veil.*
> —Sarah Kerr, ritual healing practitioner and death doula

I fully felt the shock of it all. I had never felt this way before, and the grief was heavy. Later, I was out with my dad and sister making arrangements, and I thought, *How can everyone else be going about their day as if nothing had happened? I am in shock! My mom has just died! How come the world isn't feeling the weight of this grief like I am?* My hurting little boy inside was in stunned denial over the trauma of her death, yet the familiar world around me wasn't acknowledging this trauma, it was just moving on. I was outraged and resented others who were having fun without a care in the world; how dare they go on as if nothing had happened!

I didn't have much patience or kindness for others. My usual affable self was in hiding as the deep grief of my inner child took over. I was with others who loved me, yet I felt utterly alone. I could never have imagined I would feel this pain and mournful resentment, but I had never lost my mom before. My world was turned upside down, and I didn't know what was happening or what I was going to feel next. My hurting inner child was silently screaming, *Where's my mom?! Why aren't you crying with me, helping my heart to find her?!*

It is true that we don't know how we will feel during a situation until we are in it. I did a lot of activities during this time that don't make sense now. That's how the shockwave is; it throws us curveballs. We repeat ourselves, do chores twice, or forget things all together. We experience emotional reactions we've never been through before, and feelings come up that are foreign to us. All of these behaviors and this enormous emotional shift are normal after a loss.

Disconnecting

A sense of disconnection is big part of the shockwave effect of the loss. It blasts us off course and gets our attention. Trying to absorb that something so big and significant just happened shocks the system. The shockwave isn't cuddly or familiar, it's foreign, jagged, and unfeeling. It alienates us from ourselves and others. Suddenly, it's hard to tell what is real and what is not, as we are encased in a heavy thickness, gasping for air. We are shaken out of our dreamworld and into the rawness of the loss exposed before us. We are thrust into a new world, wanting to turn away but having to acclimate to this new reality. We may reach for familiar comforts such as food or drink, but even these are somehow off and taste odd. When we feel disconnected, we try to feel connected again, to feel like we did before, but our world has changed. We feel as though our bodies have shut down, and we become the walking dead in a world that now feels weirdly foreign. We search for something to take us out of the shock, but we feel like aliens in our own skin.

As a loss event unfolds, we get swept up in its swirling energy. We become transfixed by the shock and either shut down or go into a crisis-task mode. When the event is particularly traumatic, this response becomes exaggerated and tends to focus on survival. We are caught up in the moment, hyperfocused on regaining stability or getting out of pain.

All of this is the initial shockwave, the first phase of the tender path. The shock itself doesn't usually last a long time, but the feeling of disconnection from what we knew can go on for some time. In the first few days after a loss, we try to incorporate the news that someone has died or that we lost our job or experienced a betrayal. I can tell you that, universally, nobody likes this phase and that we all want it to go away as quickly as it came on. Our world contracts to a small, tight circle, and we cling to anything comforting and familiar. Feeling disconnected commences even before we start to grieve.

GRIEF

Grief and the process of grieving feels like a rock that we keep turning over and over, expecting to find something different on the other side.

Lost, hopeless, tired, and bewildered, most of us are the walking dead following a significant loss. We have to be reminded to eat, bathe, or see what's on the schedule. Simple things feel overwhelming as we stumble along in an out-of-body sort of way. It's hard to even walk around the house because everything reminds us of the loss, and we're crying all the time. Finding any source of comfort is difficult, even though friends and family try hard to be there for us.

Grief is an active, intense yearning for whatever was lost from a death, a miscarriage, a bankruptcy. Pangs of grief are individual, natural reactions to loss. These feelings, and the action of grieving, is the response to loss. We cry for the person who has died, but a part of us cries for ourselves, as we are now left behind and sad. Grief is our love in action.

We all go through the grieving process at our own pace, and it will take however long it takes. Waves of grief wash over us and come at the most inopportune times, often when we least expect it. We feel as if the grief knows when there is a window to burst through to get us to acknowledge our deep sorrow.

Many people find it easier to stay in crisis-task or survival-task mode, staying busy with such actions as making funeral arrangements, dealing with insurance companies, staying organized, meeting with lawyers, or working on projects. For some, these activities feel normal and solid. The person feels productive and in control, gaining a sense of power even though the rug has been pulled out from underneath them. Others may shirk these duties altogether and become consumed by grief, frozen in place, and locked in denial, as these reactions feel like the safer options. The process of grieving can be emotionally exhausting and physically tiring. Self-care will help you gently move through this process.

Those hot tears streaming down your cheeks are your love in action. They are a poignant reminder of how hard we have loved.

There is a belief that we will grieve intensely during each anniversary, birthday, and holiday in the first year after a loved one dies. The first year is the hardest because we experience everything without our loved one; an empty chair sits at the table, and we miss their energy and presence. The second year gets easier, but these occasions will never feel like they did when that person was alive. Some people say the second year is harder because we know what to expect; we know how the holidays and anniversaries are going to feel without them there. This was certainly true for me, but it's still a hard truth to hold. Grieving and missing a loved one during a holiday is like making a favorite recipe without a key ingredient. It looks the same and might even taste simliar, but there's a special spice that's not there and is sorely missed. These special days get easier with time, but our hearts will be pulled by our love for the person who has died no matter how much time has passed. As the years roll by, we can bring in more ways to honor and cherish our loved one's memory to help us gently heal the loss.

If you are having trouble accessing your emotions to express yourself, see if you can, at a minimum, tap into your anger. It may seem counterintuitive, but for many, anger is an easier emotion to access and will create some movement of grief within. From anger, you may be able to move on to the more tender feelings of hurt or sadness. This can form an opening for you to go deeper within, but know that anger is not meant to be the go-to feeling, it's only to help get feelings moving.

Depression without Sadness

Is my depression making choices for me today, or am I taking charge?

Grieving is the emotional process connected to a specific loss event. To grieve is to feel sadness for a loss and for how it affects us. Sadness becomes a companion as we walk the path of grieving and helps us best express our grief. Even after we are on the other side of the loss event, sadness can circle back because it's the strongest emotion connected to that event. The sadness we feel usually heals and lifts when we work through our grief.

If you are stuck and everything feels like a loss, when every day is a bad day, when it's hard to get up and you can't find the motivation to shower or put on clean clothes, then you may be experiencing more than sadness; these feelings could be symptoms of depression. Depression usually feels heavier than sadness. Sadness is a storm that passes. Depression lingers no matter what you try. If you had feelings of sadness or symptoms of depression before the loss, these feelings will be magnified afterward. Being depressed is like wearing a heavy wet blanket every day, even when you do things that you normally feel happy doing. Take a moment to assess whether you have been depressed most of your life or your sadness is related to a specific external event that shapes your reaction.

Symptoms of depression are either situational—the result of a loss or a series of losses—or biological, when the body does not produce enough of a chemical that helps us feel steady and balanced. People with what is sometimes called biological depression usually have a long-standing mental health condition that predates the loss. To clarify, depression and sadness both produce a biological reaction in the body. If you have a predisposition for anxiety, you may feel this along with your depression.

Depression has many symptoms that shouldn't be ignored; it doesn't just go away and can last weeks, months, or years. If you see loss after loss everywhere you look and everything is hopeless, get yourself in to see a mental health profession- al, who can diagnose whether you have clinical depression or sadness related to your grief. If you have clinical depression or situational sadness, ask about antidepressants. A lot of people don't want to take medications because they either see it as a moral failing or think they should be stronger than that. Not everyone wants to take a pill for everything, myself included, but if your body needs an antidepressant medica- tion, then it may respond well to it and you'll probably feel better. The metaphor I use is, if you're down in a ditch from grief, sadness, or depression, the medication will help get you out of the ditch and up onto the road—but you will still have to walk the road yourself. Medication smooths out the path so you don't have to work so hard to feel okay, so you can more easily find your smile. You may not have to take the medication forever, just long enough to help you through this rough patch.

You can also talk to a therapist and look into alternative coping skills. There are many holistic approaches to healing these symptoms, such as energy work and homeopathic medicine, so be creative and open yourself to these possibilities. Trust your intuition and be gentle with yourself.

Lingering Loneliness

How can I still feel all alone in a room full of people?

Most people feel alone and lonely when a loss occurs, especially a significant loss. This is particularly true when the loss is one that we have never experienced before and leaves us in a state of shock, bewilderment, and confusion. We feel as if we are floating like an astronaut in space, untethered and ungrounded. When we look around, everyone else seems to be the same as they always were, but we are lost in this void, unable to clearly express what we feel.

These feelings are normal in the time immediately following a big loss, but we usually start to feel more grounded over time. If you still feel disconnected and lonely long after the loss, look at your thoughts. Negative thoughts give energy to your sad fuel, keeping you in grief. See if you can find a bright spot in your life. Bright spots can come from unexpected places, such as a burst of sunshine coming through the clouds; a good-morning greeting from your neighbor; a friend calling; or receiving a happy, unexpected surprise. As the loving writer Louise Hay says, there is an "I" in illness and a "we" in wellness. Get out with others and let your community or tribe help you heal. Any of these actions can take away some blues and feelings of loneliness. None are the complete answer, but they help to make this tender path a little gentler. Take care of yourself in the way that you know how. While it's important to connect with others, they can't fill in the blanks; we have to be creative and walk ourselves out of the mournful place.

You may be feeling anger, relief, or guilt rather than sadness. Our feelings are messengers, a built-in "weather system" that tells us what is happening inside. See if you can decipher what your feelings are trying to tell you, to see what the message is within. Don't fret too much if you're not feeling the way you or someone else thinks you should feel.

Grief as Anger

Anger is fear under great pressure.

My wise mentor Rev. Don Burt once taught me that anger is fear under great pressure. Sometimes our fears or concerns about a situation are so great that we push them down and compress them, causing the pressure to build and eventually erupt into anger. Alternating between feelings of grief and anger is confusing and frustrating. The grief feels depressing and the anger feels empowering, but the feeling of having power is not necessarily good, as it comes from a place of fear. Both feelings have their own expressions, and each needs to be honored and recognized; just be aware of not getting stuck in anger.

Those who have been given a chronic disease diagnosis or have a terminal disease often experience the grieving stage of anger. This is their fear under great pressure, as the news was shocking and surprising, and it upended their world. Others may be depressed because they lack the physical ability to do things they did before, and it comes out as anger and frustration. It's a horrible feeling when the mind works but the body refuses to cooperate, and people often mistakenly think that their physical limitations are a reflection of their worth. Feeling betrayed by their body, they turn this anger inward.

What we do with the messages of anger and fear depends on many factors. We can use them to lash out in indulgent and potentially destructive choices, or we can take the messages to heart, honor the experience, and begin to use the power of these emotions to help ourselves transform the experience. We can choose to give these messages the power to create opportunities or to destroy hope.

Sometimes we jealously guard our pain, hurt, and anger. We don't move forward or backward, we just stay stuck in a space of anger and fear. But holding on to these feelings doesn't solve anything, it just makes us miserable. If you are stuck in this anger stage, ask yourself what the loss you are carrying feels like. Does it feel like a hard, knotted rope leashed around your heart? What is the worst thing that could happen if you eased up on guarding this pain? Would you lose anything? Might you gain something unexpected? My thought is that you would probably gain some emotional freedom from releasing this pain. Read some of the releasing techniques in chapter nine, "Practical Tools for Honoring Loss."

To visualize what this anger is doing to your internal system, make two fists and squeeze them as hard as you can. Hold it longer than feels comfortable. Now release. This pressure and intensity are what the anger you're holding on to is doing inside your body. Anger takes a lot of energy to contain. Take a deep breath and imagine what it would feel like to let that go. When you begin to acknowledge loss, you begin to recognize that you're angry, hurt, sad, and lost because your parent died or your spouse wants a divorce or you lost your job. Anger is often the first and easiest emotion to access, so that is how such pain is demonstrated. That's okay; it's you, hurting. Know that there are healthy (assertive) and unhealthy (aggressive) expressions of anger, and be aware of the nature of your anger.

Taking the pain of loss out on ourselves or others through anger isn't a healthy expression. We don't always mean to do this, but sometimes we lash out at those closest to us because we know that they will love us even as we scream at them in pain. If you've been grumpy or have lashed out lately, see if you can apologize to those around you who have been witness to your pain. They have probably given you a lot of room to express yourself, but it's hard to get a dose of this every day. You could say something like this: "I realize that I've been hurting and feeling angry and frustrated lately, and I know that I've been taking it out on you. I'm sorry that it's spilling over on you. I want you to know that I'm not upset with you, it's just the situation I'm in right now. Thank you for being there for me during all of this and for creating a safe place for me to express myself."

The message is to honor whatever feelings you have because when you don't, you will feel worse. Know what your limits are. Do what you can. Learn how to express your anger in appropriate ways and not push it onto others. Be gentle with yourself as you name these natural feelings.

Cumulative Grief

Sometimes it's easier to be angry than sad. Anger is a defense mechanism that says to the world we are still strong even though we're crumbling and shaking inside.

Cumulative grief can come about when past losses have not been acknowledged or healed and the loss bucket is overflowing. Cumulative grief also occurs when multiple losses follow each other in short order and one hasn't been fully processed before another happens. For example, my mom died, then the next year my aunt, whom I was very close to, died, and then a good friend who was another mother figure died, all within less than three years of each other. Then, not long after my friend's death, our dog died. This period was very difficult for me to get through, as I had just gone through one death when another one happened; the trauma was compounding, and I felt I couldn't take any more.

This rapid succession of loss complicates and overburdens our ability to process and integrate each loss, and all of these unresolved feelings get stacked like pancakes inside our loss bucket. For those who have been in war zones, or have experienced accidents or illnesses along with death, such cumulative grief often becomes deeply traumatic to hold, and they experience symptoms of post-traumatic stress disorder (PTSD). This overabundance of loss complicates the grieving process, and it takes longer to process these feelings, as our internal resilience gets stretched beyond capacity.

If you're going through a cumulative grief cycle, please talk with a therapist to help process the grief, and use the techniques I talk about in chapter nine, "Practical Tools for Honoring Loss." Know that there is a reason you feel overwhelmed and that this feeling is normal, as you are able to emotionally process only so much at one time. It's incredibly difficult to move through many layers of emotion, and you may need more help than you would like to admit. Give yourself permission to reach out for help.

Frozen Grief

There are four automatic amygdala reactions we typically have to trauma: fight, flight, freeze, and fawn. (As you read in Diana's story, fawning is when we try to appease someone to minimize a potentially dangerous situation.) Each of these responses is an automatic survival mechanism.

In the case of frozen grief, we know what happened but we become frozen in the shockwave phase. It may best be described as PTSD but may not meet all of the criteria for such a diagnosis. I name it as frozen grief because that is how people describe what being locked in place feels like inside.

Being frozen in grief is different from resisting grief. Resistance to acknowledging or moving through grief is typically a conscious action empowered by fear, stubbornness, or pain. Frozen grief is more commonly a subconscious traumatic reaction, where we are caught in a "looping movie" dissociative state. We play the loss over and over with a great preoccupation for the loss as our minds try to understand what happened. Through this trauma response, we try to put the events in an order, try to make sense of an event that seems so horrific and bad. There are a million swirling, scattered, unorganized memories of the event in our minds, and we are triggered by the smallest innocuous reminders. It all feels intense and overwhelming, freezing us in our tracks, preventing us from moving forward or backward.

If you feel you are in a state of frozen grief, you could be experiencing PTSD. Sometimes a significant loss can trigger the memory of a previous loss or abuse, leading to cumulative grief as well as frozen grief. There are some events you can't forget, but know that you can create some distance between you and the memory. Please seek professional help if you feel you or someone you love is experiencing frozen grief, as it may indicate a larger, more complex issue.

Prolonged Grief Disorder

If you are still crying and lost in your grief years later, you may have developed something called prolonged grief disorder, or PGD. This is when the grief response goes on with the same intensity for more than a year and causes significant impairment in functioning. Often the PGD bereaved feel numb, distrustful, stunned, and in disbelief. This doesn't mean the person is grieving "incorrectly"; rather, it is a symptom of the severity and depth of the emotional impact. Depression, in contrast, is described as a free-floating and generalized state of feeling and is less associated with the loss itself. Getting help to guide you through PGD is important for your overall well-being. Sometimes we are so lost in grief we don't know how sad we actually feel.

Grief with No End

Cross-country truckers who drive, bleary-eyed, through endless ribbons of highway are known as long-haulers. Long-haulers live in a world in which the landscape looks the same, mile after mile and it seems like it will never end. An ongoing grief or loss that is not resolved and for which there is no fix or resolution in sight is akin to the unchanging life of the long-haul trucker. Examples of grief with no end include having a chronic physical or mental illness; having a child with ongoing addiction issues; and experiencing multiple losses all at once or close together, have intangible elements, and are hard to define. I see this type of grief as different from prolonged grief disorder, as long-haulers do get some relief now and then. They know they are in grief, whereas someone with PGD doesn't always recognize there is a problem, as they are lost in their grief.

I see grief with no end in the parents of an adult child who is an addict, is severely mentally ill, or who keeps making bad choices and doesn't want help. These parents feel whipped around by the chaos of their adult child's behavioral choices. The situation goes on without any clear resolution, often long after the parents and families have tried to intervene and spent tens of thousands of dollars trying to remedy the issue.

I have worked with many parents whose situation gets so bad that they need to have an order of protection issued against their own child. These parents are at their wits' end. The adult child doesn't want any help, and they keep on creating turmoil because they get something out of the drama. These sorts of ongoing losses create a sense of hopelessness in the parents, and the extreme boundary setting of an order of protection at least allows them a sense of safety. But this action doesn't bring a feeling of solace; it just creates guardrails around the unpredictable and complex relationship dynamic. The parents are still in a great deal of pain, and as they go to bed each night, they still worry about their child, where they are, if they're safe. They feel grief with no end. You never stop being a parent, even if your child has abandoned you along with all the lessons you tried to teach them.

Grief with no end is like cumulative grief but in a ground-hog-day sort of way. The grieving long-hauler parent must learn to hold this unique loss, as it is always in process and never ends. These parents and family members get used to the idea of holding a reality of, for example, not knowing where their adult child is, but last they heard, she was doing drugs and nothing had changed. Being estranged from an adult child is heartbreaking and extremely difficult for the families.

The long-hauler's never-ending grief is a lonely place, as others get tired of hearing the same story. Yes, he's still using drugs; yes, she still hasn't called us; no, we don't know where she is; no, he refuses to take his medication or see a therapist. One goal for these grieving parents is to learn the art of loving detachment and create strong boundaries within themselves, holding the unknown while still sending love.

If you find yourself in this type of long-hauler's grief with no end, please refer to the tools I have created, discussed in chapter nine, "Practical Tools for Honoring Loss," as a way to process your feelings. Forgive yourself and know that you did what you could do at the time, that you can't fix everything in your outer world so that it's tied up with a bow. If someone is not ready for the message, they won't even see a loud Jumbotron in front of their face. I will be teaching you how to set boundaries and hold the undone and the unfixable in later chapters.

INDULGENT VERSUS RESTORATIVE CHOICES

In the first shockwave of grief, we often have such overwhelming feelings that we don't know what to do with everything we are feeling. We are overcome because of the depth and immensity of the loss. Our world has been turned upside down, and often our judgment is, as well. Maybe we have never experienced anything like this before, and we literally don't know the next steps to take. When we are in such times of emotional crisis, we make choices and do things we think will make us feel better.

Our behaviors are great indicators of how we emotionally interact with loss. We all have complex emotional reactions to adversity, and we either do things that will restore us or escape into what feels good in the moment but is not a long-term solution. In other words, we make either indulgent or restorative choices.

Indulgent Choices

Some people's first response to a loss is to do something self-soothing, such as drinking, eating away feelings, or going shopping. Any of these responses in moderation may help us deal with the shockwave of grief, but overindulging in such behaviors tips the scales, and the behavior becomes problematic. In other words, some people choose behaviors that become indulgent escapes and wounded coping skills instead of bravely facing the loss, acknowledging that it is happening or has happened, and being gentle with themselves. What started as a way to comfort themselves becomes the go-to escape whenever they feel sad.

The first shockwaves of grief are sometimes too loud, and we look for things to smother and overtake these intense feelings. This is why some people have an exaggerated response to everything following the death of a family member or spouse. Their grief spins out of control in their hearts, and they lose any connection or desire to become still and ground themselves.

Indulgence comes from pain that wants to lash out. The person is looking for a quick fix, an instant remedy. Some people think that getting into a new relationship or acting on impulse in other ways is going to help, but these behaviors just exaggerate the disconnection from their healing. Indulgence is giving in to our wounded and hurting inner child and satisfying whatever it wants, even if it's not good for us. Episodes of crying, anger, or shutting down are great examples of this pain looking to be soothed. We usually don't know when we are being indulgent, we just impulsively react to a huge emotional eruption and run scared.

Overspending, overeating, oversexing, overdrinking, or anything "extra-" can be indulgent when they are in response to pain. The following are examples of indulgent choices:

Overrelying on food, alcohol, sex, gambling, shopping, or other activities for comfort

Sleeping more than you need to just to avoid dealing with reality

Going into a victim space to get sympathy from others so you don't have to begin the healing journey

Pain shopping (e.g., rereading texts or emails) after a betrayal in an attempt to find out more information

Cheating on your spouse after they cheated on you

Doom scrolling and getting lost in stories of sorrowful loss

Withdrawing and isolating from others

Not taking care of yourself; not bathing or dressing in clean clothes each day

Any one of these behavioral responses could be masking depression or anxiety, which can happen concurrent with grieving. Each of these choices is a resistance to and denial of what is happening in the moment; it's how we push back at the pain and try to get through the day. When we give in to these indulgent urges, we may at first feel that they're helping; we may even feel like the hurt part is taking revenge, evening the score with life's injustices.

The indulgent response eventually loses its magical ability to transport us out of our pain, instead becoming just another way to mask the pain and stay in denial. We eventually feel bloated and empty, and then we are at risk of getting lost in our pity party or self-loathing. No matter how much of one thing we do, the pain of our loss is still there, waiting for us to acknowledge and deal with it. You can go on and on being indulgent, but what does this lead you to, happiness or emptiness, restoration or repetition?

If you are indulging in these types of behaviors, ask yourself why you are resisting this moment. How do you distract yourself so that you don't feel what is happening? Whatever indulgence you have been giving in to, see it for what it is. If you have indulged in these choices in the past, gently look back, with a soft gaze, at these choices. Forgive yourself if you were too indulgent with your pain. Know that you did the best you could with what you knew at the time. See if you can give some gratitude to the indulgent choices, as they did help you cope in some way. As the poet and wise soul Maya Angelou said, "Do the best you can until you know better. Then when you know better, do better."

Restorative Choices

Slow down and respond with intention instead of impulse.

Restorative behavioral choices feel more balanced and are less reactive than indulgent choices. We still feel big emotion related to our loss, but restorative choices are those that are thoughtfully made instead of being subconsciously acted out. Choices such as taking walks, napping, and getting massages help to restore us. They are not always as fun, exciting, or dramatic as indulgent choices, but they build us up and restore our resilience in the long run. Making restorative choices can mean eating our favorite foods and drinking without overindulging. When we do these things within the context of being with friends and family, we go through the loss experience together and share our grief, our memories, and our healing with each other. Restorative choices feel like balanced self-care, not taking a second helping of cake or escaping into being overserved. It's the feeling of nourishment rather than gluttony.

Restorative choices include behaviors such as the following:

Meeting up with friends and getting out of the house

Looking into meditation or other practices that will help calm the mind

Connecting with a faith community

Journaling or making artwork that's just for you

Bathing and dressing in clean clothes each day

Taking a nap because you need the rest (but not an all-day nap)

Being clear with others about what you can and can't do

Being gentle and kind with yourself, like you would with a person who needed extra care

Say hi to someone and connect with their energy, as this will help get you out of your lost and foggy head space. Engaging with others and seeing their eyes and smile reminds us that we are alive and part of a community. Look into meet-up groups or other events, and push yourself to go to one, even if you just stand at the back. There are probably others standing at the back who also need to connect with others. Putting yourself out there can be hard to do, as you may want to retreat and pull up the covers. But getting out with others is important when your world has changed so much after a loss. Trust me, you will feel better if you give yourself this small gift each day.

Self-compassion and restorative choices have the same goals, and both require inner strength, as they are harder to do than giving in and indulging ourselves. They are behavior choices that help us get back to our center, with the main message being one of connection with ourselves and others. When we ignore self-compassion and restorative choices, when we indulge and impulsively act out our pain, then we delay and derail the healing journey of grief.

When considering restorative choices, ask yourself what you can do to feel more alive and more like yourself. Then see if you can make a choice that adds to your life, where you will feel a sense of wholeness afterward. If you do this each day, this energy will build on itself and it will become easier to make restorative choices instead of giving in to indulgences.

> *Set small goals for yourself to help you feel in control and acquire a sense of independence even though you're grieving.*

If you are not sure whether a choice is indulgent or restorative, ask yourself whether you are escaping from your feelings or are making a particular choice as a way to restore yourself. Another way to determine whether a behavior is restorative or indulgent is to ask yourself how you feel after you've acted on the choice. Do you have a feeling of shame or emptiness? Or do you feel like you did something nice for yourself and feel encouraged? Indulgences tend to be wants, whereas restorative choices and their aftereffects tend to be needs. Sometimes it's hard to make the distinction, especially when you are lost in pain, but I think if you are honest with yourself, you'll be able to discern the difference in the feelings you're left with after the fact.

You can still get through your grief and loss if you do not have self-compassion or make restorative choices, but the road will be bumpier and often longer. This isn't a message of one action being good or bad or that you are good or bad for choosing an indulgent choice rather than a restorative one. Just remember that there is a consequence to every choice. The message is to go through this experience with humility and an openness to learn the wisdom the experience teaches. Gentleness with yourself is key here, not perfection.

What are some restorative actions you make in response to a loss? Take a moment to sit with yourself, and be objective but gentle as you consider this. Losses are likely to come up in your future, so you can plan ahead and create a "tool kit" of choices to more gently navigate these experiences. How would you like to expand your tool kit? What changes do you need to make to prepare a more solid foundation of restorative responses to a future loss? Thinking about this now will help you to be more consciously aware of the choices you make in the future.

Following the disorienting shock of loss, we begin our walk on the tender path not knowing where we are headed. As this new landscape of grieving unfolds, we are invited into a new reality that encourages a bravery and strength we didn't know we had.

In the midst of winter, I found there was, within me, an invincible summer.—Albert Camus

BONNIE'S STORY: LOSS OF A CHILD FROM SUICIDE

Please note that this story discusses suicide in depth. If you have persistent thoughts of suicide and feel hopeless, please see a mental health professional, call the national Suicide and Crisis Lifeline at 988, or call 911.

Bonnie has a naturally cheery disposition and is a bright, funny, and deeply caring person. She is the type of person most people look for in a friend, someone with whom you could have silly adventures and confide in. A little over ten years ago, her bright light was shrouded in grief. She came to see me soon after her teenage daughter's death by suicide. Like most parents I have worked with who have lost a child to suicide, she was in a state of deep grief. Suicide is a shock that nothing in life prepares us for, as it doesn't compare to any other life experience.

After her daughter Hilary's death, this suburban mom was a walking shell of her former self. Bonnie was going through the motions of tasks she knew she had to do, as she was married and had a younger daughter to care for, but her spirit was crushed. Occasionally, I could see the bright flashes of her smile, the spirit of the woman she was before she lost her firstborn. Like all suicide survivor parents I have worked with, she was forever changed, as this unique trauma stretched her beyond anything she had ever experienced before.

Over time, Bonnie worked hard to transcend this loss and regain her center. Today she still greatly misses her daughter, but she is now firmly in her present life and no longer spins in grief. I asked her what life was like immediately following Hilary's suicide by hanging, how she transformed after this extreme loss, and what her life is like a decade later.

A note on hopelessness and thoughts of suicide. Thinking about suicide is a normal response when we are in times of great pain or extraordinary trauma. When we say, *I no longer want to be here*, *This is too much*, or, *I can't take it anymore*, we are sending the strongest message possible, to ourselves and others, that we are in great pain. No other words compare to the intensity of saying to someone else that we are suicidal. Many people who say they want to kill themselves believe that less dramatic statements wouldn't reflect the intensity of what they feel. But when I ask these people if they really want to die or just be out of pain, most, if not all, say they just want to be out of pain. Often, thoughts are only thoughts.

Can you describe what you felt like inside following your daughter's death?

I felt like my heart was literally breaking, and my entire being ached for my beautiful daughter. I missed hugging her, watching her head off with friends, and just sitting and being with her. I even missed the way she rolled her teenage eyes when she was frustrated with me. I would cry throughout the day from the pain. I remember watching the clock every night, praying for the time to go to bed so that one more day was over. Sleep was the only time the pain was gone. When I woke up, I would have a moment of everything being normal, and then I would remember what happened and ask myself if it was true. At times, I was angry with her for doing this to us, and feeling angry with her was hard on me.

Loud sounds and voices and emergency vehicle sirens and lights would startle me and send waves of panic through my body. It was hard to breathe, my heart would race, and I would get flashbacks of finding Hilary dead. She was only sixteen. I knew how she died, but a part of me that was in denial kept wondering if an intruder had come into the house and did this to her.

I was overwhelmed with fear that something terrible would happen to my nine-year-old daughter, Kendall, to the point where I moved her mattress into our bedroom. When I woke up during the night, I would check on her and listen to her breathing. I needed to keep her close to me at all times.

What were the strongest emotions you felt?

My strongest emotion was missing her in my daily life and wanting to be with her to protect her. When they lowered her coffin into her grave, I had to be held back so I wouldn't throw myself in. I wanted to go with her wherever she was.

Did some part of you die that day?

A part of my heart died that day. Never again would I be able to get through family special events and holidays the same way. They are now bittersweet. I treasure the memories, but they hurt, and I now create new traditions that do not involve her memory, which helps.

Life goes on for the living, and we still have to do everyday things. How did you get through basic tasks like bathing, eating, paying the bills, and grocery shopping?

I made lists of everything I had to do each day and used a calendar to keep dates straight. I had no sense of time. Grocery shopping was a joke because I would either forget the list at home or forget to pick up something I needed on the list that I held in my hand. I kept losing my car in parking lots. I just focused on a couple of things at a time.

How did you find the courage and strength to get through each day?

I found courage and strength from friends and gifted therapists. Friends would let me talk, and when I was ready, we would get together. They did not push me to get back to "normal" but to find a new normal. My first therapist lost a son to suicide, and she truly understood my pain and knew how to guide me through the first year.

She taught me to set small goals for myself each day and to get through each day moment by moment.

During this time, what did you need but didn't know how to ask for?

I needed my husband to connect with me and acknowledge my pain. He was so engulfed in his own pain that he could not see me or help me. I felt like I was caring not only for Kendall but for him, too.

I was blessed with family and friends to help me. Meals were provided, and the bringing of food was very helpful. It was one less thing I had to think about. I wanted Kendall to have positive experiences with friends, so I often invited her school friends over to play, although sometimes that overwhelmed me.

What changed as you went from a world of Technicolor to a world where everything was shades of gray?

Everything in my life changed. I couldn't remember to pay bills. I had no concept of a budget or the value of money. If Kendall wanted an expensive toy, I bought it. We bought a boat and a convertible car. We had important holiday traditions that no longer made any sense and only carried pain and loss. We did not spend the first two Christmases in the house. The first Christmas I didn't even decorate, and that had been one of my favorite things to do before my daughter died. Everything was a reminder of who was missing. The world became a bleak place, with shades of gray and very little color. The only thing that brought me any joy at all was Kendall.

How long did this surreal period last?

It lasted for several months.

What do you see clearly now that would have helped during that time?

It would have been helpful if neighbors and friends had spent more time with Kendall and invited her over for playdates.

As a response to this type of trauma loss, many people be-come either extremely shut down or exceedingly indulgent. During this time, what was your self-care like?

My self-care went out the window. At first, I basically sat on the sofa, read books, and ate Ben and Jerry's Cherry Garcia. I preferred to be alone. I started reading books about suicide. I had to understand what had happened to my daughter.

What did you say to yourself to get through the day, to help you move out of the cyclic thoughts and feelings that you knew were not helping?

At first, I just survived moment by moment, reacting to my surround-ings and events. I knew I had to get Kendall back to school, so I focused on that. I created a timeline of what I needed to do for her. I kept telling myself that I couldn't fall apart because I needed to be somewhere or get something done. I kept telling myself I could do it.

The loss of a child at any age greatly disrupts the family dynamic. How did this trauma loss experience affect your relationship with your younger daughter?

Kendall and I became incredibly protective of each other and did not like to be out of each other's sight. We were both so afraid that something would happen to the other. We spent much more time with each other and found that being in nature and doing crafts together was helpful. But it was hard to stay focused on getting things done for her. Eventually, the day-to-day needs and demands got us both back into a normal schoolday routine. Routine was good because I could count on it being the same. It was when unexpected things came up that we struggled.

How were you and your husband and Kendall coexisting?

My husband returned to work pretty quickly, I thought, and I made sure to take care of things around the house so he could focus on work. We still missed Hilary at the dinner table and thought of her each time we went upstairs because her bedroom door was right at the top of the stairs. We kept the door closed. It helped.

In the early years following Hilary's death, were you the walking wounded?

Yes, I was. Kendall, who is now a young adult, said that my husband and I were first like ghosts and then like phantoms.

Finding a centerpoint after a traumatic loss takes a tremendous amount of work. I picture this type of loss as kicking us way out into space, and then we have to work hard to get back to earth, to become grounded again. What did you say to yourself that brought you back to your center?

I swung about wildly like a pendulum at first. What brought me back to center was Kendall. She needed a mom to love and raise her. I loved her so much and wanted her to come through this as unscathed as possible. I wanted her to continue to have positive life experiences and grow to become a strong, independent woman. When I was able to function, that was my purpose and focus.

As part of the PTSD grieving process, we will replay a traumatic loss scene over and over, like a looping movie, and many things can trigger this movie. How did you cope with this?

At the beginning, I replayed finding my daughter dead over and over in my mind. Once the movie started, it wouldn't stop. It would overwhelm me and send me into panic mode. I didn't know how to make it stop. It could happen while I was at home, out somewhere, or with other people. It was always at the front of my mind, getting in the way of my functioning.

At what point were you no longer replaying the scene of finding your daughter and the ensuing chaos? What helped this to recede into the background?

My therapist taught me that I could just stop the movie. It had never occurred to me that I could do that. I started to practice that, and it worked. The more I did it, the better I got at it. Eventually, the movie became only a flashback or a picture of a particular scene, so then it was in the back of my mind. Today, I still get flashback pictures and a sensation in my body when triggered. I remind myself that I am safe and that it happened a long time ago, and I feel better right away.

What helped you to transform the emotions of spinning in grief into something softer?

Eventually my strong feelings of pain were replaced by a dull ache. I remember that first spring, when the flowers started to come up. I felt angry that the world and time were moving forward without my daughter. She always used to sign everything "♥ Hilary." Kendall started to insist that Hilary was sending us heart signs. She found them made of snow, clouds, and even potato chips. She was insistent that they were from Hilary. I started to find them, too. This was a turning point for me. I was more focused on finding signs than on my pain.

At this same time, I wandered into a spiritual bookshop and started reading books by mediums and how our loved ones are still with us. Circumstances led me to a psychic intuitive. Hilary was clearly present during the reading, and she told me about our past lives together. This was a new concept to me, but it rang true. It brought me comfort to know that this lifetime was not our only chance to be together. The intuitive shifted some energy to help me cope with the loss. I also found my way to Reiki and Healing Touch energy medicine, where

I learned to release pain and move forward. I always felt so much lighter and brighter after a session. I found hope again. A whole new world was opening up to me.

Was it more helpful to be by yourself or around other people?

I met and befriended another mom who had lost a teenage daughter to suicide. We understood each other and could talk about things that nobody else could understand. She was getting signs from her daughter, too, and we loved sharing our stories. She got me out of the house, and we did things together. I started making plans again.

Well-meaning friends and family probably said things meant to comfort you, but most had not gone through the loss of a child. What was said that helped you?

I was raised in a Jewish family that celebrated cultural holidays but was not religious. We never spoke about what happens to a person when they die. I had some vague sense of there being a heaven with God. I was completely unprepared in this way for losing Hilary. After she was declared dead, we were taken to a private room to spend time with her. A hospital chaplain came to us and answered my most pressing question: Where is my child? She assured me that Hilary was with God and safe. She said Hilary was a lamb of God. That brought me comfort and created a beautiful, soothing picture in my mind.

What was said that felt hollow or upset you?

As we prepared for the funeral, a pastor from the Evangelical church we attended came to our home. I thought of the hospital chaplain's words and asked the pastor if Hilary was a lamb of God. He said she most definitely was not. I then asked if she was in heaven with God, and he said he couldn't be sure because she hadn't been baptized. I became so upset and angry that I told him to leave my home right then. On his way out, he had the audacity to say that the church doors were always open for us. I told him that they weren't because he had just slammed them shut in my face.

His words planted a seed of doubt in my mind and scared me beyond belief. Where was my daughter? I needed to protect her. Maternal feelings overtook my thinking to the point where I almost hurt myself one day. I was standing in the bathroom, and there was a razor sitting on the sink. It was like I was out of my body watching myself as I reached for the razor. I was about to cut my wrist when, thankfully, Kendall called out my name from the other room. It snapped me back into reality and back into my body. I went on as if nothing had happened.

Most people who are actively suicidal don't want others to know, so they become expert at not giving any indication they may kill themselves. Afterward, most parents either take on a tremendous amount of guilt or stay in the bargaining stage of loss (should have or could have), or both. They go over and over the signs they missed, thinking they should have known better, and so on. What were the signs that, in retrospect, were staring right at you?

I always felt I was a wonderful mother; I put my children's needs first, I advocated for them, I provided them with encouragement and positive experiences, and I loved them unconditionally. After a setback with migraine headaches the year before, Hilary appeared to be thriving and enjoying her teenage life. She had her first boyfriend, attended homecoming, volunteered at a local hospital, regularly got together with friends, and was doing well in school. For me, there were no red flags anywhere. I was so shocked when I found her that day that my first thought was, "Hilary? Not Hilary!" It did not seem possible with the girl that I saw every day and had dinner with every night.

At the hospital, I was questioned by two detectives. They took me off to a room by myself and grilled me on how much I knew about my daughter's secret social media accounts. They did it in such a way that I felt ashamed and guilty that I did not know. I later found out that

Hilary had posted the quote, "You bleed just to know you are alive." If I had seen that, I would have gotten her to a therapist right away.

Did you in any way carry responsibility for Hilary taking her own life?

In the days and nights that followed, I was haunted by past conversations I'd had with her. A girl at her school had died by suicide six months before Hilary, but she was an acquaintance, not a friend. I felt guilty that I had let Hilary go to her wake with friends. Had that given her ideas? A few months later, Hilary showed me a picture of her tennis team with the girl in it. I remember talking to her about the pain and suffering the girl's friends and family must be going through. Should I have spent more time processing this with her? It never occurred to me that she was contemplating her own death. I later found the girl's name doodled on some of her school papers. This made me feel even worse.

What helped to quiet this guilt so you could move on with your life?

The questions why and what happened to her that day led to an ongoing sense of guilt that I have only just healed. When I had the reading with the medium, Hilary came through loud and strong that I was taking on too much responsibility for this. I did the very best I could. It was her decision. Hilary was filled with self-loathing, self-doubt, and self-hatred, and her head was on fire. The medium said that as Hilary's soul and body separated, she was asked if she wanted to go back. It was so quiet there that she wanted to stay. She suffers no more now. She said that I needed to work on my guilt or it would make me sick. Meditation was recommended. I installed Insight Timer, a free meditation app, on my phone. I listened to Salena Lael's Cleansing Violet Flame meditation and felt the guilt lift off my shoulders. I now remember that I have always been a wonderful mom.

The energy around this loss is tremendous. Some people bury it deep inside, where it manifests as debilitating depression or explosive anger. How did you channel this extreme trauma loss energy inside of you?

I channeled this trauma through helping others. I stayed in touch with Hilary's friends after her death. They came to the house and we met for coffee dates. I watched as they each swirled through their own grief. One of her friends attempted suicide, and then I really started worrying about all of them.

There had been a suicide by hanging at Hilary's school every year for several years in a row. I learned from her friends that the school was not addressing the problem. As I had coffee with one of Hilary's friends at the local coffeeshop, she told me that the school had thoughtlessly chosen *The Crucible* as its play that year, which includes the Salem witch hunts and death by hanging. Right above my head, pinned on a bulletin board, was a flier for the play with the illustration of a noose. I was horrified and furious. I met with the school principal and drama director about the insensitivity of their choice for all of the students who lost friends to hanging. They could not understand my concerns and were in total denial that there was a problem. A week after the play, another student hanged himself. I lost it.

Did you find a positive outlet to express your anger?

I wrote to the new superintendent about the ongoing problem with suicides, and he embraced bringing about change. There were student and parent presentations, changes to the health curriculum, and connections to mental health services in the community. I was heavily involved in these changes and recognized how much it helped me. I then created a group called Hilary's Hope. We gave teen presentations on mental wellness. The group eventually morphed into a support group for parents of children with mental health issues. It encouraged me to focus on other people and transform the pain into something positive. Hilary's death was not in vain; it now had meaning and purpose. The school district that Hilary attended now has Hope Week, a yearly program that provides resources on suicide prevention along with messages of hope and connection.

Many people create memorials to their loved ones. What ritualistic or ceremonial acts did you do to help you process your extreme grief?

Every day I wore Hilary's favorite necklace to keep a part of her close to me. I even wore her flip-flops in the winter because she once tried to sneak out in them on a snowy day, and she told me that your feet stay warm if you walk fast in the tire tracks. She was right. I used to go to the cemetery often. I had a ritual of bringing her favorite drink of a Starbucks Pumpkin Spice latte, playing her favorite CD, and leaving flowers. I felt closest to her there. On the first birthday she was gone we had family and friends meet us there, and we had dinner and a balloon-message send-off. I took her Easter baskets, Halloween decorations, and holiday wreaths decorated with her favorite colors. On the anniversary of her death, I left a note telling her how much I loved her. Eventually, we had a marker created with her picture and heartfelt messages from all three of us. I don't feel the need to go to the cemetery much anymore. I feel her presence around me at different times now and know that she is always in my heart.

Most of us don't have a reference point for the loss of a child, much less a suicide. Was there anything you experienced earlier in your life that helped prepare you to deal with this loss?

I lost three pregnancies between the births of my two daughters, but those were quite different types of loss. It was much harder to lose Hilary. I learned that it was helpful to be gentle with myself, and I knew to focus on my living child and keep going forward, even when I didn't think I possibly could. I did learn about grief through my earlier experiences, but the trauma surrounding Hilary's death left me debilitated.

I have heard a parent say they wish they could have gone in their child's place. Did you ever want to end your life because the pain of losing your daughter was so great?

I did have thoughts of wishing it had been me who had died, and I did have thoughts of wanting to end my life because I wanted to be with her so desperately.

How did you move through this?

Kendall kept me grounded and present. She needed me to be her mom and stay with her. She truly kept me alive.

Many studies show that following the death of a child, the parents will likely divorce or the marriage will be irreparably damaged. How did the loss of your daughter affect your marriage?

My marriage completely fell apart after Hilary died. It was like we both had the flu at the same time. We were desperately trying to just breathe and survive moment to moment. We each had our own way of dealing with the loss. I focused on Kendall, Hilary's friends, my suicide prevention work, Hilary's Hope, and developing my spirituality. He focused on the accumulation of things.

How did you try to work through these challenges?

He found some comfort in the heart signs that Hilary would send. I tried to get him on board with the spiritual changes in my life and how they helped, but that didn't work for him. I remember being dragged around the Boat and RV Show, shopping for a boat. This was only a few months after Hilary had died, and I did not understand the need, since I had had few experiences with boats. He had childhood memories of being at a lakeside cottage, so I just went along with buying a boat. Next, he took me shopping for a convertible car. I was not thinking coherently yet, so again I went along with it, hoping it would help him. We did have some wonderful times on the boat with family and friends those first couple of summers. But he stayed stuck and cycled around in his grief, and I couldn't take anymore. I saw no solution in sight, so I left and we divorced.

Did you ever think that it would have been easier if your daughter had died another way?

Suicide has tremendous stigma surrounding it, and I was so filled with shame that I did wish she had died in any other way. I wished it had been a car accident, an illness, or even a murder. When I told people I lost her to suicide, there would be an awkward silence followed by a look of shock and horror. I felt like I had to explain more and take care of them instead of having them care for me.

Did you feel judged by others?

I felt deeply judged by others. In my mind, people were talking about what a bad mother I was and wondering how I could have let this happen to my child.

Was this your projection, or did you in fact hear others say or imply this?

Once I was having lunch with an insensitive person. The conversation turned to another family that had had a child with mental illness problems. She said the family was so crazy that the girl killed herself. She kept on talking, but I was stunned and heard nothing she said after that. I quickly left and cried in my car all the way home. It reinforced what I was afraid people were thinking and increased my guilt and shame. After that, I only talked to and spent time with people I knew were safe and would not hurt me.

How do you frame Hilary's death? Do you say, for example, that she died by suicide or as a result of a mental illness?

After that lunchtime experience, I stopped telling people I had lost a daughter at all. It was just easier. Now when I'm introduced to people,

I say I have one daughter. I tell someone the story only when I get to know them. I personally hate the term "committed suicide." It sounds like the person committed a crime. I thought about saying that I lost her to mental illness but decided that would lead to more questions. I now prefer to say that I lost my daughter to suicide. In my mind, that is exactly what happened.

When you were finding your way back to yourself, did you think it was possible to find the self that you knew before, or was she gone forever?

I thought it would be impossible to find myself again. I was only a shadow of who I had been. I didn't recognize myself at all. I was so traumatized and deep in the pain of grief. I felt lost and afraid that I would never get better and feel like myself. I was frustrated when I couldn't take on the same activities and tasks. I never did become the old Bonnie again, but I became Bonnie 2.0, a new version of myself. Parts of me remain the same, but I have changed and grown.

Who or what did you hold on to that helped you find your way back?

My therapists, books, friends, and the deep faith I developed have helped me find my way back to center. I've learned all sorts of coping skills for my coping skills tool belt. My Healing Touch practitioner has helped me peel away layer upon layer of pain. With her, I release the old and leave filled with bright, healing light.

Many people say that times heals all wounds. Do you think that's true?

I believe that time buffers wounds. I don't think healing happens magically; you have to work at it. I was always strong and incredibly resilient. I do not bounce back from setbacks and difficulties as easily as I once did. It takes more effort and time to process things and regain my strength.

Now, years later, when you go back into the pain of your loss, does it feel different?

The constant heartache comes less often, and the waves of grief and anguish have diminished. Sometimes when I am triggered by events or the season, I feel pain. It is not as severe, and I am able to regroup quickly and move forward with my day.

You have a unique perspective on life and death because of this experience. What key message would you like to give to grieving parents who have lost a child to suicide?

First and foremost, you will get better. Keep a journal of your feelings and thoughts. It will help you to process all those raging emotions. I recommend finding a great therapist you connect with to help you walk through all the turmoil. I also recommend joining a parent support group. It helped me so much to have a friend who had gone through the same thing. I think it is helpful to stay open to signs from your child and remember that they are a lot closer to you than you think. I found Reiki and Healing Touch to be an important part of my healing process because they helped me to recenter and release pain and trauma. I found my readings with a reputable medium to be very helpful. Many questions were answered, and I spent some fun time reminiscing with Hilary. I have also created a symbolic box inside of me where I keep all the trauma, grief, and pain. Sometimes the box opens when I'm triggered, but I am able to snap it shut, set it aside, and go on with my life.

Now, more than ten years after Hilary's death, how has your worldview changed?

Before Hilary died I was pretty materialistic and caught up in the trappings of suburban life. I now focus on people and relationships. The accumulation of things has very little meaning to me.

This experience probably tested you beyond anything you thought you could manage. What emotional and mental strengths have you gained?

I was definitely transformed by the experience. I am a better listener, more compassionate, able to sit with people in pain and help them feel better. I'm less judgmental and more understanding of other people's perspectives and how their life experiences have shaped them.

I also recognize and name my emotions clearly. I use techniques that help when I am stressed or anxious. I need time by myself each day. I've learned about healthy boundaries in relationships and the freeing nature of forgiveness. I've had life-changing experiences during prayer and meditation. I've learned about the Emotional Freedom Technique (EFT), tapping, and energy healing. There are days when Hilary feels so present I can almost touch her. I doubt I would have learned all this without her death.

In what ways do you feel more vulnerable and fragile?

I feel more fragile to stress than I used to. I have days when I try to do too much and get overwhelmed. I plan my days carefully and adjust them to how I feel. I do not schedule as much in the evenings because I am just plain worn out from my day at work. I like to have a set routine and continuity in my life now; before, I was more spontaneous. I am not interested in the news because the suffering and discord are upsetting and anxiety provoking. I do not like scary shows or movies or anything that might include a hanging. I like to surround myself with kind, loving people who support me. I like repetition, reruns, and rereading books because I know how they end and so feel comfortable and safe.

How do you find happiness, contentment, and joy today?

I practice gratitude to identify the joy in my life. There are things to be grateful for even on a particularly difficult day. I look for humorous events that happen each day. I smile when I see a dog with his head hanging out the window. I laugh when my students say funny things. I smile when a young child waves at me at the grocery store. I love to think of Mother Mary, Jesus, and God giving me hugs. I love to look for signs and "coincidences" that God sends to me to answer my prayers. Kendall constantly amazes me and brings me joy as she becomes the strong, independent woman I hoped she would become. Life goes on, and so does joy. Life is not about waiting for the storm to pass. It is about learning to dance in the rain.

I do feel bittersweet joy around the holidays. I am still able to enjoy them, but they tug at my heart. When I attended Hilary's best friend's wedding several years ago, I was torn by the sadness of Hilary not being there to celebrate, the fact that I would never see her marry, and my joy for her friend. It was a very difficult evening.

What is your message for those who struggle to find hope?

I heard somewhere that life is like a tapestry. We humans only get to see the back of the tapestry, which is full of criss-crossed threads, knots, chaos, and disorder. Only God can see the front of the tapestry, full of order, sense, and beauty. Our lives are full of questions and doubts and wondering why. We have to develop faith that what happens in our lives has meaning and purpose in a way we cannot understand while on earth.

Soon after Hilary died, a friend told me that if I stayed open, there would be a gift for me in this. I thought she was crazy, but with time, I have learned that she is right. So, stay open to the possibility that something good will come from what you are going through right now. It might not be obvious for a while.

I often asked why me and why my family at first. I couldn't understand why this had happened to me. It didn't help me to ask this over and over because there was no clearcut answer. I started to question less when I got involved with my suicide prevention work and Hilary's Hope. I heard from a young woman whom I had never met that Hilary's story had kept her from taking her life. I began to think that there was a bigger story going on here beyond my own. I chose to believe that

Hilary's death led me to working with her to help others. I also developed my spirituality, which I shared with others. I believe that I will not get the answers to all my questions while here on earth, so I need to have faith and carry on loving and supporting my family and partner, and finding purpose and meaning in my work.

The greatest lasting legacy of Bonnie's transformed pain is in the form of Hilary's Hope, a suicide prevention program geared toward high schoolers. Creating this program, and speaking before thousands of people about her pain, helped Bonnie channel her grief into action. Hope Week is now a yearly program integrated within Hilary's school system. Bonnie's love for her daughter lives on to help others find hope in the darkness. Hilary's life and death have meaning.

~

Reflections on Bonnie's Story

Bonnie's journey with her daughter's death is a story of immense and profound pain that most of us cannot imagine. This experience stretched her beyond anything she'd ever known, yet through it all, she kept returning to an internal guidepost. This baseline part of her never left her, but it was battered and hard to access through her grief. Even through soul-crushing pain, a wise survival part of her kept moving forward. This helped her get through the agonizing grind of living without her daughter for another day and to seek out others who helped her find her way in the world again.

Bonnie's story is inspirational in that she never gave up, even though her marriage dissolved and she had moments of wanting to die so she could be with Hilary. You read how she couldn't process her daughter's death at first because she was inconsolable and lost. Attending to and understanding the pain would come later, as early on she had to focus on getting through the numbness of the day and going to sleep at night only to wake up and remember the awful nightmare she was living in. She was fighting to stay alive and present for Kendall to keep her life from being derailed.

The raw emotional trauma that Bonnie experienced is an unequivocal life changer. She was forever changed by this trauma and had to redefine who she was on the other side of this event. The coping skills that she utilizes help her live with her wounding. She's not healed from this, she's not the same as she was before, but she is healing every day in ways that she had never imagined. Today she finds it easier to smile. She is healing and walking her own tender path.

Parents of a child who chose suicide are truly the walking dead, shells of their former selves, at least initially. Their will to live on for their other children or family is often the only reason many don't take their own lives. None of these parents or family members could have imagined the incredible emotional pain they experienced as a result of their child's death, and they wouldn't wish this pain on their worst enemy.

If you have lost a family member or friend to suicide, know that your grief journey is unique to you and that even though you feel alone, you are not. There is strength is talking with others who have held this unique pain. Reach out to the community of people who have experienced this type of loss and who understands what life is like after the suicide of a loved one.

Having lost a patient to suicide, I know firsthand how his death in this manner devastated me and brought up tremendous pain, anger, confusion, guilt, and questioning within myself. I had been working with him for about a year. He came in one day for his regular appointment, carrying his newborn. He appeared to be doing well and had a calm, happy demeanor after having been in a long period of depression. We had a good conversation and talked about his adorable baby, and I thought he was on the upswing. The following Monday I received a call that he died from suicide. This was a terrible shock. My heart sank, and I replayed our last meeting in my head. What had I missed? What hadn't I seen? He hadn't talked about suicide. Had his baby distracted me from these signs? But, of course, he didn't want me to see any pain, as he knew something I didn't know.

A suicidal person will sometimes have a burst of energy right before they kill themselves. They know they will soon be out of pain, so they appear to be relieved and happy. But my patient's elevated mood didn't stand out as a forewarning when I saw him. I wanted him to feel better and was glad to see him happier, which might have been why I didn't see his mood as a red flag. To think that a devastating decision underlies a moment of peace or relief is counterintuitive to the observer, but the suicidal mind is a mind with a sickness.

Healing after someone's suicide feels like empty grieving, as the survivors are missing parts of the story. We think that if we could just find that missing puzzle piece, then their death would make sense and we would be more at peace and have a sense of completeness. The confounding twist of this type of grief is that we will never have that puzzle piece, we will never know. This missing link requires us to extend ourselves into a place of holding the unknown. For me and others who live on after someone has taken their life, the path of grief healing is not easy, but it does get easier to hold. I have a gentle place inside of me that holds his bright smile, energy, and essence. I don't hold on to his suicide.

If you think someone is suicidal, don't be afraid to ask them about it directly. If you are suicidal, know that you can reach out and people will be there to help you. Be clear with others about your feelings, and tell them you are thinking about harming yourself. Remember that most people who are thinking about self-harm don't really want to die, they just want to be out of pain. Thoughts of suicide are normal; it's the loudest message that you can give yourself and others of how much pain you are in. Remember that you are not alone.

⁓

This is such a heavy topic that most people simultaneously are intrigued by it and avoid it. When you are feeling calm and centered, read through the following questions and allow the gentle answers to arise.

- Did Bonnie's story stir up some feelings that you didn't know you had regarding suicide?
- Do you know someone who decided that suicide was the only path they could take out of their pain? How did you respond?
- What do you look at differently now?

Take a break from reading and let the energy of Bonnie's story move through you. Take from her story messages of strength, resilience, and healing. Bonnie's strength is inspirational. Know that you, like Bonnie, can move through tragedy and trauma and go on to live a productive, happy life. ♥ Hilary

*Finding a glimmer of hope when we are broken
open is a treasure. Know that you can find hope
in the most unlikely places if you pay attention
and become open to the possibilities.*

～

Bonnie's charity of choice for her story contribution is Erika's Lighthouse, a beacon of hope for adolescent depression. Learn more at www.erikaslighthouse.org.

～

Additional Resources

National suicide hotline: 988

Shattered: Surviving the Loss of a Child, Gary Roe, Wellborn, Texas: Healing Sources Publishing, 2017.

Beyond Tears: Living After Losing a Child (revised), stories as told to Ellen Mitchell, New York: St. Martin's Griffin, 2009.

Life After Suicide: Finding Courage, Comfort and Community After Unthinkable Loss, Jennifer Ashton, New York, NY: William Morrow, 2019.

CHAPTER FIVE

The Stretch

Yeah. I mean, acknowledging is easy. Something happened or it didn't. But understanding . . . that's where things get sticky.
SARAH DESSEN

When the shockwave after a loss occurs, we are slammed into a new reality, and we impulsively just want to get through it. The second phase, the stretch, follows this initial period of shock. The stretch is the walk through an unknown land, a brave new world, with new language, new ways of thinking, and new feelings that we don't understand as we adjust to what is now missing from our lives. We are reluctant explorers in this bleak landscape, whether we like it or not. We want to go back to the familiar, which is still warm and close but receding from us each day.

In this phase, we feel like we are being stretched beyond belief. We say to ourselves, *I don't like that this loss just occurred* or *I'm scared that this happened and I don't know what to do with it yet.* We are moving out of shock and trying to figure out what happened so we can return to emotional safety. We are slowly acclimating our emotional selves to this new loss experience. Each step we take feels like we're going backward. We easily get triggered, remember the loss, and then feel our raw feelings. We think we're getting better, only to be asked, How are you today? and then we are a puddle of tears. The stretch is an emotional roller coaster; one moment we're crying, the next, we're laughing. One moment we're numb, the next, we feel raw.

This phase is the invitation to learn how to stretch and grow into deeper parts of ourselves as we hold our grief. It is the invitation to move on with life, which is often a big leap. It is during the stretch that we decide what we want to do now, how we will go about doing it, and when. We are moving toward feeling solace, but there's much more to experience before we get to that point.

SETTING THE TERMS

How we greet loss greatly determines
our emotional experience of it.

During the stretch, we begin to determine how we feel, and establish the terms of our relationship to the loss experience. We realize we are overwhelmed and wonder how we can get back to center. The feelings we have inside are like an impatient child; they're not going to give up until we give them recognition. Once we acknowledge these immense feelings, they don't have to work so hard to get our attention. Some days we can be productive, and sometimes all we can do is spin in grief and stare out the window. Painful sorrowful thoughts and feelings have a way of pushing in and ruining a good day.

We want to get back to feeling in control, stop feeling so emotionally wobbly, and become clear-headed again. The following are some ways we can begin to internally acknowledge this uncomfortable truth:

- I hate that this has happened, and I'm scared.
- I'm mad that this has happened, and I don't like it.
- I want to run away.
- This is unbelievable and upsetting.
- I guess this was bound to happen one day.
- Now what?

We initiate the stretch by acknowledging these normal thoughts and feelings. Even if we are upset or scared, we can acknowledge these feelings by saying to ourselves, *I don't like that this happened, but I will try my best to use all the tools I have to move through this experience and out the other side. If I can't do this on my own, I will ask for help. I will be gentle with myself.* When we have worked hard at developed good coping skills, a strong belief in ourselves, a positive support system, and proven resilience, then we say to ourselves, *I can do this.* Through this perspective, we set the terms for moving through the loss experience. All of this helps us to initiate and engage with our relationship to the loss.

If we don't have a strong sense of self going into the loss experience, then we will feel lost and will need to work harder to find sources of strength. These sources can be found through counseling or being around others who are wayshowers of positivity. Ignoring this opportunity for healing leads to a greater chance that the feelings of doubt, rejection, and fear will linger and perpetuate a state of depression or uncertainty.

Certainly, many people ignore losses in their lives, but these are often the same people who are sad and don't know why. Their loss bucket overflows with disregarded pain.

Moving through the Stretch

I'm not yet to acceptance, but I'm no longer in denial.

Moving through the stretch is a process, as is the entire loss experience. Some of us move through this part of the tender path with grace, but we often find unexpected barriers on the journey to healing. We resist reality when we hold back the truth of the loss with all of our strength, hoping it doesn't get closer. We reject reality when we discard it, and we ignore reality when we turn our backs on it. All of these reactions are defenses, when we pull the covers up and retreat into a shroud of shadows. They are parts of the emotional mechanism that drives the indulgent choices we sometimes make after a loss. They are avoidance and active denial in full bloom. We often subconsciously know we are engaging in these natural reactions as we try to cheat the truth and pretend it will magically go away. The quest becomes how to recognize when these defensive reactions are happening, bravely transform them, and join with the flow of the loss instead of treating it as the enemy.

Resisting the Stretch

Denial fuels our resistance, as it is the thin cushion between us and the stark reality of the loss. We think we are being clever as we resist the stretch, that we are fooling the loss, but this hubris quickly evaporates as the daily march of life goes on. Subconsciously, we are spinning in fear. We know what has happened, but our minds try to pretend otherwise and find all sorts of ways to distract us with our wounded expressions.

Here are some of the many ways that we resist the stretch:

We disregard responsibilities and find distractions.

We don't help our siblings clean out our parents' house to get it ready to sell.

We don't look for a job after being let go.

We don't develop a plan to deal with mounting debts.

We put off a partner's request to talk about an issue with our child.

All of these are ways that we shut down, push away, and say that we are going to stay in denial because we can control that. We have all done this at one time or another, but we know that this works only temporarily and that life has a way of shoving reality back in front of us. Many of these are akin to an indulgence. Ultimately, we have to deal with the loss. Not making a choice is still a choice.

I have had some experiences in my life where I felt like I was thrown into the deep end of a pool and had to hold on to two bowling balls while treading water. I didn't know what to do, as I was out of my depth with the situation at hand. I wanted to stubbornly resist the reality, but I knew I couldn't push it away. Ultimately, I found an inner strength and faith in myself; I knew that I was going to figure this out and that if I couldn't, I would ask for help. This is when everything shifted for me. Once I said I would ask for help if I needed it, the pressure lifted immediately, and I joined with the flow. I no longer felt alone. I became engaged and curious, at one with the journey. I was stretching in a way that felt like encouraging growth.

If you are going through a loss experience now, look at how you are acknowledging the loss and how you are resisting. Hold the resistant aspect of yourself; know that this is your protection system working overtime to keep you safe. See if you can gently guide yourself to do small things that will help you face the loss. You don't have to dive all the way in, just give yourself permission to begin to look at it. Ask yourself what you could do to begin to look at parts of this resistance. You may need to work through your more complicated feelings through journaling, which you will learn about in chapter nine, "Practical Tools for Honoring Loss."

Rejecting the Stretch

Grief is patient. It waits for us to find the courage to face the pain.

Rarely do we want losses in our lives, but this inevitable part of life helps us appreciate that which is still around us, that which we can touch, feel, and experience. Many people simply reject this elevated perspective of impermanence, however, and want things to go back to the safe and the known. If we reject the loss and pretend it didn't happen, chances are that it will take us much longer to integrate it into our lives.

Rejecting the stretch is different from resisting it. Some people don't feel like they should or even can mourn after a death or other significant loss. For whatever reason, their narrative is that they deserve to be miserable, lonely, and lost. They reject the idea that they can heal from their loss, as their self-esteem is wrapped up in it. This victim narrative, which often originates in childhood wounding, keeps them lost, hopeless, and isolated. They send a message to others that no consolation will heal their loss. I liken this to them sitting in a bathtub filled with cold, dirty water. It's time to get out, but they stay stuck, sitting in that tub, rejecting the reality and rejecting the healing. Sadly, they are comfortable in this place, as it is familiar.

Some people have an intellectualized, pragmatic response as to why they can't or won't give themselves the space to mourn. They say they can't dwell in the past, they have things to take care of, they can't just feel sorry for themselves, explaining away why they don't take the time to mourn. Others can understand this logically, as it makes sense that we all have to get on with life. But this response shortchanges the grieving process, and most likely their grief will get crammed into their loss bucket, ignored and shut down. This is yet another way that we isolate ourselves from our grief work and reject the opportunity to heal in the stretch.

These "practical" reactions to loss are often learned from older relatives or parents, but they may hide the real reason; some people do not feel worthy of giving themselves the space and time to grieve. For them, grieving feels like a selfish act; they think they should be stronger and able to deal with the loss. They judge themselves for feeling bad. This internal emotional self-abandonment can come from a variety of sources. For example, if they expressed emotion as children, they were shut down, ridiculed, or minimized. A fifty-year-old man once told me that when he was a boy, his father told him he was useless. He now realizes how this event derailed his view of himself for most of his life. He wasn't allowed feelings, so he rejected many opportunities to heal because of this earlier loss within him. Once this kind of thinking is internalized, the child, later the adult, clamps down the expression of emotion. Either they don't feel worthy of emotion or they never learned how to express it. They are uncomfortable when emotion comes up, as it's foreign to them. They feel overwhelmed, so they shut that down right away. This is one of the many origins of inner child wounding.

I see this pattern most often in those who grew up in an emotionally unavailable household. They have no frame of reference for how to express emotion, so they push it down and away. They usually get angry rather than feel sadness or other feelings that make them feel vulnerable and exposed. Vulnerability equals weakness to them, and they feel a great need to protect themselves. Anger and defensiveness feels like a safer emotion, as they feel more in control. They probably saw their family of origin express these emotions.

The man who was told he was useless when he was a boy lost access to his emotional range. His concept of self was thrown off course, and the carefree, authentic freedom in how he saw himself was ripped away in one statement. It wasn't until almost five decades later, in therapy, that he acknowledged this projected hurt from his dad. He was able to reconnect to his authentic self and symbolically give back to his dad the painful wounding that he had projected onto him. He gave himself the gift of emotional freedom. He healed the loss of not being in touch with his emotions.

Ignoring the Stretch

FEAR is an acronym for "face everything and recover."

Ignoring the stretch is playing a game of hide-and-seek with the loss. When we are in denial, we try to hide from the pain of the stretch, but the loss and pain are there whether we want to accept them or not, and will eventually find us. Denial is a fear response, much like the magical thinking of children who tell themselves that if they don't acknowledge something, it's not real. Those in denial ignore reality and create an alternative that doesn't include the loss.

Sometimes ignoring the stretch is easier than identifying with the loss or finding positive support. We think it's better right now to bury it and pretend it doesn't exist. We all make choices based on how we feel about a situation, but it's important to remember that this is just something we are experiencing, it's our reality at the moment.

If you know you are in denial and ignoring the stretch, if you don't want to touch it or look at it, be gentle with yourself and remember that this is normal. In time, you will ready to pick up and examine the loss, feel the emotions that surround it, and ease into the stretch. You will alternate moments of sadness with a clear perspective. This is natural as you integrate the loss.

Can you think of a time you resisted, rejected, or ignored the stretch? This is how we derail and delay the grieving process, which is why I bring these forms of denial into the larger discussion. Gently observe yourself, and use this new knowledge to inform future choices. You can use the honoring techniques described in chapter nine, "Practical Tools for Honoring Loss," to learn how to hold this pain as you heal.

CHANGE AFTER LOSS

There is change that inspires growth, and there is change that is loss. Change that inspires growth is when one door closes and another opens. Much of how we interact with change depends on our emotional landscape leading up to it. Examples of change that inspires growth are a job transition, a spouse who is unhappy and wants to go to counseling, and a serious but treatable disease. Each of these changes carries an invitation to step up and stretch, to open ourselves up so that a bigger part of us can embrace the change, to feel inspired to expand ourselves to new horizons. During the stretch, we reorganize our lives to accommodate the loss; we stretch to include it in our narrative.

Contrast this to a change that is final, such as a divorce or the death of a family member. This type of loss experience opens us to an entirely different kind of change. There is a simplicity in dealing with a death when compared to dealing with an ongoing loss experience, for example. A a death is final. There are no potential alternative outcomes; this is it. Dealing with a death stirs up many unresolved issues, as most people don't realize that they are walking around with unre-solved issues related to a previous death or loss.

Another example of how we acknowledge change is when we recognize that we have emotionally outgrown a friendship or need to let a relationship go when growth has become too divergent, when we recognize that we are making ourselves smaller to fit into their world in order to maintain the relation-ship. Too often people stay in relationships that are no longer working because they don't want to lose the friendship. When this happens, they usually are replaying unhealed wounding instead of acknowledging the loss of what the relationship once was and the need for a change. This is codependency. When we break free of a codependent relationship, real growth and change can occur.

The stretch takes us to the threshold of our relationship to the loss. This is where the real work begins.

The stretch is an ever-changing and dynamic experience, and we move through the stretch at our own pace. Whatever the loss experience, we need to adapt and stretch in order to align ourselves with the goal of joining with the experience. The objective is not to just get through and done with the loss experience, it is to be purposeful on each step of the journey.

Ask yourself what you need to do today to be in service to yourself. What can you do today to be in service to others? If we stay purposeful on our journey with loss, we will feel empowered, enlightened, and have a sense of oneness with the experience instead of feeling separate or disconnected. When we are one with the experience, we have a feeling of connection, drive, power, and agency. Even though it is a stretch, we are engaged.

Be Gentle with Yourself

Be gentle with yourself as you journey through your grief. You may be having a good day and then the funeral home calls and says that ashes are ready to be picked up, or the lawyer calls and says the divorce papers are ready to sign, or the doctor's office calls to say the test results are in. These sorts of situations feel like intrusions. They immediately bring us back to the loss, and we are thrown back to square one with our grief. But grief triggers are not about what we've lost; they are gentle reminders of the love we carry within. When they happen, they show that we are further along than we think, as what we feel at this stage is the push and pull of the grief as we move through it. We are beyond the shockwave. The great sorrow and fear we feel during the stretch are growing pains of our healing. Be gentle with yourself, as you are moving mountains inside of you right now.

Self-compassion, self-love, empathy, and a sense of resilience are essential tools to help us weather the weight and overwhelming feelings throughout a loss event. Self-care can be as simple as gently saying to yourself, *It's normal that I'm sad after my spouse died,* or, *I'm really upset and mad that I lost my job,* or, *It's okay that I'm feeling what I'm feeling.* Remember your resilience and that you have been through difficult experiences before. What did you use to get through them, and will those same skills work today?

Self-Compassion

Empathy is when you put yourself in someone else's shoes and feel what they are feeling. Compassion is when you want to do something about the pain.

Most of us neglect compassion for ourselves and are rarely taught how to give ourselves this grace. We are taught how to be compassionate toward others, how to give them comfort, attend to their needs, and be supportive. Yet, all of those kindnesses we give freely to others we neglect for ourselves. We punish ourselves, deny ourselves food or water, shut down and withdraw, go to our cave to sulk, or go to our depression nests. If we are lucky, others attend to our needs and show us compassion, but we are often too sad and don't have the energy or willpower to be gentle with ourselves. The denial of self-care and self-compassion—I'm just too sad to be good to myself—can reinforce the idea that things are really bad and that our self-neglect somehow proves it. Sometimes we simply don't have the energy to be kind to ourselves, as we are spent and exhausted.

Many of us try to stay strong and fight through a loss event. We want to show ourselves and others that we are still independent and in control. We aren't gentle with ourselves; we push ourselves beyond what we have to give. The best of us goes to work, where we put out all of our energy, and only the spent leftovers come home, exhausted. People who are going through a tough time may be able to do this for a bit, but then things start to break down. The stretch invites us to surrender to the flow and find an internal strength.

If you're watching someone go through this cycle, be gentle with them, as this is their way of learning to accept what is happening. See if you can offer some ideas for self-compassion, and maybe they will pick up on them. If you are going through this cycle, see if you can find small ways to extend compassion to yourself. They don't have to be big or grand gestures, just small ways to help yourself on your healing path. This will help you create a sense of grounding.

Here are some examples of gentle self-compassion through restorative choices:

- Take a nap when you need one.
- Set small goals for yourself; this will help you feel more in control.
- Set boundaries; don't talk with someone if you don't have the energy.

- Eat foods that are good for you.
- Be gentle with your self-talk.
- Give yourself permission to feel your feelings.
- Give yourself permission to let others help you when they offer.
- Ask for help.
- Take walks and give yourself words of gentle encouragement.
- Give yourself permission to know that not everything can be tied up in a neat bow.

Trying to push through an experience because you feel you don't have the time, the need, or don't feel deserving of self-compassion will probably come back to bite you. You may have the energy reserves to push yourself through, but is now the time to be a hero? Is this an old inner child wounding pattern of overcompensation, stubbornness, or not wanting to feel vulnerable?

One example of overextending ourselves and giving away our energy is in retelling our loss story over and over. Well-meaning friends and family want to know what happened, but they don't know that we've already given that same update to four other people that day. It takes tremendous energy to update people when we are going through a transformative loss experience. The retelling can be retraumatizing and zap what little energy we have to heal. If you find yourself in this type of situation, see if you can gently ease up on overextending yourself. You've probably done a lot of pushing through things in your life, so maybe you can try something different this time. Quiet the inner critic who pushes you beyond your energy reserves.

We can extend kindness to ourselves by having a clear set of internal boundaries. These are promises or commitments we make to ourselves, where we say, *This is what I need to do for myself today* or *This is how much energy I have.* To set a boundary for others, you can simply say, I appreciate your concern for me, and I want you to know that I'm following up with my doctors and taking care of myself. I don't have the energy today to go into everything, but, hopefully, we can get together in a few weeks and I can tell you more. Or, Thanks so much for your concern. Would it be okay for you to call my daughter so she can give you an update?

Hope and Resilience

When facing the unknown,
hope is as reasonable as despair.
—Martha Hickman

Resilience is the ability to bounce back from a situation and move on with our lives. It is the ability to stay afloat in the middle of a storm, the response that helps us to navigate a tremendously difficult time and still feel intact. It is the strength we call on to help us through the stretch energetically. Self-compassion reinforces resilience because we are giving back and replenishing ourselves so we can call on an internal strength.

A key ingredient that fortifies resilience and encourages strength in a storm is a sense of hope. Hope is when we call on our trust in ourselves, or something outside of ourselves, to be a beacon toward where we are moving. Hope and resilience work hand in hand to help us weather a storm, and we can't achieve much in life without either. We sometimes have to strive to find hope, especially in times of great struggle. We do have the ability to generate hope within, but it can also be inspired by something outside of ourselves.

Hope is a wonderment, love, and trust. It's when we give ourselves the gift of dreaming of a reality that we want or need to happen. Hope is the prayer of a parent whose child is going in for surgery or a job applicant who really needs this job to help their family. Hope isn't grand; hope is soft and sometimes silent. We can find hope if we believe in ourselves, someone else, or something outside of us. We can find hope in the smallest of gestures and the quietest of moments. We need to become still inside to access hope. This is when we gently ask where we have found hope in the past so we can draw on it now.

Hope is there even in the darkest hour. If you feel lost and without hope, search inside to find a spark, an internal light, that feels bright and encouraging. Give yourself permission to hold on to that spark, even when your inner critic or depressed pessimism wants to squash it. Hold it gently in your palm like a small bird, giving yourself a sweet kindness and compassion. If you don't have a strong sense of resilience, you will probably need to rely on other people to help you stay focused and take care of responsibilities after a loss. If you need hope, consider who in your life carries a positive outlook. Can you lean into them? Ask them how they stay positive when they have lost hope; you may be surprised by their answers.

Resilience is the engine, and hope is the fuel. We need to refuel after we've been through a lot. Resilience is finding the strength to face a situation head-on. It's doing those things that need to be done but knowing our limits. It's having an internal belief system that we will get through this loss. It's giving ourselves gentle reassurance and encouragement, reminding ourselves of how we've overcome things in the past, and pulling on the strength of others to help us find our internal strength.

We all have our own level of resilience based on our personality, family of origin issues, life circumstances, and outlook.

Some people can quickly access this resilience after the first shockwave of grief and loss as they go into task mode and get the situation under control. Not everyone has a strong sense of resilience, though, as this quality is an extension of our personality. If no one in your life modeled aspects of resilience and fortitude, then you may not have a frame of reference for these behaviors. However, resilience is also a skill that can be learned. To build a strong sense of resilience, look at times you were challenged by a situation and persevered, when you made something happen or got through a difficult situation. Think of a time when you were stubborn or passionate and wouldn't let a situation be ignored or neglected, and use this memory to remind you of your resilience. You are stronger than you realize.

Resilience is gently holding pain and honoring it, not beating yourself over the head with the pain to prove you're strong.

Resilience is holding courage and vulnerability at the same time. Leaning into pain helps to stretch us and show ourselves how strong we are, but the key is to lean in just enough for it to be a good stretch. Resilience is not leaning into the pain until we break. Many people—mostly men, I find—lean too hard into the pain as an ego response, a way to show that they are strong and can take it. The difference between an ego response and resilience is that an ego response tries to claim personal power, while resilience is a give and take, the ability to navigate and bounce back from a situation while respecting the reserves we have. When we are resilient, we can rise to the occasion and then give ourselves some breathing room. If you find yourself leaning into the pain harder than you need to because you want it to just be over, then ask yourself why you are doing this. Are you trying to prove something to yourself?

—

The stretch is challenging for everyone, as we are asked to grow and change in ways that we didn't ask for. It's waking up and feeling pretty good and then remembering in a flash that our loved one is indeed dead, and the somber cloak of sadness envelopes us once again. Remember that you have resilience. You can hold this pain, you can move through this stretch, and you're going to make it. Surround yourself with people who are positive and hopeful, as this will influence your outlook as you rise to their level of perspective. Their behaviors and expressions will help you find a brightness inside.

Throughout this book, you are reading stories of how others called on their resilience and self-compassion to journey through their loss experiences. Use their stories as examples of how to explore these parts of yourself and to help you develop your tool kit of self-compassion and resilience so you can move forward with a sense of strength and agency when loss events occur. You are stretching and growing in new ways than you could have ever imagined before. Be amazed and impressed with your daily courage as your resilient hopefulness magnifies. However your loss lands on you, or you move through the stretch, it will be in your own time. An invitation to solace awaits on the other side.

The shape that loss takes within us over time varies.
Our wholeness is revealed as we incorporate
the loss into our life tapestry.

NICOLE'S STORY: UNINTENDED PREGNANCY AND LOSS

Nicole is a wonderful woman with an open heart and a great laugh. She is a divorced mother of two teenagers. When she was eighteen and just out of high school, she discovered that she was pregnant. After careful thought, she decided to not take on the responsibility of a child at that point and terminated the pregnancy. In time, she went on to marry the father. They had two children and then divorced after twenty-one years of marriage. Some time after the divorce, she discovered she was pregnant again but had not planned on having any more children. Just like when she was eighteen, this pregnancy came out of the blue, but unlike then, Nicole lost this child through miscarriage after six weeks.

Deciding to have an abortion is often a difficult decision and usually constitutes a significant loss in a woman's life. Some in society convey the message that having an abortion solves the problem of an unintended pregnancy, but the resulting loss and a woman's emotions around it are often left unacknowledged. The same is true, and maybe even more so, for miscarriages and stillbirths. Women have reported to me that this experience was hushed away, minimized, or dismissed, the loss never acknowledged for the mom or the dad. As a result, many women doubt their feelings of loss or feel they are wrong if they have any emotions around their experience.

Rarely are these experiences acknowledged or honored as a loss. Some women see the end of a pregnancy as part of their life story and have worked through their feelings, while others are tormented by it. Today, Nicole has worked through her feelings regarding her abortion and miscarriage and is living her best life, surrounded by friends and engaged with her work. What follows is Nicole's perspective of walking through two different unintended pregnancy experiences.

(Note that unintended pregnancies are those that are mistimed, unintended, or unwanted at the time of conception.)

*When you were eighteen and discovered you were preg-
nant, what your first thoughts and feelings?*

When I found out I was pregnant, I was scared, shocked, and completely overwhelmed. I grew up in a religion that said you were a
murderer if you had an abortion, so I was extremely scared, and
scared to tell the father. I knew he would not want to have a baby at
the time and that I could not have a child alone, so I felt I had no other
option. My family already was not supportive of me, so I felt alone
except for my boyfriend and some friends.

*When you decided to have an abortion, what were your
feelings leading up to the procedure?*

I was in a complete fog and could not comprehend how I was going
to go through with it. I felt alone. I would just cry, and I felt I had to
keep it a secret lest others judge me for it. I also had a hard time
with thinking that God was going to judge me and that I was now an
unforgivable person.

Were your friends supportive of your decision?

I told only my boyfriend, my boss, and two friends. Oddly enough,
those two friends had gone through the same thing just before me
and so were supportive, but they were also going through their own
healing and coming to terms with their choice. My boyfriend was a
little more supportive, but he was not very in touch with his feelings.
He chose to tamp them down and felt I should do the same. So,
even though I felt I was a sinner and could not be loved because
of what I was doing, I found myself turning to prayer and guidance
from above.

*Did you acknowledge the abortion as a loss, or did you see
it as something you just had to do to take care of yourself?*

I definitely felt it was a loss, although I did not speak of it to anyone except my boyfriend. I just kept it inside and tried to deal with my emotions as best I could.

Did you consciously process this major event, or did you just get on with your life?

I mostly tried to just get on with my life. I kept it hidden from everyone except the few who knew but who would rarely talk about it. The clinic I used had protesters out front all the time, and yet the day I went, there weren't any. I chose to see this as divine help. I prayed and thought of the baby a lot.

We forget how young eighteen is, yet here you were, having to make an adult decision. Did this feel overwhelming?

That is so true, we do forget how young that is. This decision felt totally unreal and completely overtook my thoughts all the time. I believe it is what moved me to try different things. I didn't go to college because I took beauty school throughout high school, so I had already started my career at that point. I was near the end of beauty school and training to become a hairstylist, which had been a dream of mine since I was very young.

Did you have any experiences earlier in your young life that prepared you to make a decision about your unintended pregnancy?

Up until then, I hadn't done much that you would consider wrong. I tried to live my life well and not fall into alcohol or drugs like a lot of teens do. I relied on faith and prayer and my connection to my spiritual beliefs and knowledge.

What did your eighteen-year-old self need to hear?

I needed to hear that I was not alone and that I would not go to hell for making this choice.

Did you feel that a part of you was lost after the abortion?

I definitely felt it change me, and it also changed my connection to my boyfriend. I did not feel the open love for myself that I had had before the experience. I know I shut down a bit and got hidden and lost within myself. I began to tell myself that this was something that others went through all the time and that if I could push it away, it wouldn't be so bad.

Was your boyfriend involved in the decision-making process?

He was the one to say he wanted me to have an abortion. He paid for all of it and felt it was 100 percent the right choice for both of us. My mom was pregnant at seventeen and had the baby, and my parents got married because of it. I didn't want to become them, nor did he.

What acting-out behaviors do you feel were related to this loss experience?

I had plenty of acting-out times afterward. I tried many different things to mask the pain and loss. I also grieved a lot throughout my twenties. The father and I would rarely talk about it, but I would feel better when we did.

Was there a wayshower for you, someone whom you could lean into and gather inspiration from?

Not until much later in my life, after I had my other two children. She was a shaman friend whom I was working with. She channeled my son's soul and helped me to forgive myself, him, and the whole experience. Then she continued to help with the healing and releasing.

How did your unintended pregnancy affect your sexual relations?

It absolutely affected me at first. I began to not like having sex. It felt dirty to me after the abortion. He, too, was thrown off by it and had the thought that it could happen again. Eventually, I started healing and accepting sex and choosing to experience it again. We knew we were not going to choose pregnancy again until we were sure, so we took extra precautions to ensure it wouldn't happen again until we were ready for a child.

Many in our current society have polar-opposite views regarding abortion, including the view that abortion is a shameful event. How did you work through your perception of yourself from this perspective?

At first I chose not to see that at all. I was keeping my secret 'til death, and even after. But when I chose to allow myself to feel and see and understand what I went through, I changed my perspective.

How did you transcend these feelings to become more whole?

I saw how I could heal and choose growth from the experience and share it with others. I knew if I could help women see the experience from all views, it could be of great service. In order to do so, I had to tap into it all to feel it, forgive it, and love it so I could make space to heal. This process isn't a race but a flow of faith and love.

How did you find your center again so you could grow into a functional adult?

I accepted the wholeness and truth of my experience and began to see a higher perspective. I also saw and connected to the soul, who began to show me his side as well. It was all quite healing and loving.

After you married, did you embark on having a child in a conscious, purposeful way, or was it something you left to chance?

Once we decided to have a child, we both felt we were ready, and my beautiful daughter was immediately conceived. You never know how soon the Universe will comply. I was so honored and grateful to be pregnant. I really gave my all and did my best to comply with my doctor's orders. My daughter was born happy and healthy.

Were there any shadow feelings from remembering the loss at eighteen?

No, by this time I had grown and been through healings and forgiveness and different perspectives.

Have you ever done a ritual or ceremony to honor the child you decided not to have?

I did do a healing ritual, where I spoke about the baby and gave love and gratitude for him in front of others, who were doing somewhat the same thing for their own loved ones.

How do you think of this unborn child today?

I see this child as always with me, loving and supporting me. I believe that souls continue to grow, whether they are here in the physical body or in the astral. It's part of the blessing and the purpose of all we went through together.

What would you like your younger self to know?

Looking back, I would tell my younger self that all will be well. You have not done anything wrong, nor are you alone. I believe now that the choice was never fully mine. It was the soul's choice not to come through, yet it provided for me and my boyfriend, who became my husband, the growth we both needed. That experience has led me to where I am now in my life. Without it, I would not have learned the forgiveness, compassion, and understanding that I have. I know that that soul is always with me, guiding me and loving me at all times, just as I know it is receiving the unconditional love I have for it.

One study shows that one in four women will have an abortion before the age of forty-five. What would you want a woman to know if she is thinking about having an abortion?

I would tell her that it is her choice and that no one can judge her for it. I firmly believe that no matter what the choice, the soul is aligned to this decision. Ensure that you are giving love to yourself, and seek guidance if you begin to feel lost or swallowed in your emotions. You are a worthy woman making a choice that is neither good nor bad but is aligned to your life in this moment. Feel into the choice and choose with love, for yourself and all involved. You cannot choose wrong. You are love and never alone.

Some women who have had an abortion never tell anyone. Some walk with a phantom pain of sadness, having never consciously acknowledged their loss. Some won't even mention it to medical providers. What advice do you have for women who never talk about this loss?

I would say that any and all feelings you have are valid. But as someone who has come from a buried depth of the same experience, I can say that you are lighter when feelings are released. Even if all you can do is write all the feelings you have down on a sheet of paper, do it. You will be releasing and clearing the emotions so they will not weigh on you or overtake your thoughts. Be gentle with yourself.

Many women who have had an abortion struggle with how to weave it into their narrative. How and when did you incorporate the fact that you had an abortion into your narrative?

I began to incorporate my abortion into my story only after the work with the shaman. But still, only a few people would hear it from me. I consider it a sacred part of my life. It was a big growth for me. Since then, I have shared my story in my services of mentoring and guiding people who come to see me. Many feel no one understands unless they have lived it. Even then, each experience is unique.

Later in life, after your divorce, you were dating a man and became pregnant, essentially a parallel to your unintended pregnancy at eighteen. What feelings came up for you?

The feelings that came up for me were, first, shock, then complete love and joy. I honestly didn't think about or link any feelings to the earlier pregnancy. I truly loved my partner and was blessed and excited to share this with him.

How far along were you when you realized you had a miscarriage?

I was five weeks along when I discovered I was pregnant. About two weeks after that, I felt a shift and took two or three more pregnancy tests to be sure. I am very in tune with my body, so I was becoming more aware of the internal shifts, until the day we rushed to the ER, where the miscarriage unfolded.

What were the feelings that swept over you?

I was sad and confused but also completely understood that there was higher reason to all of it. Also, the energy of the soul absolutely came through. As the miscarriage was happening, the entire hospital lost power and all of their computers shut down. This was no surprise to me, and a higher confirmation.

What feelings came up when your miscarriage was confirmed?

During my pregnancy, I was receiving messages about the soul and the energy and light I was carrying. I felt honored and knew that all is always in perfect alignment with our souls and selves.

Did this event feel like a loss?

I did feel a small loss at first. So did the father.

Did you tell others about your miscarriage?

We did tell others, especially since we had told some people that we were expecting. We asked them to hold space and prayers for the soul and for us. They sent love and support, sometimes silently.

Why do you think some people don't talk about miscarriages or stillbirths?

I think for some the pregnancy doesn't feel real because they never physically see the child. I also think that they don't realize it can have an effect on them, for the same reason. Sometimes they haven't told anyone that they were pregnant in the first place, so they don't feel the need to share it.

After your miscarriage, what did you do for self-care?

The miscarriage took place one day after my forty-fifth birthday. I already had plans to leave town three days later for an advanced training course in my field of mediumship. After connecting to self and spirit, I decided I should still go. It was in a remote place, and I knew there would be healing on multiple levels.

Did you do a ceremony or ritual to honor the miscarriage?

I had a ceremony on a small beach near where the training course was, where I honored myself, the soul, and the father for the experience.

Is there a place for a man's feelings in the narrative of the pregnant woman?

Of course. For a man who didn't physically experience the pregnancy but felt along with the mother, it would be of great importance for each of them to work through the loss, alone and side by side. Just knowing that they are honoring the baby and the experience would bring a higher, or perhaps more aligned, balance of the whole.

What would be helpful for a woman to receive from a man to help her go through this loss, and vice versa?

Love, that is all that is needed. Love through all the feels, and time, are most helpful.

How does your faith in yourself, or a power greater than you, shape how you went through these experiences?

The divine knowing and the connection of both souls' energy have helped me tremendously. Also, the support from my partners, friends, and Spirit.

What helped you transcend these experiences to become whole again?

Mostly, my connection to self, my inner knowing and guidance, has helped me beyond measure. Honoring and experiencing each feeling fully. Forgiveness, if needed, and love, always. Faith, and knowing we are never given more than we can handle.

How do you see yourself differently as a result of these experiences?

I see that I went through life and soul growth experiences that have helped me to become the beautiful, loving, strong woman I am today. Growth goes on beyond what our eyes can see. I see that I am always under divine guidance and, most importantly, that I have never done anything wrong. Every action is always in full alignment to our soul's purpose. I am grateful and blessed. I will always be connected to these souls, both in spirit and while I'm in physical being.

Hopefully, my story resonates with someone. I live my life in service to being of love, divine help, and support, for Source, All, and Me. Thank you for honoring and allowing my experiences here. We are blessed and eternally grateful. Blessings of love and peace.

~

Reflections on Nicole's Story

Nicole was brave to go to this deep, sacred place within and share her story. For many women, an unintended pregnancy is filled with conflicted emotions and shoulds, shaming, and judgment. Choosing abortion was a big and heavy decision for such a young person to make, especially from a lonely place. Nicole clearly states how her idea of herself shifted once she knew she was pregnant, as well as after the abortion. We learned how, after the loss and during her stretch, Nicole went through an indulgent phase. She had a natural adolescent response to such a big event, one that many, in fact, choose when they are moving through a stretch phase. Nicole's story is one of great courage, faith, challenge, and a belief in herself. The stretch she went through after her abortion helped and encouraged her inner strength, but she didn't realize how courageous she really was until long after the fact.

We often don't fully process these intense experiences until years later. Once we have lived some life and have more space between ourselves and the experience, we can look back and recognize how we were feeling. In the moment, however, we are overwhelmed and often just want to get through it, to not feel it. The prefrontal cortex is still developing at age eighteen, so having a bigger perspective of such events is very hard to do at that age.

Many women who choose to have an abortion are not offered the help they need to process this unique grief. They leave the clinic feeling that they followed through with a choice they felt they had to make. Rarely are these complicated feelings processed or worked through. Often, these women are left alone in their sorrow, as other people in their lives don't know what to say or how to provide comfort. These women grieve but often in silence. Some women want comfort, and some want to be left alone. Some who come to see me have held on to this knowledge for so long that they finally need to tell someone in a confessional way. This silent shame is a huge emotional burden for many women, but it can be healed, as Nicole shares in her journey.

Perhaps you have gone through a situation similar to Nicole's or someone in your life has faced this choice. Whatever your thoughts are about abortion as a response to an unintended pregnancy, Nicole reminds us of the depth of personal struggle many women go through when they are faced with this choice. She also gives us a deeper understanding of the souls journey in this unfoldment. Through this expanded perspective her message is about having compassion for others who have to make decisions about their bodies that many cannot imagine facing.

After I was born, my mom became pregnant with her second child. The baby died in her womb at eight months. My mom was to deliver in a Catholic hospital, and their unjust policy required her to carry her now-dead baby to term. Then, when the baby—my brother, James—was delivered, they denied this child a baptism. My mom was adamant that her child be baptized, especially after such a traumatic pregnancy, and they finally relented. My brother is buried on top of my great-grandfather's grave and is waiting in spirit for my sister and me.

All pregnancies involve and stir up emotions. The decisions that mothers- and fathers-to-be make are not easy, and they are not done thoughtlessly or carelessly. Anyone who has worked in healthcare will tell you that more people than we realize have had unintended pregnancies, stillbirths, miscarriages, or abortions. Each person who walks this path has to face their own shadows of pain before, during, and after the event. I have compassion and love for any person who lives this experience.

- What emotional reactions do you have to Nicole's story?
- Did her story bring up long-dormant feelings?

If you know someone who has had an unintended pregnancy, stillbirth, miscarriage, or abortion and they bring up this topic, ask them if they'd like to talk about it. They may be ready to hold this experience in a new way.

⌒⌣

Nicole's charity of choice for her story contribution is the Delta Spiritual Foundation, which brings people together to further the advancement of spiritual study for the highest good. Learn more at www.deltaspiritualfoundation.org.

⌒⌣

Additional Resources

Planned Parenthood provides birth control, sexual identity and gender support, abortion, medical services, and much more. Learn more at www.plannedparenthood.org.

The organization Unintended Pregnancy provides information on the choices for an unintended pregnancy. Learn more at www.unintendedpregnancy.com.

Support after Abortion is a nonprofit that works with more than eight hundred agencies to individualize the care that a person impacted by abortion receives and to find the hope and healing they deserve. Learn more at www.supportafterabortion.com.

CHAPTER SIX

Moving toward Solace

I know now that we never get over great losses; we absorb them
and they carve us into different, often kinder, creatures
—GAIL CALDWELL

The third phase of the tender path, moving toward solace, is
when we move from a time of anguish and a river of tears to a
time of soft sorrow and then clarity, confidence, and comfort.
It is when the void from the loss settles in. Solace means that
we are finding comfort and consolation, not that we have
everything figured out and we're better. It is the expansion
of our emotions into a new plane. It is gentle self-care and
self-compassion as we bring a healing balm over the deep
ache. The situation may not be resolved—a divorce is not
final, a bankruptcy is still ongoing—but we are acclimating
and finding a place for this new reality. As we move through
the stretch, we are making space for the solace. The raw heart
pain isn't as searing or sharp as it used to be. The longing becomes a dull ache. The heart now longs for healing more than

it wants to retreat into sorrow. We learn from the stretch that we can't marinate in the sorrows of the past or project them into our current situation, as doing so impedes our movement into solace.

From a place of solace, we can more easily see where we once held the wounded feeling of loss within us. We are on the far side of the loss, looking back. The question becomes who we are now, as this is a time to honor the transition and the change we've gone through. We have new wisdom from the job loss, the injury, or the diagnosis. We know more now.

Many people in the throes of grieving cannot imagine feeling a sense of solace, as such relief from the pain is neither intuitive nor immediately within reach. Rather, solace is a consolation that we walk toward on the tender path of grief. We enter into a softness around the pain and the space within. As the shattered pain of grief lessens and we feel calmer, we begin to embrace solace, moving from sullen isolation to joining with life. We transition from hopelessness to hopefulness. We breathe, we unclench, we expand.

The time of solace is the invitation for us to transcend the stretch and the pain, to gently move to a time of reflection, living, and movement.

We don't arrive at a place of solace; we gradually assimilate and meld into this feeling. Solace is the culmination of many efforts of resilience and self-compassion. It is the result of wrestling with resistance, then gently holding, rejecting, and, finally, claiming. We know we have entered into solace when we start to experience more positive feelings and activities.

We are able to more easily breathe, and we experience more space between the waves of crying or deep sadness.

We eat better, go out with friends, and feel more confident.

We again find comfort in the familiar, and we engage in gentle exercises, such as yoga or walking.

We work or volunteer to feel a sense of place and purpose, and we feel hopeful about the future.

We dream of new opportunities and adventures, perhaps even taking a vacation.

We treat ourselves to a home renovation or another project we've wanted to do.

Many of these activities are similar to those of self-compassion that you read about in chapter five, and that's exactly the point. These actions are balanced and have a feeling of readiness, of *now is the time*. They are not indulgent, nor do they have elements of escapism. These choices are grounded in the sense that we've done much of our grief work and are now on the other side of it. We are not "over" grieving, but we begin to feel lighter and more like ourselves again. We more easily hold the loss without becoming a puddle of emotions. Tears may still well up when we talk about our prognosis or a loved one who has passed, but we're able to get through the conversation with a greater perspective. This is when we hold the loss in one hand and hope in the other. Our healing lives in the now.

An example of this perspective is when we see an object or an experience that someone who has died would enjoy and we think, *Oh, they'd love this*. There is a pang of sadness and melancholy, but it's not devastating. This is how we know we have entered into a space of solace. There is more breathing room between the pain of grief and feeling more healed. The triggered memories are poignant and sweet instead of awakening a deep heart pain. We learned to comfort ourselves in the stretch and regain our sense of self. We can dream again, imagining possibilities, as the future doesn't seem as bleak. We are wiser from having gone through the experience. We know more about ourselves and life and love. We are able to hold a tenderness for ourselves, as we have gone through the fire.

I have lost both my parents, but the parents of some of my friends my age and younger are still living. I don't like knowing what's coming for my friends when their parents pass away, the grief they will walk through. But I do know that because I've walked this path, I can be there for them emotionally in a way I could not have been before. Because of my own place of solace, I can create a safe container and hold space for them as they begin their walk with grief. These are some of the gifts of grief and loss that I can share with them. Solace brings us to a place of wisdom, a sacred space within. This phase holds extraordinary power, as it is the incubation of rebirth. We move from what we saw as regular life into a space of activated growth and energy

Times of solace give us the breathing room to wonder about where we would be in our lives today if the loss hadn't happened, or what we'd be doing together if someone who died were still here. We can imagine where we'd be if we hadn't gotten the divorce or if there had been no betrayal or job loss. Solace is a time that opens reflection within us because we are no longer weighed down by the heaviness of grief. We can stare out and imagine that if it hadn't happened, our lives may have turned out differently. Solace is another way we integrate the loss into our tapestry. We can compare it to other situations and to where we are in the present, integrating this perspective into our lives. This exercise serves as a benchmark for being able to appreciate our lives today. Know that your heart has expanded to hold the lessons your grief has taught you.

We are always looking back into our history of triumphs and traumas and reexamining the losses. We try to figure them out, turning them over and holding them, asking ourselves who we are now, even years after a loss. We reassure ourselves and reintegrate what the loss means as we remember what we went through and how we came out the other side. We can examine a loss today because we now have insights we weren't ready to receive before. Each step we take in life is built on the triumphs and traumas of our past.

As we feel more solace and comfort within us, we can move from going through the motions to living life again. There is freedom and perspective in solace, where we touch our divinity and step into a personal power that we have never felt before, a place of truth, wisdom, and knowing. Transforming loss fortifies us, making us stronger than before.

SHIFTING PERSPECTIVE

The minute you start seeing your obstacles as things that are made for you, to give you what you need, then life starts to get fun, right? You start surfing on top of your problems instead of living underneath them.
—*Ashton Kutcher*

A man called me one day and asked if he could bring his wife, Sharon, in to see me, as she had just been diagnosed with cancer and was paralyzed by fear and anger at herself for having gotten it. After we spoke for a while, I recognized that Sharon was a strong and practical woman. I offered her the idea that she could experience this disease in one of two ways. She could continue to be mad at the cancer (cancer feeds off anger), or she could work with her body, entering into a collaboration of compassion with it toward the best possible healing outcome. She immediately said she didn't want to be mad at herself all the time, that she'd already been doing that. So, being pragmatic, she asked me how she could change her perspective.

We talked about the options of embracing or fighting the cancer. She had never considered this first option before. By holding on to, being mad at, and mourning the loss of what she knew of her life pre-diagnosis, she was holding herself back from the possibilities of how she could embrace her new reality. She was focusing all of her internal power in the wrong direction. After careful thought, she decided to develop a path toward a more positive, hopeful, and encouraging connection to her diagnosis. She wasn't giving in by removing herself from her battle with cancer; rather, she was using all of her available energy to connect with love and hope instead of fear and limitation.

Sharon still didn't like that she had cancer; in fact, she hated that she had cancer and that she had to go through the treatment. The cancer diagnosis had ripped apart her known reality, and she had felt totally out of control. But changing how she saw herself in relation to the cancer gave her the gifts of power and control. The process of being kind to herself, and of taking responsibility for and honoring her feelings each day, gave her focus, hope, and direction. She took on this change in perspective, as she had gone through enough dark days of mourning and anger to know that she was ready to move on.

At the end of the hour-long session, Sharon turned to her husband and said, "I think I can do this. I feel better." His eyes welled up with tears as he saw the engaging, optimistic fire in his wife's eyes that he knew so well. Her cancer reality was still the same as it was at the beginning of the session, but what had changed was her relationship to her reality. The diagnosis had thrown her off-center, but by shifting her perspective, she was able to get closer to her center and re-connect with her personal sense of power. The only thing that happened was that Sharon shifted her perspective. She was still in her stretch but was moving toward solace.

Why is it that at the beginning and the end of life we are authentic and live in the now, while in between we forget and put importance on things that really don't matter?

Dr. Kübler-Ross writes of extending positivity and hope: "What all of our patients stressed was the sense of empathy which counted more than the immediate tragedy of the news. It was the reassurance that everything possible will be done, that they will not be 'dropped,' that there were treatments available, that there was a glimpse of hope—even in the most advanced cases." We have all heard how we need to "fight and beat" a diagnosis, but when we look at this as a fight, we set ourselves up for a battle. Sharon thought she was fighting cancer, but she was fighting with herself. If you are in this situation, look at how you can change your perspective and your language to more positively impact your healing journey. Words have mean-ing and energy to them, so give your body (or the circumstance) gentle strength instead of engaging in a battle with yourself. You are still working to heal, just with a different energy wrapped around the experience. Strength comes from merging and engagement with our reality. Say to yourself, *I'm doing everything I can in my power to help myself heal. I love myself.*

Those who have faced the prospect of death are forever changed. No longer can they feel immortal, invincible, or impervious. All of these are illusions, but our ego, our hubris, doesn't want to believe this inevitability and pushes it away. I've seen this in my patients, particularly in cancer survivors because they have faced down death. If there is anyone who is fearless, it is someone who has faced the specter of cancer and stayed positive, doing everything they could to heal within. They are truly fearless heroes. Once someone has been to that threshold, their worldview changes. Objects or situations that were once precious are now just things as what's really important comes into focus. They begin to see love, togetherness, closeness, and kindness as important parts of life. Everything else fades into the background and is put in its proper place. During the final days, all of the noise and undulations of life are reduced to poignant and profound I love you's.

I was visiting my mother's lifelong friend, who was literally a day or two away from dying. She lay in her bed, having taken all the energy she had that day to clean up and put on a new nightgown for a visit from my sister and me. She wanted to be there with us, to see us, but she was a shell of her former self and apologized, saying she didn't look like herself. I said, "But you're still you." With a half-grin and a laugh she said, "Yes, I guess so, I'm still me." She was still the delightful woman we had always known. Her energy and life force were still vibrant and available even though she was only days away from death. I realize now how she was providing us, and herself, with tremendous solace, giving the gift of her life force one final time.

Positive Claiming

Our journey of loss into solace travels with us over the arc of our lifetime. We always hold the loss memory alongside the joyful ones.

Positively identifying with a disease, diagnosis, or other such loss is reflected in someone who is ready to actively engage in moving into and through the experience and is looking for support. They talk about their diagnosis or loss in a positive and future-focused way. They see the loss as something they are experiencing, not who they are. They have done enough of their grief work that they aren't lost or confused about the loss nor in denial about their feelings. They have a strong sense of agency to move on to the next stage. Generally, they are looking for others who have a similar mindset to help them through their journey. They may join organizations focused on a cure and start to wear a ribbon or T-shirt or get a tattoo that is the symbol of that journey. They use the strength of that community to help them find the internal courage to work through their loss or go through treatment. The community helps them to know they are not alone. They fully embrace that this is what they are experiencing, and they are going to get through it and go on to create the best possible life. Instead of wallowing in and overidentifying with a loss or disease, they live in the now and acknowledge what is happening—they claim their reality. This is their positive expression and a way that they help themselves work through the loss. Through these actions, they create an internal platform on which to build a sense of solace. Their positive outlook becomes a big part of their healing. We can embrace our personal journey with loss, or we can be in a battle with it.

Not everyone needs this kind of support to help them through their journey. For some, their belief in themselves, their faith community, or their family and friends helps them feel strong. Others have a strong sense of self and an internal process that gives them the encouragement and strength they need. They can go within to find their motivation and drive, using their resilience to move them forward. If you are in this position, recognizing what you need in support is vital.

Our relationship to loss evolves over time if we indeed embrace and accept the loss. If we resist, push away, or fight it, the emotional energy around it will not evolve but become stagnant, stuck, and stunted. People who overidentify with a disease or loss often use it as a shield, enabling them to stay in a sad place or garner sympathy from others. This victim stance inhibits their healing and is usually demonstrated in other aspects of their life as well. If you know someone who does this, be gentle with them. Recognize that they are interacting with their disease in this manner for a reason that makes sense to them on their tender path right now. Overidentifying with loss keeps them spinning in their stretch, hindering the welcoming of solace. Self-love, compassion, and resilience move us into a place of solace, from where we can gently look back on our loss journey and see how far we've walked in the deep shadows of our grief.

Embracing a loss or a disease is not about celebrating or being happy about it. It is about finding a place inside where you can honor the experience, hold it, and pay attention to what your body and emotions need each day.

Emotional Landmines

All I did was open a drawer, and a million memories tumbled out. I had to shut it fast and tight, hoping to not be swallowed up by my mournful feelings.

Long after we have moved through the stretch, sometimes even years later, we may experience what I call emotional landmines. These are the objects, sights, sounds, smells, or touches that trigger a flood of memories about the loss. They happen unexpectedly, and we are immediately transported back to the loss event. Emotional landmines aren't always associated with loss or trauma, but they usually are.

One of the most common emotional landmines happens after the loss of a parent, when the family starts to clear out the house and get it ready to sell. This practical task of dislodging treasured items becomes supremely difficult once we start to uncover and explore the emotional landmines hidden throughout the house. In the excavation of someone else's life, we see them differently and learn what they held important and dear. Although difficult, this arduous task can be part of the healing process and help us to gently unfold our feelings of grief.

If you've ever been through this experience, you know what it's like to come back into your loved one's extremely quiet house and look around. You see how they lived in the house, where they put their glasses at night or where they placed the special gifts you gave them. You feel like you're walking in a molasses of memories, and it takes more effort to breathe. What was once their house becomes a shrine, and it's hard to disturb those carefully placed treasures. Each item, no matter how trivial, becomes special. It's a mournful ritual, and sadly, it's one I've done a number of times.

After my grandmother died, I went through her house, opening drawers and closing them right back up. Her powdery perfume filled the room, and for a brief moment I thought she was there. I didn't want to change anything because she was the last person who put things in that drawer in that particular way. I didn't want to disturb the illusion I was creating in my head that she was going to come through the door to ask me how I was. My innocent dream was that if I could leave things the way she left them, then she would live on. I didn't want to break the spell. Each drawer and closet contained a lifetime of treasures and memories safely tucked away, and discovering them felt overwhelming. Each object held her intentional energy.

It was impossible to leave everything intact since we needed to sell her condo, so my parents and sister and I all had to take a deep breath and unpack a lifetime of memories, keeping some items and dispersing others. It doesn't feel like it at the time, but this task is a cathartic archaeological dig. Ultimately, the treasures that I kept from her house found a new life in my house. They console me and bring me solace. My grandmother is with me every time I hear the grandfather clock chime.

Sometimes the landmines are inside of us, the losses we discover stored away in our loss bucket or have forgotten about. When we open that drawer or cabinet or bin, the landmines come spilling out. I was putting some things away and inadvertently opened a cabinet where we had stored our old dog bowls and dog collars, and I got an immediate wave of missing our dogs who had passed and their furry faces. I shut the door and started tearing up. I hadn't planned to open that cabinet and feel that rush. I didn't want to go to that sad place, but I just did. Life took me there, reminding me of my loss. Sometimes these emotional landmines are too overwhelming and we need to close them up again, but eventually, we have to face them for one reason or another.

Be gentle with yourself as you come across landmines on your loss journey. See if you can make restorative rather than indulgent choices to deal with the pain. If you're holding on to something that the person who died last wore, treasured, or touched, and you don't want to wash it or give it away, then store it for a while. You may regret forcing yourself to get rid of things as a way to move on, as this is a hard way to go through this time of loss. I know from firsthand experience that you will know when the time is right to clean or give away a treasure to someone who will cherish it as much as your loved one did. Memories and the love of the departed live within us, not in the items they collected that we hold on to.

If you need to clean out a space after the loss of a loved one, do the easy stuff first, like removing items that you don't have a strong emotional attachment to. Get rid of expired food, junk mail, and unsentimental objects first. For more emotionally charged items, have a friend or relative with you as you go through drawers, cabinets, or closets. Talk about the fun times and shared memories. Resist the temptation to have someone else do this cleanout for you. I've known too many people who had someone else do the cleanout. They didn't keep anything from a loved one's house and later regretted it.

If you don't want to disturb how your loved one had items placed in the house, take a picture of the space so you can remember how they it arranged. At first, you may not be able to get rid of or give things away, and this is natural. In time, your wanting to hold on to those things so you don't forget your loved one will gently fade. The gift of solace is that we don't grasp or cling to stuff as tightly; we begin to let go of the need for the object to hold their essence.

Eventually, you will realize that your loved one lives not in those objects but within you, which will help you to pass them on to someone who could use them today. Be creative in thinking about other family members and friends who might like certain items. Imagine how your loved one's treasures can live on with other people. Celebrate your loved one with the items they treasured, then pass them on. No matter what you want to keep from your loved one's house, those items will lose their magic once they are taken out of the house. Yes, you may keep that painting, chair, or table and know it was theirs, but it won't have the same sparkle as it did when it was in place in their house. Keep what's really special, and let the other things go with love.

ACTS OF CEREMONY

Endings are beginnings that let the light into heartbreak.

Every culture has a ceremonial process honoring the deceased through funeral rituals and practices. With solemnity and dignity, the acts of ceremony surrounding the death of a loved one play an important role in providing a sense of solace. If the deceased is a member of a faith community, there will probably be a set funeral rite that is followed. This ritual may include a wake or a time of witnessing and praying for the deceased person. The bereaved acknowledge the death and see their loved one in a casket or the cremation urn alongside pictures of the person living their best life. There may be prayers or other forms of funeral rites as well as a service or mass.

Afterward, there may be celebrations of a life well lived or a period of mourning. All of these rituals and ceremonies have a place and a purpose in helping us to grieve and to heal.

There are many ways of honoring a loss, and doing so is important so the loss doesn't get tossed into our loss bucket. Acts of ceremony help us to prepare to hold a sense of solace within. Any form of ceremony, large or small, marks time and signals to the subconscious that an event happened and needs to be honored. Honoring can come in such simple acts as lighting a candle or saying a silent prayer. These small acts help us to prepare for the conscious acknowledgment of the grieving process.

Rituals give significance to life's passages. Without these ceremonial rituals, we would have no reference point to signal that a meaningful shift of creation and loss has occurred. They are opportunities for people to share in the common bonds of grieving and honoring. There is a trend today to move away from or streamline and sanitize established funeral rites and ceremonies. Many companies give three days or less for bereavement leave. I call this "corporatizing" grief. There are also many sociological shifts that direct the amount of time we "should" spend grieving. Whatever the reason, recognizing the value inherent in rituals is important.

When we do not acknowledge grieving rituals and cycles, we limit our healing progression. For example, when I was six years old, my maternal grandmother, whom I was very close to, died. My parents felt it best that I not attend her wake and funeral, that I was too young to go. I respect my parents' choices, as I know they were looking out for me, and I probably was too young to go. But now, decades on, a part of me is still subconsciously looking for my grandmother. I think that by not going through these rituals as a little boy, I didn't experience the same kind of solace I would have if I had gone. This may not have registered even if I had attended, or it may have been too confusing or upsetting, but a part of me wonders.

I compare not going to my grandmother's funeral to what I learned from attending funerals as I got older. I had many older relatives when I was growing up, so as they started to pass, I went to many wakes and funerals. I began to take in the ebb and flow of life and death. As a child, I learned how to navigate weddings and birthday parties, and the ritual of funerals eventually became a regular part of life just like all of the other family ceremonial experiences.

The wake, which is the visitation at the funeral home, is a unique experience. Here you are in this really nice building, and there's your dead relative in a box bathed in pink, foamy light at the end of a room. At our family wakes, I usually saw relatives whom I rarely saw otherwise. One time I was shocked to see one of my uncles, a big man who had been in the military, break down crying at my grandfather's funeral. It was one of the first times I saw a man cry, and that was when I realized that adult men cry, too. Seeing my relatives together and sad was unsettling and overwhelming, but I learned that feeling sad, crying, and expressing mournful grief were normal. They modeled for me how to grieve and how to honor the deceased through ritual.

Some of the best things my sister and I did at both our parents' wakes was to bring some of the stuffed animals, toy boats, and other knickknacks that they had collected to offer to people who wanted an item to remember them by. We didn't want them, and there was a lot of stuff. Years later, people still comment on the keepsakes they took away that day. These are the little things that help us heal and bring us solace.

I use my example of going to wakes and funerals as events that taught me about the importance of ritual and ceremony and how they provide solace. Going through the ceremony speaks to a deeply emotional part of us that marks this time and says, yes, this person has died, and yes, time is moving on even though they died. Acts of ceremony—telling stories, laughing about shared memories, and saying words of remembrance—bracket our experiences, highlighting them in our tapestry. They honor the person's life and who they were to us. Being with family and friends, reminiscing, and seeing that others are just as sad and mournful helps us to accept the reality of the loss. We create a shared treasure box of memories through honoring as a group. We feel comforted being among our tribe.

After our dad died and my sister and I were cleaning out the house (we took four huge loads out of the attic alone), we would stay there overnight after working all day, which was our own way to say goodbye to the house. Months after the funeral, once we had fixed up the house and had it ready for sale, we had a disco party in the basement. Many friends and family felt a deep connection to the house, and this was a wonderful way for us to celebrate all the good times there. This experience was magical for my sister and me, as it was like a big, warm hug from our mom and dad. It was a great send-off and a beautiful way to honor our parents, the love they gave us, and the beautiful house that had sheltered us for fifty years.

There have been times when I wasn't able to make it to a funeral and instead took time to go for a walk in nature, saying prayers or intentions for that person's soul. I created my own way to honor them, to remember who they were to me and our experiences together, to thank them and bless them on their journey. I intentionally made space to honor them. Other examples of acts of ceremony include planting a tree in honor of your loved one, making a mandala on the sand, creating a memory stone with your loved one's name on it, putting one of their treasures in a special place, or having a cake or a party to celebrate their life on the anniversary of their birthday or passing.

Acts of ceremony connect us to the loss, to each other, and to ourselves. We feel the love and support of others, as we know we are not alone in our mourning. The subconscious speaks in symbols and images, so when we go through a ceremonial action, we see and acknowledge this time, marking it as a special moment in our lives. Think of this the next time someone you know has died and the funeral is scheduled. You go to support the family, but you also go for yourself. This person, in whatever capacity, had a place in your life. Honor them and yourself. There's an expression that we don't regret the funerals we attend, we regret those we don't.

Whatever sort of ceremony you choose to honor a loss, it's important to connect with why you are performing the ritual. Perfection isn't necessary, as your desire is to bring meaning and solace to your grief process.

～

Walking the tender path is a deeply personal journey, one we all have to take in our own way, at our own time. The shockwave is when the rawness and loudness of the loss are inescapable and indescribable. Our world is thrown upside down as we spin in denial at the thunderbolt of traumatic news. Then we enter a time when we are stretched beyond our capacity. We feel a lump in the throat whenever the subject of the loss surfaces. Every day, we learn uncomfortable, unknown details, or a life-and-death decision point is barreling down on us as we stretch and absorb the shock.

As time marches on, we name the loss and put our grief into action. This recognition and holding of the pain is the push and pull of acceptance and rejection, which makes the stretch a most challenging part of the tender path. Then we slowly, gently, and quietly begin to merge with the solace. The solace wraps our discomfort with a warm blanket and a sense of knowing and wisdom of the burdensome path we have walked. Solace brings the lightness of a new dawn, a sense of accomplishment, a confidence. We become sage survivors of a purgatorial misery.

Joining and holding grief doesn't mean we are lost or consumed by it. Rather, we befriend and get to know this new part of our lives. I liken this to being reluctantly assigned a seat next to a stranger whose language we do not speak; we still feel compelled to get to know them. This is our journey with grief: a new acquaintance whom we know nothing about but whose language we learn and whom we get to know well. The tender path has much to teach us.

Grief has taught me many things about myself, unapologetically showing me how far I can stretch and come back to my center. It has taught me to hold throbbing, lava-hot heart pain until it simmers to an ache and then cools to a feather-soft, bittersweet memory.

DAVID'S STORY:
LIVING AUTHENTICALLY WITH A CHRONIC DISEASE

My buddy David is one of the strongest men I know. He's the kind of guy you'd call at three in the morning if you needed help. He can hold space for your pain as well as be with you to celebrate your accomplishments. He's the brother we all wish we had. The deep well of his heart is felt by all who know him. I was fortunate that David and Brandi asked me to officiate their wedding, which was a memorable, fun-filled day. (Brandi's story follows chapter two.)

David was diagnosed with facioscapulohumeral muscular dystrophy, or FSHD, in his midthirties. Receiving this tongue-twister of a diagnosis was a shock to David and the rest of us, but what was even more incredible was that he had had this degenerative disease his entire life, but it had been overlooked or misdiagnosed.

Most of those with FSHD are diagnosed in their mid-to-late twenties, after years of having hard-to-explain symptoms. This is a slow disease that robs people of the use of muscles in their face, shoulders, upper body, and legs. It takes away everyday things like washing your hair, being able to reach the top shelf, and the ability to smile. Those who have this disease learn to live with it by making adjustments so they can still do everyday things. For many, it progresses to the legs and feet, weakening the muscles. A quarter of those end up in a wheelchair at some point as the disease progresses.

Ultimately, his diagnosis gave David a sense of purpose. This sounds counterintuitive, but as you read his story, I think you will see this inspiration. The following is David's experiences with this degenerative disease as well as my own reflections and feelings, as his friend, on learning of his diagnosis.

Most people can't imagine what it would be like to receive a chronic disease diagnosis. What was speeding through your mind when you were told of your diagnosis and the prognosis?

I thought my life was over. My thoughts raced to, *I'm never going to be able to do the things I want to do with my life, I'm never going to be able to walk my girls down the aisle, I'm going to be a burden to my wife and she's going to have to take care of me, I'm going to end up in a wheelchair, I'm going to live a short life and will die early.* It was an overwhelming sense of darkness and clouds closing in on me. It was a bleak outlook, and I walked out of the doctor's office with my wife (fiancé at the time), got in the car, and just sobbed. Brandi was positive and had a *let's figure it out* mindset and tone, but I wasn't listening. I started to shut down.

What was your emotional experience like after the diagnosis was confirmed?

I don't have a lot of distinct memories about the time right after my diagnosis. We made some phone calls to family on the drive home and even stopped at my parents' house to share the news with them, but I don't remember that at all. My wife was always the positive force and optimistic, the one who kept the faith for us when I couldn't find it.

Did you immediately go into fact-finding mode, or did you become avoidant and shut down?

I did do some research on FSHD, so I didn't totally shut down. I remember having a hard time saying "I have FSHD." I had a hard time taking on the disease as mine. I guess it was a form of denial. I knew I had it, but saying it out loud made it real, and admitting it to people did the same thing. I didn't want to be looked at any differently or seen as sick. I didn't want to be defined by my disease, and I certainly did not take it on as part of who I was.

At the appointment when I got my diagnosis, my doctor asked me how I felt about participating in clinical trials. I said I was on board because there is no cure for FSHD. On the day of my diagnosis, my doctor reached out to the University of Rochester in New York, which is one of the leading research centers in the world on FSHD, to see if they needed anyone with FSHD for any studies they were conducting. We quickly heard back that yes, they needed someone, so we began the process for me to enroll in a clinical trial.

I began reading information, news, and stories of people with the disease from the FSHD Society. I also looked for news of a chapter in the Chicago area so I could meet others with FSHD. After six months, I reached out to the FSHD Society again to inquire if there was a group here. I was told no one had stepped up to start one, so I told them I'd do it and began the process of creating a chapter of the FSHD Society.

I don't remember the time or place the shift happened, but it flipped from this being a disease I had to having a sense of responsibility to play an active role in FSHD, to help advance what we know about my disease, and to connect with others that have it.

Was there a "before" David, a David 1.0, and then a David 2.0 after the diagnosis?

I guess the easy way to say it is that my hopes and dreams have intention now, whereas when I look back before the diagnosis, they look amateur, almost childish and naive. David before the diagnosis was just floating through life and seeking my larger purpose in the world. My hopes and dreams had an air of immortality to them, dreams that didn't take into account age or my body. My FSHD diagnosis gave my life a sense of purpose. It created a sense of gratitude that I can do the things I want to do, to enjoy them in the moment and not take them for granted. Once I arrived at the acceptance phase, I began to see my own mortality and how our future is not guaranteed. My hopes and dreams have an asterisk by them now, knowing in the back of my mind that FSHD is here in my body and it's going to do what it's going to do.

I'm a runner and have been for more than thirteen years. I would love to say that I'll be eighty-five and still running, but some of that isn't up to me. Yes, I can remain healthy and get out and move my body, but it's also possible that FSHD will progress to a point where I can't run anymore. It's about controlling what I can control and focusing my energy there.

What helped you through the acceptance of this disease?

The biggest thing to help me settle into my new reality was meeting others with FSHD. This moment still stands out to me, more than six years later. I worked to create a chapter of the FSHD Society in the Chicagoland area and set up our first meeting. Once everyone was there, I remember sitting down and looking into the eyes of others who had my disease. It was the first time I had met anyone with FSHD face to face. As we did introductions, I learned that this was the first time for everyone else, too.

For the first time, I felt I was truly being seen as having FSHD. This unspoken acceptance and acknowledgment of "I see you" passed between all of us, and it was truly powerful. This might have also been one of the first times I identified with or said that I have FSHD. To be in that space with others who had my disease made it real for me. It created a sense of community and belonging for everyone in the room. I also had the emotional pride of being the one who had created this for others, that I helped us all feel this collective moment of being seen in a way that none of us had experienced before. I felt a tremendous honor and privilege to be able to create that for us all.

I was also able to see the spectrum of ways that FSHD affects people. My FSHD is mostly hidden, as I have the ability to do most of the things I want to do, but there were people in that room who were in wheelchairs or used a walking device. There were people who had lost facial muscle, and you could tell when they spoke. This created a complex emotional moment for me, of gratitude that the disease had affected me the way it had so far and that I was still able to do most of the things I wanted to do. But it also created a picture into what my reality could be down the road, a visual reminder of what my life could look like. That brought a perspective to me about being grateful for the abilities I had and to appreciate them while I had them.

It also created moments of feeling like I had it easy. In fact, I still feel that way at times. In that moment, and even today, I have feelings of impostor syndrome, that I have "FSHD light" (there isn't such a thing), and that others who are more severely impacted look at me differently and judge me. In their presence, I feel guilty about labeling myself as having FSHD because I can still do most of the things I want to do, while they have trouble speaking or swallowing or can't walk. That feels entitled and privileged at times, and I shrink myself down in their presence because I have it easier than they do.

What became super important after the diagnosis?

Anything physical became important to me. Every run I take, at some point I have a moment of reflection about what others with FSHD would give to be out here running. It becomes a reminder to me to soak in the moment and be grateful that I still have the ability to run. Pushing myself physically took on a sense of importance, to be able to do things in spite of the disease. I still wanted to run long distances and to take long hikes and carry a heavy pack just to say I could. But I was also mindful to not put myself in situations where I could get hurt or be unsafe.

What became trivial or insignificant after the diagnosis?

What became insignificant was having good muscle definition in my body. FSHD meant that I was never going to have pecs or super-defined biceps and triceps, so I had to let go of the desire to look good physically. What also became trivial was proving myself physically, that mindset when you're moving a couch and say, "No, it's fine, I got it." I didn't do that anymore. I let go of others perceiving me as weak because I couldn't lift that couch or carry something heavy. I was more okay asking for help, and I let go of how others might perceive me for that.

This is a genetic disease, so what feelings did you have about getting FSHD in the hereditary lottery?

I've had moments where I wish I hadn't gotten this diagnosis, but overall, I'm grateful for it. It's created perspective that wasn't there before. FSHD has made me a better person and a better partner, father, friend, and advocate.

Do you ever wonder what life would have been like if you had just lived with your unique body quirks, not knowing that the genetic timer would eventually go off and activate FSHD?

I've never wondered what life would look like if I had just gone through life without a diagnosis. I probably would have put myself in unsafe situations that I wouldn't do now, like lifting heavy things over my head or working out and getting frustrated that I wasn't developing muscle and wondering what I was doing wrong. It was Brandi who pushed me to get things looked at. She noticed how my body was doing things that weren't quite right and suggested we get that checked out.

How did this new information affect your relationship with Brandi?

Our relationship grew stronger because of the diagnosis. She never lost sight of the positive and the *we'll figure this out* and *it's going to be okay* energy. Even when I didn't and couldn't see it, she never wavered. She never made me find my path or forced me to move when I didn't want to. She allowed me to find my way out of the initial dark place I was at and move to this place of acceptance.

We were always a team before the diagnosis, but we grew stronger and closer because of it, and I never felt alone in my disease because of her. She was right by my side, and I knew I could always count on her. She kept her head on straight when my brain went foggy after the news. She helped me dig into the research and work to solve our next steps.

How did the ripples of this new reality begin to affect your job?

At the time of my diagnosis, I was running a logistics department for a major retailer and would have to pull pallets or pick up heavy boxes from time to time. After my diagnosis, I began to think that I couldn't keep doing that anymore. I began to be mindful about the physical things I was doing and was careful to not put myself in danger.

Roughly a year after my diagnosis, I changed jobs and industries and took a corporate desk job, where I have flourished and succeeded more than I ever could have imagined. While I still worry about progression and getting worse and needing to ask for accommodations, I feel much more supported in this organization to receive those without any implications of blowback. I've shared my FSHD story with my company, and was well received. I'm also involved with an employee resource group that focuses on people with disabilities and their caregivers, and I have taken leadership roles at both a local and national level.

How did it affect your friendships?

When I shared the diagnosis with my closest friends, I was nervous because I didn't want to be treated any differently or be seen as sick. But all I got was love and support. They check in on me to see how I'm feeling, they show up to volunteer at events for FSHD, they raise money, they share my story. I could not have asked for better friends.

How did your parents and siblings react to the news?

My family reacted to the news with the equivalent of oh, that sucks. While I know they care, they're not capable of holding space for things like this. I was raised to not rock the boat, and when things get hard, we need to make things okay as fast as possible. My diagnosis was overwhelming for them, and I think my parents probably have some guilt, as it's a genetic disease.

Nothing has changed in our family dynamic. My disease is not talked about, and no one asks me how I'm doing or how I'm feeling or if I'm noticing any progression. I had to amend what I seek from them so that I'm not let down by their apparent lack of caring. It would have been wonderful to have my diagnosis bring us together, but it hasn't, and I've accepted that.

How did you determine how you were going to experience this disease?

The big shift in my mindset came about six months after my diagnosis, on the plane ride back from Rochester after my participation in the clinical trial. My wife went with me on this trip, and as we met with the world's leading doctors on FSHD, we learned that I was the last participant in this study. Now that I was here, they were going to be able to finish the study, which had been going on for three years. We learned that they were very close to shutting it down because they needed one more person but hadn't had any luck getting anyone—until my doctor emailed them asking if they needed anyone else for any studies. They immediately said yes and worked to get me out to Rochester as fast as possible. Being in this space, surrounded by nurses, staff, and doctors who were so happy I was there, was surreal. I would play a role in helping advance the scientific knowledge of FSHD.

My wife was right by my side the whole time. She saw me crying while I was journaling on the plane ride home and just let me be. It was in those journal pages where I started to use the term "my disease," when the fact that I had FSHD became a part of me and integrated with my identity.

How did you transform the darker thoughts that came up for you?

Before that trip, I kept FSHD at a distance. I was scared to bring it into myself and make it part of who I was, but knowing I was playing an integral role in advancing science for my disease, and feeling like I was more significant than I realized, blew open my heart and mind. What came in was a firm sense that I had FSHD and it was part of who I was. But it would not define my life, it was not all I was.

I had a responsibility to participate in my own rescue and volunteer for research to advance what we know about FSHD. I would make it my mission to connect with others who have FSHD to make sure they didn't feel alone in this, too. FSHD affects only about a million people worldwide, so it's a small group of people, globally speaking.

Did you look to others with the disease for coping skills, or did you invent things on your own?

I do look at others with FSHD who have lost the ability to do the things that I'm able to do, which gives me some perspective on how they can remain positive despite the things FSHD has taken from them and how it doesn't stop them. I also rely on Stoic philosophy, which I've been studying for years. Its core teaching is focusing on what's in our control and what's not, and how we choose to react to those things. I strive to embody that Stoic principle in all I do so that I can be the person I want to be.

I can't control that I was born with FSHD, but I can control how I react when feelings of sadness or "poor me" enter into my mind. I choose to focus on staying active the best way I can with the abilities I have now so that I can keep my muscles active and strong. I choose to connect with others who have FSHD, to share experiences and help each other.

As we get older, most of us check in with ourselves when we get out of bed and evaluate how our body is that day. Is this something you do?

No, I just live my life and go about my days. I only notice when I can't do something or when I feel like I've lost range of motion in my shoulders, where I'm most severely affected. But overall, I don't focus on checking in with myself every day on what I can or can't do. Thankfully, I don't experience pain with FSHD, which is wonderful, as many others with FSHD do experience pain.

However, over the past couple of years, I've noticed a loss of muscle in my right thigh. My brain automatically goes to FSHD, but it's also possible it's just muscle loss from not running as much or not working out. There's always a low-level worry in the back of my mind that a decline is coming. So I continue to stay active, run, walk, and help in any way I can.

Do you look at your chronic disease as a loss?

Initially, I characterized my diagnosis as a loss, that my life and this future I had created for myself and how I envisioned my life to look were taken from me. But the more time goes on, the more I realize that FSHD is not a death sentence. Yes, it can create some real hardships for me and my wife, but I will be okay.

What advice do you have for those who are having an internal battle with their disease to help them transform this reluctance and fear and move beyond them?

In the moments after a life-changing diagnosis or loss, the last thing someone wants to hear is that it's all going to be okay and that they'll move beyond this. That can feel incredibly dismissive. I think every person needs to navigate their own path, and there's no right or wrong way to do it. The strength, comfort, and love from others makes the journey easier and less lonely. I think it comes down to accepting that you can't control what happened to you, but you can control how you react to it. Perhaps the most important thing is that this path invites the people in your life to come by your side and navigate this path with you, arm in arm.

My hope for everyone who experiences any kind of loss is that you can choose to react to the loss not by hiding it away but by keeping it with you. You have a choice in how your life is going to unfold. When we take our loss in one hand and our fear in the other, we can remain in control and bring those pieces of ourselves with us into the light. A friend of mine said something that's stuck with me: you can look at your disease as something that's been taken away from you, or you can pivot and figure out how you can work with it.

Most of us want to be independent, to take care of things and be in control of our lives. What are you no longer able to do, and what is your emotional response to this?

I'm able to do most things despite FSHD. The disease mostly affects my shoulders, so it's hard for me to reach things up high or carry heavy things away from my body. These tasks have been hard for me to do for as long as I can remember. Before my diagnosis, I just thought I wasn't strong enough and would push through these hardships. Now, knowing what I know, I ask for help to put the dishes away or get heavy things down from cabinets.

Do you see yourself as differently abled, or this is just how you are?

Yes, I see myself as differently abled. I know I'm technically disabled because muscular dystrophy fits in that category, but I also hold that term loosely for myself because I'm still able to do all the things I want to do.

What are some things that you do differently now?

I won't cross the line and do anything stupid where I could potentially hurt myself, but I hate admitting that I can't do the little things that I need help with. There's an ebb and flow between when I'm okay asking for help and when I have an attitude of *I'll do it my damn self.*

I anticipate needing to change the way I exercise. I've started to think about what I will do if I lose the ability to run or hike. I'd hate to give up running, but I've already thought about taking up biking if I can't run anymore. If I need to start using assistive devices to walk, that will change the way I interact with the world. I don't know what that reality would look like, but those kinds of thoughts cross my mind. My body is actively overproducing a protein that's killing and destroying the muscle in my body, and that muscle is never going to come back.

How did the diagnosis change the way you look at your body?

The diagnosis answered some questions I had about my body. I had never been able to build chest muscles and never knew why. I thought I wasn't eating right. I bought books on weight lifting form and tried to focus on it. I could never bench press a lot, and I felt like a wimp when I asked for a spotter at the gym for ten-pound weights on either end of the bar.

I don't like the way I look in the mirror, and I hate being at the beach or pool because my scapulas wing out so much that I think people will think I look weird. My scapulas winged out from my back before my diagnosis, but I thought that was normal. I now know that it's the telltale sign of FSHD. Now I ebb and flow in the acceptance of the way I look without my shirt on. There are times I really don't care and times that I hate it and don't want anyone to look at me.

Many people who have a chronic disease want to be seen as themselves, not someone who has a disease. What matters to most of us is that we are seen for how we feel inside. How important is it to you that others know or not know that you have FSHD?

I'm definitely guarded with who I tell about it, and it's certainly not the thing I lead with when talking about myself. I try to assess the kind of person I'm with before determining whether I share with them. If I perceive them as someone who can hold that space for me and can match and hold that vulnerability, then I'll share it when it's appropriate to do so in conversation. But if not, then I'll keep it to myself.

Many people who are given a chronic diagnosis go into a victim space. What are your thoughts about people who hide behind their chronic disease or use it to curry sympathy or special treatment?

This is a hard question because what they need to hear and what they'll be able to hear are quite different things. People who take on the narrative of the victim typically do that for the attention. Until they do the work to unpack the reasons behind their need to receive such attention, nothing I could say would break them out of that. I've experienced people in the FSHD community who fall into that victim mindset, but I don't view it as my job to break them out of that cycle. I'm going to instead focus my energy on the people who want to move forward in spite of FSHD, who are willing to listen to others' experiences and hold space for each other so we can form a community of lived experiences, where no one is better or worse than anyone else.

What are some of your greatest fears as a husband and father, knowing that this degenerative disease is progressive?

I fear being a burden to my wife and kids should I progress and need a wheelchair or assistive devices or can't work anymore. I have fears that my wife will need to care for me, and that's not the life I want for either of us. I'd much prefer to keep things the way they are because we've learned how to navigate that and I don't want to be a burden on her.

How has FSHD changed the way you interact with your children?

I try to be a role model for them about how you can step up in the face of such news. From leading the chapter here in Chicago to planning and executing a fundraising walk to sharing my story of FSHD to my entire company, I try to be an example of how news like this doesn't need to be suffocating, that it can be turned into fuel to propel you forward on your life's path.

It is said that those who walk through fire are transformed into a stronger version of themselves. What are some of your personality or character traits that were transformed by this diagnosis?

It's enhanced my resilience, perseverance, gratitude, generosity, intention, determination, leadership, and confidence. It took all the things I already was and amplified them, and they continue to grow and evolve.

After a loss, a lot of people will ask, why me? Did you ask this question?

I believe things happen for a reason, and going back to Stoic philosophy, I can't control what happens to me, only how I react. So, knowing this is a genetic disease, I know I didn't do anything wrong, and I've had it since I was born. I have just decided live a life of purpose and service. I choose to use this disease as fuel to propel me forward and help me become the best version of myself. That's the kind of life I want to live and the person I want to be.

~

Reflections on David's Story

I am so appreciative of David for giving us a window into what his journey has been like, especially in those first few tender hours after he received his diagnosis and his ongoing journey of self-discovery. He took us to an intimate yet frightening time in his life, when his idea of himself changed in an instant. As his story unfolded, we saw how he would have moments of strength and then get lost in his fear. Yet throughout, he reiterates that the diagnosis gave him a sense of purpose. I think holding on to this idea of purpose and meaning provided David with an internal drive and perspective to help him through this experience. I cannot imagine the strength he has had to find to hold a future that may include physical disability.

As David says, we can look at being given a chronic disease diagnosis as something that's been taken away from us, or we can pivot and figure out how to work with it. His sense of self was fortified by the disease diagnosis, which encouraged a stronger version of himself to show up. I'm so proud of my friend and how he joined with his loss in a wise and pragmatic way. He elevated the experience to be one of living in the now and appreciating all he has. He embraced the experience and used it as an opportunity to live his life with a sense of purpose. He joined with others who share his positive attitude in a community of lived experiences, as he calls it. This was a remarkable and truly inspirational reframing and perspective shift.

David's progression through his journey beautifully illustrates the three phases of the tender path. From his initial shock to the long stretch of integrating and forming his positive relationship to the diagnosis and prognosis, David more fully embraced his purpose-driven life. He took an active role in living with FSHD instead of giving his power over to the disease. He was always a thoughtful man, but now his experience shifted this quality into high gear, demonstrating even more gratitude, more appreciation for the small things in life. He embodies moments of solace as well as times when his FSHD challenges him to stretch. He holds all of these complex emotions at once as he engenders a new reality for himself. David's story is a powerful example of the great courage it takes to be vulnerable. He models for us how to hold both realities at the same time.

I would want anyone who has been given a diagnosis of a chronic disease to read David's story. My wish for them is to have his almost superhuman ability to rise above the situation and find strength and hope within themselves. David is one of those people who inspires others to do better and become the fullest version of themselves in each moment.

My personal reaction to David's diagnosis

I met David at a men's weekend retreat more than ten years ago. We immediately connected on a deep, heartfelt level and saw ourselves as kindred spirits on a healing path. I knew David before his diagnosis and before he married Brandi. As I wrote at the beginning, he's the brother we all wish we had. He is kind, generous, and never pushes himself or his agenda on anyone else. If he does have an agenda, I imagine it would include his family, running through the woods (which he calls his "church"), and probably coffee.

I listened as he told me of his diagnosis, but inside I was trembling and scared for what it would mean for him. I wanted to be present and stay calm for him. I could tell it was hard for him to tell me he had been diagnosed with FSHD. A part of me was in disbelief, surprised and shocked at this unexpected news. After he explained more about what the disease looks like and the prognosis, I was quieter inside. I was no longer scared that I was going to lose my friend; he wasn't dying, he just had an uncertain path in front of him. This news triggered my own journey of integrating and holding his loss, even though David was the one going through it.

Once the diagnosis settled in with him, my impression was that something inside of him calmed down. All of the questions he had about why his body didn't respond to exercise or develop muscle definition, and why his scapulas poked out of his back, were immediately answered. He now had the words for what makes him unique and special in the world. I saw a newfound confidence come over him, especially when he opened the local FSHD chapter. Not only was he finally given a name for what his body had been going through his entire life, but he also embraced a larger idea of himself. I see that his diagnosis energized him in many ways, but he had to go through a process of loss to embrace the new reality before him. I see David stretching into and with this experience. I now realize that his optimistic response and attitude toward his diagnosis helped set the stage for how I integrated this news. He modeled for me how to hold his new reality.

David's story reminds us of the millions of people who go through life with a chronic disease, whether seen or unseen. It's important to recognize that we never know the pain someone else walks with even when things look easy for them, and to not question why someone who doesn't look disabled needs assistance or gentleness.

David's story of loss is unique in the fact that he had been living with his chronic disease his entire life but didn't know it until his diagnosis. When the disease was named, he was able to enter into a place of knowing, but he also had to grieve an uncertain future. He shows us how to hold tenderness for ourselves when we are given news that is overwhelming. He is a strong wayshower and a brave man.

- What do you take away from David's story?
- Have you ever been given scary news about yourself or a loved one and had a big reaction?
- If so, what did this news bring up in you?
- Do you think you have fully processed everything from that time?

There may be some residual emotion quietly sitting there, patiently waiting for you to examine it further. Be gentle with yourself as you go down memory lane and reprocess some old wounding related to your or someone else's journey.

～

David's charity of choice for his story contribution is the Facioscapulohumeral Muscular Dystrophy Society. Learn more at www.fshdsociety.org.

～

Additional Resources

The Invisible Kingdom: Reimagining Chronic Illness, Meghan O'Rourke, New York, NY: Riverhead Books, 2022.

Surviving and Thriving with an Invisible Chronic Illness: How to Stay Sane and Live One Step Ahead of Your Symptoms, Illana Jacqueline, Oakland, CA: New Harbinger Publications, 2018.

What Doesn't Kill You: A Life with Chronic Illness—Lessons From a Body In Revolt, Tessa Miller, New York: Henry Holt and Company, 2022.

PART III

Growing through Grief

CHAPTER SEVEN

Loss and the Inner Child

*We shall not cease from our exploration, and the end of all
our exploring will be to arrive where we started
and know the place for the first time.*
—T.S. ELLIOT

Throughout our childhood we accumulate memories from
events and emotional experiences that define our sense of self
and our view of the world. We always carry the sum total of
these memories, and if we are fortunate, we can look back
on them fondly. However, the bad experiences during these
formative years often stand out more than the good times
because we interpret and feel these times as losses. These
negative feelings and memories stay with us and influence
the narrative we carry about ourselves, especially if we have
repeated losses. Even though we all experience both good
and bad times, the negative stories are often the loudest and
become heavy on the heart. The feeling of sadness we carry
is usually not related to one specific time or traumatic event

but is an accumulation of hurtful episodes, throwaway comments, emotional slights, and fallout from our boundaries not being respected. These small slights are recorded by the inner child along with the big emotional traumas. The emotionally mature part of us moved on from these childhood losses, but the impulsive, reactive part still spins and recycles this pain. It is an emotional slice of our past that is frozen in time, and the inner child stuffs this weighty, unacknowledged pain into the loss bucket. This helps to explain why many people feel bad about themselves or have a sense of loss but don't know why they feel this way. The loss and hurt they carry stings as if it happened yesterday and feels heavy on their heart. This is especially true for significant traumas such as sexual, physical, and emotional abuse. These losses create deep, lasting emotional scars and greatly derail the child's emotional development. We can certainly have traumas as adults that emotionally impact our functioning, but when this happens in childhood, the impact is usually profoundly deeper.

The wounded or lost inner child is the part of us that didn't grow up emotionally; it holds on to the unhealed losses that contribute to a false narrative that we are less-than. When triggered in adulthood, this unacknowledged wounding typically shows up as a protector by stepping in front of the responsible adult self and making decisions using outdated childhood responses. The wounding gets triggered by something similar to a childhood wounded experience, the inner child comes to the "rescue" and we react in a big way or shut down and withdraw. Afterward, our mature adult self has to clean up what the inner child reflexively projected onto everyone else. *Why did I have such a big reaction?* is a common thought after such an impulsive response.

Growing up, we don't know how to acknowledge loss because we are in the middle of our family dance of hurt or trauma loss. We are in the swirl and trying to emotionally survive, so we can't take the time or don't have the perspective to name a loss; it just is how it is. Trauma losses such as suffering childhood abuse or neglect, or having to emotionally shut down to care for others in the household, become normalized, pushed down, stuck wounding. There is no space for acknowledging loss because life becomes about emotional survival, not emotional acknowledgment or a deeper understanding of self. The child's lack of boundary setting means that ongoing losses in the household become the child's carried loss; the child doesn't know which losses are theirs and which are someone else's. Emotionally wounded parents don't see the dysfunction, so it is not addressed. The child assumes a great responsibility, and it's all mixed together in a carried family loss bucket.

CAUSES OF CHILDHOOD WOUNDING

Until I learned about boundaries, my wounded inner child used all the codependent tools learned in childhood to try to make my outer world feel safer.

Many people, myself included, will say they didn't experience any big traumas in childhood, that there was no overt abuse, that their parents loved them. But no matter how well-balanced and functional a family is, there are events that happen in childhood that get compacted in our loss bucket and impact our sense of self. These events can be, for example, not making a sports team, being dumped by friends, seeing parents have issues, being neglected or emotionally abandoned, or having an accident that creates a physical limitation. Any one of these events impacts how we see ourselves and our world and whether we interpret life with a sense of loss or one of abundance.

This dynamic becomes even more exaggerated and overwhelming for the child when a parent goes through a loss and doesn't have good boundaries. When this spills over, the child feels the immensity of what the parent experiences, and because children are naturally empathetic, the child wants to help. For example, if the parent loses a job, the child feels like they lost a job and then carries the anxiety of needing to find a new one. If one parent wants a divorce, the child is immediately thrown into an adult world with real-life consequences and losses, often feeling protective toward one or both parents. The wounded parents' issues splashes onto all of the household members, and the child takes on the concerns from the lack of money, job loss, or addiction issues. The wounded parent unknowingly transfers this wounding onto the child, and the intergenerational trauma loss commences.

The loss is felt by the whole family, but most parents are in such a state of turmoil themselves that they do not put the experience into a context for the child. The child doesn't understand that these losses are a normal part of adult life and that they are not for the child to solve. The child feels overwhelmed and may start to catastrophize, believing that all will be lost and the family will become destitute. The child feels this loss in a greater way than the parent because the child doesn't know how to solve the problem, and it all feels overwhelming. A child's family is their world, so any event feels big. This lack of boundary setting between the parent and child, called "enmeshment," often triggers internal panic and overconcern within the child. This can lead to lifelong anxiety, overcompensation, a fear of lack, and a feeling of inadequacy. Feeling uncertain, the child becomes focused on emotional safety and survival.

The gift of loss reveals what is important in our lives. In time, this wisdom rises to the top and we gain clarity.

Without the loss situation being put into a context, the wounded inner child deeply feels this emotional hurt, becoming alert and on the lookout for the next loss event or trauma. This hypervigilance creates a defensive posture, and there is no luxury for introspection, as the child has to grow up quickly to protect themselves and the family. Having to grow up too fast results in being what is called "parentified"; many firstborn children of dysfunctional households carry this badge. The now-parentified child learns to ignore, overlook, or not acknowledge slights, rejection, abuse, ghosting, gaslighting, boundary violation, or hurt. These boundary violations and loss experiences are explained away and incorporated into the child's, later the adult's, false narrative of lack: *That's just how things are.* These hurtful episodes add up over time. Dysfunction and chaos are normalized because that is "what we do in this family." If addiction or mental illness is a major factor in the household, the child begins to see this element as the enemy, the nemesis that takes their parent "away." The child loses the close, emotionally safe connection to the parent and instead becomes more focused on the parent's emotional landscape than their own. The child abandons play and neglects self-care, losing out on regular childhood experiences. Their main job is to take care of the family, reading the mood of the room and making sure the dysfunction is kept under control. The loss bucket fills with misperceptions, as children are great observers but lousy interpreters of this family dance.

Inner child wounding can also originate when the parents always argue or are divorcing. This unstable relationship dynamic creates great distress in the child and begins to shape how they trust and interact with the world. If the parents don't explain that they are the ones going through the problems and not the child, the child will take on some level of responsibility. This is why it is important for parents to say that they are arguing about their own issues but not because of the child, and for the child to see the parents apologize to each other. Parents need to define the boundary of the emotional upset because a young child doesn't have that reasoning ability. Parents who are dismissive or intellectualize away the problem for the child, as in, *You don't need to worry about this, go out and play*, often create more confusion for the child. When the losses are never put into context for the child, the child begins to make up ways to feel in control and safe, such as by acting out and physically trying to assert control or by withdrawing and self-soothing in an internal world of reading or playing video games. Often the child develops what is called an "anxious attachment" to the loss and is then always on the lookout for chaos or drama. When there are no emotional guardrails, the inner child wounding takes hold of the loss and claims it. A child's world is very small, so any changes to the status quo represent a loss of the child's perceived reality. The child needs to have losses explained in a way that is age appropriate so they have a reference point and can establish their own connection point to a loss that is happening in real time. This will give context and lessen the wounding connected to the loss.

The inner child's loss bucket eventually becomes overfull, and the child, later the adult, is confused as to why they have feelings of anger, anxiety, sadness, or inadequacy. All of these unexpressed and normalized loss experiences get mixed up, becoming a generalized feeling of depression or anxiety. I often ask people why they feel such great anger, anxiety, or sadness. They will stare blankly at me, not knowing why; they just know they feel a loss. This is a reflection of how their inner child learned to pile up the losses and pack them away because there was no time to examine, much less express, feelings. They grew numb to the dysfunction and neglect of these repeated losses, which became the background noise of their existence. They learned how to compensate and pretzel themselves around their wounding, resigning themselves to the idea that this is just how things are.

The child begins to own a false narrative of I'm bad, I'm no good, I'm a loser, I will never be happy. This incorrect interpretation becomes a misperceived fact. The child doesn't know how to express these feelings around loss because they were never encouraged, allowed, or shown how to heal in a healthy way. The child takes everything in and runs it all through their filter of self-perception. If this filter is filled with falsehoods, they incorrectly interpret what is happening and often assign blame to themselves. As previously mentioned, these unacknowledged losses later come out in impulsive or reactive ways, such as shutting down, lashing out, or abusing others—all of the wounded tools of expression the child learned from the influential adults in their lives. This was how the parent reacted to a loss and modeled this behavior for the child, how the pain of a loss was indirectly expressed. The loss wasn't named; instead, the parents covered it up with fear, anger, and, too often, alcohol or drugs. The loss was minimized, ignored, and dismissed in the hope that it would go away.

In a dysfunctional family environment, there are unspoken rules about not pointing out losses, as this identification magnifies the inherent shame that always simmers in the background. This is the sometimes dad, in and out of a child's life; the neglectful alcoholic mother, who doesn't show up for school or sporting events; the abused child, who carries a bruised victim energy to school and becomes the target of bullies. Any one of these situations can lead a child to feel a loss at some level, but when they are a daily reality, they are rarely categorized as a loss; that's just how it is. The previous day's abuse melts into the next day's routine. The daily losses become a dissociated, numbed feeling that distorts the child's self-image and the wounded story they tell themselves.

Wounded people view the world through a wounded lens. They literally don't see someone else as being wounded or hurting, seeing instead that everyone is in the same boat. They often perceive this wounding as normal, or don't see it at all. Only through a healed lens can we can more clearly see another's wounding. The wounded parent may have many unacknowledged losses, so the child will believe that it's their job to carry these losses forward. This multigenerational trauma takes tremendous effort for the child, later the adult, to overcome, acknowledge, and heal. Most parents do the best they can with the tools they have, which explains many things, but it is not an excuse for childhood wounding.

INNER CHILD WOUNDING AND RESISTANCE

The loss of self-confidence and self-esteem can be a slow drip over time, leaving us feeling flattened. But all of that is an illusion others put on us, leading to our misinterpretation of reality.

Unresolved inner child wounding doesn't go away, it just gets wrapped in adult responses. When we look closely, these adult reactions have all the markings of a child's limited emotional reasoning. Resistance during the stretch on the tender path of grief is usually unhealed wounding from childhood coming forth in the forms of yelling, screaming, shutting down, ignoring, or throwing tantrums. These responses feel natural because we did them before; they are the wounded responses in our tool kit. Our emotional wounding gets triggered in our adult lives and activates all of these old reactions. For example, if we don't want to respond when an aging parent needs us, we may be responding with the wounded inner child feeling of never having received enough nurturing and love. The wounded part of us doesn't want to give to them what we didn't receive—a tit for tat. Or, if we have an inner child wounding of not feeling good enough and then we suffer a job loss, that particular wounding of less-than is triggered and shuts down the job search, reacting to our lack of self-love, respect, or trust. This may seem like an outsized exaggerated response to others, but it feels justified, normal, and realistic to the wounded, hurting person.

Whatever the inner child wounding, it often gets triggered during the shockwave and stretch phases of the tender path, activating this old hurt and loss. The feelings you have as an adult mirror the feelings you experienced as a child in the same sort of situation. This is why you may cry harder or want to run away from others when these feelings are triggered. This is your inner child having a big emotional reaction. If you are aware of the hurts that you carried into adulthood, this information may help you to gently begin coaching yourself through your loss experience. Here are some words of affirmation that may help you overcome some of the resistance:

> I know this is hard, but I'm going to take it one day at a time. I don't need to be perfect, and I don't need to know

everything. I give myself permission to ask for help when I need it. I know that if I take care of myself and stay grounded, then I can get through this. My life flows with an ease and grace. I am loved.

If you feel an internal resistance to healing, ask yourself the following questions:

What unresolved wounding from my past is holding me back from joining with the stretch and dealing with my loss?

What internal belief system did I learn as a child that is working against me now?

Am I taking ownership, or am I blaming others for my issues?

What internal belief system did I learn as a child that is helping me?

What part of my narrative, my story about myself, is real and useful?

What part of my narrative is holding me back?

For most of us, the inner child is stuck until we consciously recognize our wounding and embrace a healing path. Well-rehearsed trauma drama will keep repeating until we can name it, then claim it. Even with all of the losses a child encounters, children are survivors and incredibly resilient. A child may have grown up in a family with a lot of trauma, but the resulting wounding can be healed in adulthood. If you connect with these feelings, know that you can heal this false narrative and that you are an expression greater than this small, wounded idea of yourself. Once you begin to unpack these elements, the childhood origin story of your emotional development will become clear. Being aware of and naming the emotional loss you experienced as a child will open up a healing path for you.

A big part of healing work for the inner child is mourning the loss of a childhood you never got to experience. You may mourn the figurative loss of a parent who had mental illness or addiction issues, or the loss of a parent who was there but not emotionally available. You may acknowledge that all of your physical needs were met, but the one thing you really wanted was never fulfilled: to feel their love.

Know that when you begin to connect with your childhood losses and name them, other losses may come forward in your consciousness. One loss may spark the memory of another, and all of a sudden, you're in a maze of emotions you haven't felt in years. This is normal, as the heart and mind want to heal. You present these losses to yourself, pulling them out of your loss bucket as you give yourself permission. You may need to address some unhealed wounds before you can truly begin your grief journey, as the issues may be commingled. I especially see these old wounds come forward when a person hasn't mourned the previous loss of a friendship, relationship, or parent dynamic and then that person dies. A seasoned therapist can help you untangle what feelings you have related to your present-day grief and what is related to past wounding. Healing yourself is completely doable and within reach, and your inner child will be grateful. Look to chapter nine, "Practical Tools for Honoring Loss," for more examples of how to work through and release this heart pain.

Mourning a present-day loss may be entangled with a previous loss from childhood. This interweaving of loss is normal and is a subtlety that gets overlooked on the tender path because the present-day loss is loud and big.

In my book *Healing Your Lost Inner Child*, I take the reader deep into this work through the HEAL process, teaching you how to guide the lost inner child from an emotionally confused, frozen space to being connected and integrated with the authentic self. What losses can you identify that your inner child carries for you? What losses did you experience as a child that have informed your idea of yourself? Is there room for healing or acknowledging these losses so that you don't need to carry such a heavy burden? If you feel your inner child is carrying unacknowledged loss, work through the exercises in *Healing Your Lost Inner Child*. You can heal this wounding and connect with your authentic self, like the thousands of others who have used this process.

For now, say this intention to help give yourself some gentleness:

> I now realize that I have experienced and carry unacknowledged losses that felt normal to me at one time. I now realize these losses were painful and difficult for me to go through. As a child, I worked hard to keep myself and everyone else safe and to make the family as functional as it could be. I know that I always try to do my best and that I can learn to heal my pain of loss so I don't have to carry this pain into my future. I am loved.

Personally, not everything I experienced in childhood led to my wounded codependency. There were good things that shaped my sense of self, my work ethic, and my ability to be kind and caretake others. However, I had to unlearn a lot of things from childhood, such as giving my power away, feeling insecure, being disconnected from my authentic self, and being overly involved in trying to help others. Boundaries helped me to restore what I lost in childhood. Boundaries always help us to have a stronger sense of self, respecting and loving ourselves when others can't or don't know how. Boundaries create verbal and nonverbal guardrails so we feel emotionally safe in our relationships. You will learn more about boundaries in chapter ten, "Helping Others through Loss."

Know that your inner child holds the keys to unlocking the deep wisdom that will help you heal your losses. All you need to do is pay attention to what this part is telling you. When we own what's ours and see the wounding we carry that belongs to others, we give the losses we felt as a child a voice. This begins our journey toward emotional freedom.

> *What I lost in childhood I have received back*
> *a thousandfold through my love and respect*
> *for myself. I generously give to myself*
> *what I now realize I need most.*

ROBERT'S STORY: A LOSS OF INNOCENCE

You have learned from other contributors' stories how they experienced a loss and found hope and healing along their tender path. The following is my story of a unique hidden loss that happened over the course of my formative years. My story may seem contradictory because I felt completely loved, my parents were kind and fun people, and my family life was happy at times. However, there were times of tension between my parents, and therefore, the household. There wasn't upset all the time, they didn't yell every day, but each day held the potential for a distressing situation that could appear out of nowhere (from my child's perspective).

Being empathic, I felt this unpredictability and had to develop my own tools to handle the emotional turmoil I felt. The last thing they wanted was for us to have problems, but ironically, their hurts were often the source of our pain. This is my story of how I developed wounded tools to cope and my inner child perspective of those times when our home life was turbulent.

My story starts when I was twelve years old, my younger sister was five, and my parents had been married for thirteen years. The four of us didn't want for many things and lived a middle-class life in the early seventies. My sister and I were lucky, as our parents truly loved us and did everything they could to create a life that they felt gave us the most advantage and opportunity. They were our biggest champions; they supported us wholeheartedly and gave us the freedom to dream. We were cared for and nurtured, and we knew they were proud of us. We were never physically or sexually abused, although I did experience emotionally abusive episodes.

My parents had stable jobs with consistent incomes. They wanted my sister and me to have opportunities and adventures that they didn't have growing up, which made our life experiences much grander than those of our friends. We had great weekends on the boat with our friends, and we even took what we all jokingly talk about as a "Chevy Chase vacation" out West. We had many fun times together as a family with warm birthdays and sparkling holidays filling our souls with love. This sounds ideal, but I lost something over the course of my childhood. I didn't know how to name it at the time, but I felt it deeply.

Simmering in the background of our family life was the relationship stress between my parents, which was projected onto the household. My parents were products of their time, when emotions weren't talked about. Unpleasant, uncomfortable, thorny issues were avoided and pushed down, usually coming out in passive-aggressive or explosive, verbally aggressive ways. This polarity created a lot of confusion within me growing up, as it caused emotional whiplashes—one day things would be good and they would say I love you to each other, and the next day there would be a lot of yelling and discord. Throughout the majority of my childhood, I became preoccupied with trying to figure out this wounded dichotomy and make sense of the emotional roller coaster. I had a tenuous grasp on the feeling that home and family were consistently emotionally safe. My mom and dad were so lost in their wounded pain there was no way they had the perspective to put any of this into context for us.

I lost a sense of being free and open with my emotions, as I was shutting down and becoming hyperfocused on their emotions. I was trying to control an outcome by changing myself, not realizing that this was out of my control. I was a good codependent-in-training. I lost myself in my efforts to make my childhood family as functional as it could be. My home life could be filled with love and laughter one moment, and then a dark mood would descend out of nowhere. My dad was anxious and filled with worry most nights and drowned out this noise with alcohol. I couldn't figure out this cause and effect. What was happening in my world? I began to lose the sense that everything was okay, as it didn't always feel okay and I didn't know when the next outburst would happen. I didn't know if I could trust what I was experiencing. My mom responded to my dad's moods by complying and making everything nice with meals and the house, but her efforts often didn't have much of an effect. As a result of this uncertainty, I lost a sense of predictability in the reliability of my home. I wouldn't know this consciously until I began my therapies in my twenties, but these periodic, pernicious losses built up over time and eroded much of my playful side.

These types of losses accumulate, and we form a constellation of wounded responses. While I didn't experience overt trauma, I learned the classic, child of an alcoholic responses, to my dad's drinking. His alcohol-fueled mood was the main actor, and we all supported this wounded, addicted dance. Problems supercharged by alcohol played a big role in our nightly dramas, misshaping my sense of safety, identity, and trust.

Most days after school, my sister and I would sit in the family room watching TV, and my mom would be in the kitchen. The garage door would go up—Dad was coming home. This was my signal that I was on duty. I would feel a nervous excitement, simultaneously looking forward to seeing my dad and feeling a pit in my stomach from not knowing what his mood would be. Gone was a sense of just being a kid because now I had to pull up my extensive emotional "mood matrix" to decode his mood. I sat on the edge of the couch, taking everything in as he walked up the steps. I emotionally braced myself and became grounded in the room by seeing the paneling on the walls, the braided rug, and the plaid furniture. How heavy were his footsteps walking up the stairs? Was his posture slumped over or upright? Furrowed brow or open face? Joking or sullen? I deciphered all of these things to determine my next steps as I tried to control my outer world so my inner world felt safe. I had already lost the ability to be carefree and joyful at my dad's homecoming. I had lost the freedom of a childhood without responsibility, concern, or care.

I changed myself based on how I interpreted his mood. I emotionally contorted into a pretzel to try to soothe and abate his mood, as my mom modeled for me. If I was successful, he and my mom wouldn't argue, she wouldn't be upset and cry, my sister and I would be emotionally safe from harm, and dinner would be pleasant. If I failed, my dad would demand to know how school was or find something that was wrong or see a bill on the counter that he didn't like. I lost myself in his world and how my mom reacted to his mood.

I wanted to be swallowed up by the walls or wished an escape hatch would open on the linoleum kitchen floor, but I had to stay in the mix. If I retreated to my room, my dad would yell for me to come out and be with the family. He wanted us to look like a happy family even as he yelled at us and slammed things around. He blasted his emotions out onto us, as they were probably too intense for him to handle. I pushed down my feelings, my guts in a knot. I pasted a semi-smile on my face and went rigid. I was losing trust in the idea that we were a happy family. How does a happy, loving family have these experiences? I doubted myself and was losing my connection to self-worth and self-love.

Today my dad would be considered dependent on alcohol, but like many men his age, this was his medication, his main way to cope. I had a love/hate relationship with his drinking, which I was figuring out as a boy. The first beer took the edge off and calmed him down, and that helped. But if that was followed by whiskey and more beer, then things could get dicey, loud, and incredibly unpredictable. Utensils scraping on a plate or his not liking something my mom said would throw him into a rage. Where was my sweet, loving, smart, creative dad, and who is this tired, anxious man who, fueled by drink, lashes out in pain? I looked at his angry, inebriated face as if to ask, *What have you done with the man who loves me?* I was so confused and lost in all of this churn.

When my mom did stand up to him, he yelled over her, not letting her express her emotions. Or he would gaslight her, making random things her fault and himself the victim. Her answer was to be quiet, try to calm him down, make peace, and retreat into her well-established enabling behaviors. She was teaching me how to navigate his anger, give power away, and how to not have any boundaries, putting his needs before my own. I lost a bit more of my identity each time I didn't set a boundary. I concluded that if I were perfect and did everything they asked, then they wouldn't argue. I was learning the role of the family peacemaker and I thought I was the problem. That was my wounded inner child interpretation. I didn't have anything else to go on, and I was incredibly confused with this wheel of moods, this roller coaster.

My mom, needing to vent, would overshare with me details of their relationship that were too much for me as an adolescent. She confided in me, telling me how overwhelmed she was and that she didn't know what to do about him. The irony was that I knew, from a child's perspective, everything she was going through because I was living it with her. I was aligned with her and saw her in pain, which broke my heart. Some days, because of everything I was learning from her, I felt like I was married to my dad and had to deal with all of his stuff. I wanted to help my mom, so I listened and offered my limited teenage wisdom to ease her troubles. I think she saw me as an ally, as being in the trenches with her. I saw the love between them, but it didn't always square with their behaviors toward each other, which confused me.

As a codependent-in-training, I had few boundaries. I didn't know where I ended and my mom began, and this overshared information was overwhelming. I knew I didn't have the solution, but I really tried to help. What I lost in this enmeshment was a sense of being a kid. I lost the separation between my life as a boy and my parents' adult world. I was thrust into their world at random times. She would cry to me about my dad's behavioral choices and what he said to her. Inside, I was screaming *I don't want to know about this*, but I couldn't unhear what she said, and I couldn't abandon her in her time of need. I loved them both but didn't know what to say to save their relationship and make everything all better. I didn't have time for play, as I was the live-in teenage therapist. I lost a hierarchical sense of seeing them as parental figures because I felt like a parent. I needed to find the answers, like an adult would, so I could solve their problems.

With my childlike carefree innocence lost, I was now privy to this adult world. Using my wounded tools of being the caretaker, fixer, and peacemaker, I worked hard to stop my parents from arguing and to protect my little sister from the emotional fallout. I thought that she would get out of the chaos unscathed through my efforts. It felt like a job, and I was always on call. After all, I had an extensive "mood matrix" that I could pull up at any time to determine the emotional weather report. I couldn't just be at home; I had to be hypervigilant. I began to see myself and my friends differently, as the turmoil and confusion colored my world. I was shutting down and becoming resentful and jaded. Like a tablet in a glass of water, my sweet innocence dissolved until all the fizzies were gone and the water was still and empty.

No matter how hard I tried, my parents were still upset with each other at times, and I felt like a failure. All of this was overwhelming to me, and I internalized the pressure with intestinal problems and by withdrawing, shutting down, and being quiet. Gone was the relaxed feeling in my body; now my gut was screwed up in knots. Whenever they asked if I was okay, I would just trail off, responding that I was fine. I didn't want to add to their problems; they had too much going on. I never thought of hurting myself, I just wanted to be out of this pain but didn't have the right tools. My wounded, hurting self incorrectly interpreted that they were upset with me, as I didn't have any boundaries between their problems and mine. My mom was hurting, I was sad, my dad was angry and anxious, and I was frightened for us all. When I listened to music, the only songs that resonated with my heart were the sad ones.

My efforts were exhausting, and I now see how much I had to give up and how much carefree play I had to discard because I was so preoccupied with how the household was functioning. I often stared into space at school, and I think now that I was dissociating from the emotional trauma that went on at home. School was more predictable and gave me a break, but at home I was always trying to process what was going on instead of focusing on my schoolwork. I lost out on some fundamental knowledge that I had to learn later. I became preoccupied with reentering the emotional landscape of our family when school let out. My inner child wounding establishing a firm place in my loss bucket.

As an escape from the house, I went deep into the woods down to the creek, which was my refuge, my place of self-soothing, with no one else there. Being by myself was the best because I didn't have to read someone else's mood and change myself for their comfort. I stayed in the woods as long as I could, making dams in the creek for the tadpoles and crawdads, until it started to get dark and my dad whistled for me to come home.

I felt restored by my escape, but then there was the walk back home. Whatever sense of peace I had evaporated with each step as I walked back home to the family I loved, not knowing what I was going to encounter, what I would have to answer to, or the work I was going to have to do to balance everything out. I held my breath as I opened the door, as I didn't know what the mood would be like, how I would have to change myself to fit into their world and make things better. Now I see that during the walk back home, I reunited with the heaviness of loss in my loss bucket. My escape into a carefree nature world was overtaken by feeling the need to be emotionally responsible for an outcome. I loved my parents and felt the burden to make all of our lives better. I had to fix it.

As I became an older teen, as I started driving and becoming more aware of events in the home, I began to lose respect for my dad. I understood the big picture better, and I didn't like what I saw. A curtain had been pulled back, and whereas before I felt like I had lost something undefined and ephemeral, now I could name those feelings: I felt angry, disheartened, resentful and depressed. I was trying to determine what kind of family we had; should I be proud of my family or disillusioned? What story should I tell myself about me, about us? Whatever illusion I had before was gone, and this reality was much worse; it was raw, unvarnished, and painful. I felt like an impostor when I smiled for family pictures.

My mom still shared what was going on between her and my dad when I was in high school. I remember telling her in frustration that she needed to divorce him. That was painful for me to say, but I didn't know what else to tell her. I was completely bone dry of whatever wisdom I could offer, and at this point, I think I was looking for my mom to set boundaries for herself and all of us. I was looking for her to stand up to my dad. My mom was a strong woman, but the marriage vow was a sacrament to her, and she could never leave him. When she tried to set boundaries and say no to him, he didn't respect her no. I imagine she stayed in the relationship because she loved the best of him and out of a sense of obligation to keep the family intact. My sister and I would have supported my mom if she had left my dad. Of course, none of us wanted this kind of loss. When the times were good and loving, it was wonderful, but the emotional burden of the tension building and the pot boiling over was a lot for us to handle.

I didn't have much to say to my dad during my mid-to-late teen years. I respected that he was my dad, but I didn't respect his emotional outbursts or behavioral choices. I loved him but hated his behavior. I couldn't have verbalized this at the time, but I can name it clearly now.

I was becoming a young adult and had a car and after school jobs, but I felt like a little kid inside. My inner child wounding was showing up by my shutting down, withdrawing, trying to fix other people, and giving my power away. We were all lost in this cycle, and no one knew the way out. We were all using our wounded tools to cope, but none of the tools we had were the right ones. This is what I mean when I say we all come by our wounding honestly. It sounds like a cliché, but we were all doing the best we could with what we knew.

I was relieved when I went away to college. I packed up my codependent tools and left home. I felt like I retired from a job. I no longer had to be the person in the middle of this family dynamic, trying to make it work. But every time I visited my family, I felt a heavy, molasses-like, codependent cape descend on my shoulders as I reunited with the peacemaker role I played in the family. I moved of their house after college, and the distance gave me breathing room to sort myself out from the mix. I began to feel more myself and less glued into the family jigsaw puzzle. But even though I was feeling more myself, I didn't know who that was because I had curated myself for others, not me.

I began therapy in my midtwenties, and only then did I begin to understand my inner child wounding and my lack of boundary setting. I was learning the lost inner child parts of me. I learned of the roles I played in the alcoholic household; as the family peacemaker who tried to control things and how seriously I took that role, and the role of the hero trying to be perfect for my parents, making everything better.

I began to understand my mom and dad from an adult's perspective. For a long time, I resented how much like my dad I was. I didn't respect or love those parts of myself that were like him. I pushed back any time someone said, "You're just like your dad." Over time and through years of therapy, I learned how to respect and love myself and, in turn, to love and respect my dad. I also learned how to love and respect my mom's oversharing and the enabling choices she made in their relationship dance. My deepest heart never stopped loving them, even at the height of the turmoil.

My sister sees our childhood from a different perspective; she thought the back-and-forth with our parents was ridiculous. Now we both see that I protected her from experiencing the full range of what I experienced; I shielded her from the blast of turmoil that I felt intensely. I created an emotional buffer between she and they with my wounded tool kit. She could see our parents clearly from outside of the bubble, as though looking into the fishbowl. She spoke up more often, pushed back, and found her voice earlier than I did.

My sister was focused on a world with horses, where she could play unburdened. She had an inborn passion for horses and horseback riding, which is all-encompassing. Mom and Dad would ask her to make decisions around her horses, which they had no knowledge of. As I turned inward, she turned to a world that took her in and taught her how to handle, saddle, and ride a large animal. She says now that finding harmony with a horse is a meditation that nothing can interrupt. This connection allowed her to escape the family's burdens completely.

My sister's view of the world is that she can control a twelve-hundred-pound animal, so "you" are not going to be a problem. While she was less affected by the turmoil in our household, she was still exposed to the yelling, and she lost the innocence of family harmony. She says she, too, was emotionally shaken by our parents' unpredictable behavior, which was so out of character from all other aspects of life with them. Like me, my sister went away to college to find her place in life. Upon graduation, she was determined to be independent and self-reliant. We both became successful in our careers and were not burdens on anyone else. We never wanted to go back to this broken family dynamic, which never changed. As young adults, if we stayed too long in their house, our wounded parts would activate and we would inadvertently find ourselves sliding back into the churning family dance. Without us there, our parents went through the wounded cycles on their own, spinning in their familiar dramas.

When I look back to the sixties, seventies, and eighties through this window, my heart is tender for both of my parents. They were deeply loving people and had many friends who loved them. It is too simplistic to make my dad the villain in this story, as he's not. Nor do I see my mom as the victim, as she had a strong internal sense and made clear but painful choices for herself and the family. My dad's anxiety wasn't addressed until much later in life. My sister and I wonder how our lives would have been if he had gotten on medication sooner instead of trying to fix the problem himself. He was a compassionate, loving man who gave freely of his time to charities and helped others without the need for recognition. He was always thinking of what my sister and I would enjoy, what he could build for us, or an experience he could create. When my sister and I married, he loved our spouses. He was sweet and loving toward my mom, calling her by her nickname, Miss Precious.

This is the side of my dad that I cherish, and why I never emotionally left him. My mom was unconditionally loving, gentle, and kind, and when she and my dad were in a good place, life was grand between the two of them. She had many girlfriends who were like sisters to her, and she loved when the extended family was all together. While my story is of loss, we also had an abundance of nurturing, caring, loving, fun, tender, gentle times as a family, and I'm grateful because this is the love and hope that I call upon in times of need.

My parents remained married until they died. At their best, they showed me how to hold and receive love. I felt cherished and unconditionally loved by them. The good times eventually outweighed the bad. The bounty of love won out over the collateral damage of loss.

Respecting and loving myself opened new pathways for me to respect and love my mom and dad. Before that, I felt a sense of loss, as I looked at them and our family through a lens of how dysfunctional our homelife was. I used to only see the "bad" stuff and all the things I describe in this story. Looking at my family in that way kept me stuck and in a victim space. I walked with a narrative of loss and lack. As I became more healed, I could see the complex dimensions of their relationship, everything they did for us, how they showed their love, and how they were always doing their best with what they had. I realized how they were co-creating their relationship reality, how they each played a role. I learned to hold a space for the good and the bad, to not lump it all together but to honor all of the parts that make the whole. I examined and healed all of those wounded responses, feelings and experiences I had stuffed in my loss bucket. I saw my mom and dad's dimensionality and contradictions and imagined their personal emotional struggles.

I realize I didn't lose anything tangible in my childhood. What I lost was something much more precious: the untroubled sense of being a kid. I know that if I could have verbalized all of this as a boy, my parents would never have wanted me to feel any of it. It would have been painful for them, but I believe they would have examined themselves and worked toward healing. They would have tried many ways to fix the dynamic if any of us could have named it because they loved my sister and me and wanted the best for us.

I realize now that I grew up way too fast. I became overly responsible for things that I shouldn't have been responsible for, and I was privy to many adult problems I shouldn't have known about. As a boy, I was almost always stretching and adapting to the loss, fitting myself into the paradigm of the family and pushing any of my boundaries aside to smooth things over. I had moments of solace, but I was quickly pressed back into the stretch in my parentified role. Through a lot of conscious effort over the years, by following my HEAL process and other therapies, I have reconciled and healed this loss within me. I refer to myself as a codependent in recovery, practicing my boundaries everyday.

This is ultimately a love story, as my sister and I were always close with our parents, and we didn't get lost in their wounded dance when we became adults. We were done with that predictable, tired show, and we always knew how it would end. We shifted our perspective away from the codependent family patterns. We showed up for holidays with our mom and dad, but now we had boundaries. We healed ourselves as much as we could so as not to be a part of that codependent world and so we could love them as adults.

My sister and I went on to create loving long-term relationships in our adult lives. We enjoy our lives fully and can express ourselves freely. The codependent burdens we had are healed, and we are stronger for it. I learned how to give myself permission to play and be goofy. We worked through our childhood woundings and stopped the intergenerational cycle that we had learned so well. We both went on to larger lives, but we always came back home and always loved our parents. The perspective of my family and myself that I have today helped me heal these deep inner child wounds. We feel soulfully blessed to have the parents we had.

In writing this story, I had to examine deeper parts of my childhood than I had looked at before. Even with all of my self-work and my work as a psychotherapist I had to dig deep, as this was a heartbreaking, soul-stretching story for me to write. I surrendered to the process and gut-cried as I wrote, even though I've talked about all of this before. That is how the grief journey is; we are always turning over the loss and discovering new, unknown parts that help us understand ourselves better. Each time we hold and name a loss, we heal a little more, and eventually, we can examine the same loss story through an expanded and healed lens.

Your family dynamic may have looked different from mine; maybe you had it much worse or better than I did. When you feel calm and centered, gently ask yourself the following questions.

- What were some things that came up for you when you read my story?

- What perspective do you now have on your formative years?

- Have you looked at past events or situations as losses but now see them as part of the larger tapestry of your life, each experience supporting the one that came before and the one after?

Take some time to let these new emotions find a place inside of you. Be patient with your tender feelings and this new perspective. Be gentle with yourself as you heal.

Why things are the way they are is never a simple explanation. We are complicated creatures. When we open ourselves up to possibilities, we uncover the hidden gems of love, trust, and respect.

Additional Resources

Healing Your Lost Inner Child: How to Stop Impulsive Reactions, Set Healthy Boundaries and Embrace an Authentic Life, Robert Jackman, St. Charles, Illinois: Practical Wisdom Press, 2020.

Healing Your Lost Inner Child companion workbook, Robert Jackman, St. Charles, Illinois: Practical Wisdom Press, 2020.

Healing Your Wounded Relationship: How to Break Free of Codependent Patterns and Restore Your Loving Partnership, Robert Jackman, St. Charles, Illinois: Practical Wisdom Press, 2021.

Adult Children of Alcoholics and Dysfunctional Families, www.adultchildren.org.

CHAPTER EIGHT

Deepening the Work

My grief says that I dared to love, that I allowed another to enter the very core of my being and find a home in my heart. Grief is akin to praise; it is how the soul recounts the depth to which someone has touched our lives. To love is to accept the rites of grief.
—FRANCIS WELLER

There are many subtle nuances of the grief journey that aren't often discussed but are universally felt. Our responses to grief say a lot about where we are in the integration of loss in our life's tapestry, revealing how we examine our loss through rejection, resistance, acceptance, and finally, the joining with our grief. These reflections can happen at any point along the tender path. Even when we are lost in our grief, at some level we are always in negotiation with loss and working to find a place for it to live within us. We try to make meaning out of this normal emotion of suffering as we travel the wilderness of life and make our way on the tender path toward balance and solace. The deeper reflections of loss discussed in this chapter are a master class in grief work, when we feel the loss in ways that are hard to explain to others. We may think there's something wrong with us because we don't hear other people talk about having the reactions that we do. These are the aspects of grief that reveal our multidimensional interaction with this emotion.

If you are grieving now, you may find that no one else understands your grief, how you are grieving, or your grief journey. But this is okay because your tender path needs to make sense only to you. You are developing your personal response to your loss, and no one else can do that for you.

What's Wrong with Me?

Loss has its own rules. We begin to realize that we have to adjust to the rules of loss and the feeling of being out of control. Once we acknowledge and stop pushing against this uncomfortable truth, we can join with it and be in its natural flow and unfolding.

Sometimes we don't have a reaction to a loss that we think we should have, perhaps feeling only a little sad or even neutral. We think, *I don't feel the way I think I should be feeling. I know it's a loss and a bad thing that just happened, so why do I not feel anything?* We are confused and embarrassed because we don't have an expected reaction, what we think we "should" be feeling. Over the years, people have sheepishly confessed to me that they didn't feel bad when someone died. They wonder what's wrong with them, if they are callous or unfeeling, and they feel ashamed of their nonreaction. They don't know why they feel guilty or have a sense of relief or freedom when a loved one dies. I have also seen people have dramatically mournful reactions to the death of someone with whom they had a deeply difficult or contentious relationship. Our emotional reactions always teach us about our wounded and healed selves.

If you don't have a reaction you believe you should have, know that "should" thoughts lead to a negative-thinking paradigm. Shoulds restrict us to an obligatory path that we feel we can't get out of, which reinforces a victimhood narrative. Your feelings are your feelings, so the reaction you have is what you have. It's personal to you, and no one else needs to know what you're feeling or not feeling unless you want to share this with them. Comparing yourself to how other people would react isn't going to help you find the answer. You may not immediately understand your feelings, but that doesn't make them wrong.

Two factors often contribute to an unexpected reaction. The first is our relationship to the person or loss. For example, if you had an estranged or arm's-length relationship with someone who has died, you may feel conflicted or not feel the loss deeply. The second is when we have shut down or restricted ourselves from feeling deep feelings in order to protect ourselves. This usually indicates a prior trauma history, where we had put up emotional guardrails to protect ourselves from incoming attacks. People with this history will often have a limited reaction, if any at all, to a loss.

If you have a hard time finding a greeting card that fits your unique relationship to a person when they are living, you may not have the emotions you think you should have when they die. This reaction indicates a complex emotional relationship that has many frayed ends and unresolved issues. Gently notice and hold space inside for this conflicted emotion. Know that it's hard to hold love in your heart for someone who has hurt you. This is a normal protective response. A part of you is probably working hard to figure all of this out.

If you have a reaction different from the one you expected, spend some time writing symbolic letters, and see what comes up. (You will learn about symbolic writing in chapter nine, "Practical Tools for Honoring Loss.") You may be surprised to learn that there's a part of you that's been long dormant and now has a voice. Give yourself the gift of self-expression, and know that whatever you are feeling is normal and that your feelings will not overtake you. Be gentle with yourself as you uncover the reasons why you have a reaction different from the one you expected.

Our reactions to loss are unique to us. They are not about a moral failing or not having enough compassion. We can heal these complicated relationship dynamics once we are ready. Forgiveness is a gift we give first to ourselves, then the other person.

WELL-MEANING PEOPLE

Casseroles and cards are fine, but others don't know what I really need and I'm afraid to tell them.

Those who are close to us know when we are in pain, and seeing us hurting is hard for them. They may offer suggestions and distractions to help us feel better and move on. Sometimes their expressions work and are indeed helpful, giving us a sweet comfort when we most need it. A friend making easy-to-reheat food or doing a small chore that we are unable to do means so much. But sometimes the efforts are clumsy or even self-serving, meaning they want us to feel better (happy) so they don't have to worry about us. Perhaps they haven't gone through a loss like the one you are experiencing so they don't have the tools or the language to be able to help you. Our friends and family aren't mind readers, so they will often give or do for us what they want, not what we need.

In the most well-meaning and well-intended ways, our loved ones bring their ideas of what will cheer us up. This often results in expressions and actions that don't provide us what we need. They don't know what to say, for example, so what they do say comes out wrong. If they have lost loved ones, our loss may trigger their unresolved grief, and we end up having to take care of them. They may make changes for us or tell us what we need to do as if we have no decision-making abilities. Friends will bring food or offer to help with kids or obligations, which can result in our having to do more to organize and manage all of this help. Be honest and check in with yourself to see whether the assistance you get is helpful or is making more work for you. Perhaps the most common result of all this well-intended assistance is that it comes immediately and all at once instead of being spread out over time, to those quiet moments months later when we really need it.

Offers and actions of assistance usually come from a place of caring, but they can still feel or sound controlling and directive. They can be unhelpful at best and rude at worst, when others try to gain control over our situation because their fears are activated. They feel like they are making a difference by taking control of our lives. They leave feeling satisfied that they "helped," but we feel more depleted than before.

If a friend, family member, or coworker offers well-meaning suggestions that don't fit you, simply say, "I appreciate your thinking about me. Right now I need to do some things that have worked for me in the past. I'm taking each day as it comes and not pushing myself through my experience. Knowing that you care is a great comfort, and it's reassuring to know I can reach out to you when I need to." This statement says a lot in a small package. You are acknowledging their suggestions, but you're also setting boundaries. You are clearly stating that you will decide what's best for you in the moment, and you are putting guardrails around the interaction by saying that you will reach out to them when you need some help. This is good demonstration of self-care and self-compassion. Instead of just taking what others think will help, you are discerning what you need. You are checking in with yourself and being thoughtful and careful as you move through this time.

You may want to talk with others who have been through a loss like the one you are experiencing. They will be able to help you identify the supplies and resources to make this journey easier.

It's wonderful that people care for us, but too many people jumping in at once can be overwhelming. Instead of telling multiple people what you need, appoint one person as the organizer and give them the instructions to present to others. You only have so much energy following a loss, so guard it jealously, as you need all of your reserves to help yourself heal.

Crickets

We reflexively tell people that we're fine, but we aren't fine; we are far from it. We feel gutted, lost, and searching for something that we can't identify or name as our subconscious searches for a safe harbor from our fears and our mournful selves.

Direct help is needed at the time of a loss, but we need help most after the chaos and commotion has subsided. There seems to be a two- to three-week window when everyone gathers around for support. This then tapers off and goes quiet. After the flurry of activity ends, we are in the stretch, and this is when we most need people around us. This is when we need food dropped off or to be taken out to dinner or go on walks with others. We need this gentle comfort as the days, weeks, and months march on and we reorient to this new normal. This is when we feel truly alone, when the house is super quiet and we feel our emotions the most intensely. The adrenaline rush from the shockwave has receded, and we enter the stretch with sorrowful feelings that tear us up inside. Connection and encouragement help us to feel grounded and safe, but it's hard to ask for these things months later because friends and family pitched in so much directly after the loss. We don't want to feel like a burden or be perceived as needy. The reality is that we all need to feel comforted, especially in the first year following a death.

If you need support in the months following your loss, then bravely reach out to others or find a support group or community where you feel connected and not alone. I know it's hard to put yourself out there, but you're not being selfish when you ask for help, you are expressing a basic human need. Those who are able to step up will be there for you, but not everyone can be who you need them to be. Advocate for yourself, and be patient and persistence as you heal.

Discounting Loss

Comparing ourselves to someone else is a game that can't be won. You are somewhere on a continuum and will always be doing better than some and worse than others.

"Oh, that's nothing. I've had it a lot worse." Maybe you've heard this from a well-meaning friend, but when we experience a loss of any kind, it's not comforting to hear someone say that they've had it worse, as if it's some sort of trauma competition. Such behavior discounts and dismisses our loss, as they are implying that we shouldn't feel bad and should get over it. This could be their way of trying to help us gain perspective, but it sure doesn't feel good. Others want to imprint or project onto us how they would feel about a loss, and thus, how we should feel. This is partly from good intentions and partly that they don't want to see us hurting, as that hurts them. They want us to get through this so they don't have to carry these feelings.

Of course, we also discount and minimize losses to ourselves. We say things like, *It's not too bad* or *I've been through tougher things before.* This is our way of trying to find resilience, but what happens to the feelings around the loss itself? You know it by now: these unacknowledged and minimized losses get piled into the loss bucket.

If you or someone else minimizes or discounts your losses, say something like this to yourself: *I know this happened, and I'm sad and hurt about it. I acknowledge the important feelings I have right now around this so that I can recognize them, heal, and move on. Every feeling I have is important, and I'm learning how to honor my experiences so that I can heal. I am stronger than I realize.*

Overidentifying with Loss

When losses frighten us, they can overtake us with their big loudness, and we begin to think we *are* the loss, especially in the shockwave phase. I have cancer. I am disabled. I am a widow. I am an addict. I am divorced. I am alone. I am an orphaned adult. These statements are used as a shield of protection or a badge signaling to the world that something enormous has happened.

Overidentifying with a loss happens when the loss becomes a major part of how we see ourselves. It's when the diagnosis, the situation, the adult child who has lost a parent, or the one who was betrayed, for example, becomes what we present to the world. It's what we lead with when we enter a room, the first thing we talk about when someone asks how we are. We are, essentially, lost in our loss. The loss swallows up and claims our identity. We then carry this identity into the stretch, and it's all we want to talk about. Such overidentification can be a momentary thing, but some people hold on to it for a long time.

When we don't know what to do with everything we feel, we can become transfixed by the diagnosis or the situation and use it to claim victimhood or get sympathy or attention. We may use it as a deflection, as in, don't see me, see me as this label. The overidentification becomes a smokescreen so we don't have to talk about anything else or look at the next steps we could take. This avoidant behavior may indicate that we don't want to explore any deeper feelings yet, or we may not know how to relate to what's going on with us and use this as the first step in emotional discovery. We may hide behind it because we don't have the emotional energy to be strong for ourselves. We may use it as an excuse to get out of doing things we don't like or to avoid situations. We are stuck and spinning in this view of ourselves. When we overidentify with our loss, we may take longer to move through the stretch phase.

Overidentifying with loss is understandable when our normal life routines and schedules become hijacked by, for example, doctor appointments, insurance paperwork, scans, procedures, or protocols that are all new to us. It can be hard to find ourselves when we are overwhelmed and learning about a new diagnosis or dealing with a loss of a spouse, as the loss dictates everything in our lives.

If you overidentify with a loss, know that this expression makes sense for now, that you are forming a relationship with the loss that works for you. You are trying things out and getting used to the idea of your new reality. Overidentifying may even reinforce old childhood wounding that feels familiar. You may hold on to the idea that you are the loss, guarding it in a way. If you are stuck in this identity, gently ask yourself how you can find balance in your life. Just observe yourself as you reflect on your emotional landscape.

INCONSOLABLE LOSS

If you've never been through a loss like this before, whatever your loss, you may feel completely alone, which is normal.

You learned about inconsolable loss in chapter two, when a loss is so great that nothing will relieve the pain. If you are sitting with the deep and sorrowful grief of inconsolable loss, then consider seeing someone to talk to about it. Having someone witness your work is a way to honor your feelings and, I believe, help you heal. When others honor where you are in your grief process, you will feel seen and acknowledged. If you are allowed to just feel what you feel, then you will know someone is truly listening to you and not as overwhelmed as you are. You don't need anyone to give you platitudes or try to talk you out of a feeling. You need to be allowed to spin in the depths of your grief as another person creates a safe container and know that all of you is welcome to show up.

Having consoled many parents who lost a child, I can say that a big part of my job is creating a safe space for them to reflect and hold their pain, to be with them as they sit with their sorrow. Just my being with them and their deep pain gives them a moment to feel it. I find that this act of honoring can help them to lessen the self-punishment and decrease the loudness of the grief inside. They see that I can hold their pain even as they are writhing in it. They see I'm not crumbling with their loud grief pain, so they can lean in without crumbling. We sit with and hold the pain together, creating a safe container for emotions, where all of them is welcome.

Once I prepared myself and began to work with grieving parents, I started to carry what I call an emotional signature that signaled to them that I could hold this unique, soul-crushing pain. This emotional signature is part of creating a safe container and is felt subconsciously by others once we have done our own work. Honestly, if I hadn't prepared myself, their intense grief would have cracked me open. Once I prepared myself at a deep, intuitive level, these parents knew that I could hold and would not buckle under the immensity of their sorrow.

It's important to create a safe container for your grief so that you can begin to understand its dimension and wisdom. The people who can hold this space for you are witnesses to your grief, your sacred journey. They can hold space while you push up against a colossal wall of pain and ask why. This is why you want to find a therapist and a medical provider who have experience in the area of your unique loss. They need to be able to hold a rock-solid, safe space for you as you travel to internal lands and come back with insights and healing.

It may be helpful to interview several therapists to see if they have worked with your particular loss issue before and to learn what their treatment plan would look like. Don't be concerned about asking the wrong question because their answers will help you to determine whether you can put your confidence in them. Therapists hear all kinds of stories all the time. Don't hold back with what is on your mind and heavy on your heart. They are trained to help you with specific clinical tools and techniques to guide you on a path to wholeness. Friends may be great listeners, but few friends have the training to give you an objective response and perspective for your problems. Your friends may not know what to do with the emotional weight of what you have to say. They may even be relieved to know you are seeking out a therapist.

THE LOSS OF A PET

The loss is only the beginning of the journey toward healing.

Feelings of great sadness and grief over the loss of a pet are very real. Our pets give us total and unconditional love, and when they are gone, a huge vacuum is left that is hard to fill.

I know firsthand the deep sorrow over the loss of a pet. My partner and I have had five dogs over the last thirty years. Each one of these fur babies has had a significant place in our lives and hearts. Pets take up a big part of our hearts during their way-too-short time on earth. They fill us up with unconditional love and attentional energy whether they have fur, feathers, scales, or fins. They bring a unique perspective into our human world, reminding us to live in the moment and take each day one at a time.

When a pet dies, a part of us and our household is forever changed. When they pass away, the house becomes quiet and still. Just as with all types of loss, it is important to honor this loss. Today there are many ways to memorialize pets so that we are comforted by a part of their presence. You can create a stone marker with a paw print in clay along with their collar, for example. Just having their picture around is comforting. If your pet is alive today, treasure these moments. The time that you are soaking up their love now will fill your heart when they are no longer sitting in your lap or in the living world.

Someone who doesn't have a pet may not understand why the loss of your pet is such a big deal. They may not be able to imagine how the death of your pet is like losing a family member. What this friend is telling you is that they aren't the one you need to look to for a sympathetic shoulder.

I believe our pets check in on us from the other side. This may sound strange, but I've heard from other pet owners stories similar to those I've experienced in the still of the night. I have felt a weight, soft and silent, on the bed next to me as the energy of one of our dogs curled up between my legs. I think this is their way of connecting with us and letting us know they are not far away, that they're just on the other side of the rainbow bridge, waiting for us. Allow yourself to feel their love in your heart. They are always with us.

If you need to put your pet down, know that one day too early is okay, and one day too late is painful for them.

⌒

The personal journey of grief takes us to deep places within that hold our sorrow, our pain, and our wisdom. Through this process on the tender path, you are learning how to recognize your special connection to grief and loss. When we recognize and name parts of our path, we can walk with greater ease and fulfillment toward a place of wholeness. When we acknowledge our feelings, they are not as scary and dark as we may have thought. It's not easy, but when we speak our truth and name our pain, we welcome a feeling of wholeness where anguished sorrow once lived. We learn to recognize where we are in the moment, what we need, and how to bring balance back into our lives when a loss has confiscated our known world. Reach out to others for help, as there are grief support groups, grief yoga groups, and any number of ways to connect with others who are in the same space that you find yourself. You are not alone.

Throughout our lives, we will have opportunities to sit in our pain. We can't escape it. If we try, it will chase after us, inviting us to hold and nurture it. Listen to its song.

KATHY'S STORY: ACCEPTING A CHILD'S JOURNEY

Kathy is a wonderful Renaissance woman who has two adult children, works in nature, and gives great soulful hugs. Those in her circle are lucky indeed. When you are in a conversation with her, you feel as if you are the most important person in the world. She is present, emotionally available, and has deep wisdom. Once you get to know her, she is incredibly strong, has good boundary skills, and sees others with clarity and kindness.

About ten years ago, one of her adult children, who was married to a woman and had a young child, told Kathy that she no longer identified as male and wanted to transition from her assigned male biological sex at birth to female. (I will refer to Kathy's child as she/her from here on.) She had given her transition a great deal of thought and shared with her mom that she was ready to take this huge step. As Kathy's daughter moved forward with her transition, Kathy had to reset her own narrative as a mom.

Kathy found herself in the situation, as many parents do, where her child wished to express herself different from what Kathy had imagined for her. Every parent goes through some version of this dynamic, where differences between the parent and child can lead to tension in the relationship, especially as the child becomes independent from the parents and their expectations. This can be compounded if there are broken respect or trust issues between parent and child.

This is her story of how she found a deep wisdom to help herself as she navigated her daughter's transition and gained a deeper understanding of her child.

As a matter of clarification, the term "transgender," or the shortened "trans," is an umbrella term for people whose gender identity and gender expression differ from cultural expectations based on the biological sex they were assigned at birth. Being transgender does not imply any specific sexual identity. "Cisgender" is when one's gender identity corresponds with one's sex assigned at birth, transgender is when they do not correspond.

"Gender identity" is an inner concept of oneself as female, male, a blend of both, or neither. It is about how individuals see themselves and what they call themselves. "Gender expression" refers to one's external appearance, behaviors, clothing, body characteristics, voice, and other cues; these expressions may or may not conform to society's associations of male or female.

While gender identity is how one feels toward oneself, sexual identity is the way one feels sexually toward others. "Sexual identity" is an inherent or immutable and enduring emotional, romantic, or sexual attraction to other people. An individual's sexual identity is independent of their gender identity.

"Gender dysphoria" describes the feeling of discomfort or distress one feels when their gender identity differs from their sex assigned at birth. This term focuses on the discomfort as being the problem, not one's gender identity.

Note: All of these concepts and terms are fluid and evolving. The terms used in this story are sourced from Mayo Clinic Family Health Book, HRC.org, and other sources.

When your adult child came to you and told you about her desire to transition to female, what were your first thoughts and feelings?

I am going to start by referring to my child as my daughter because one of the biggest things I've come to understand is that I never really had a son, always a daughter—my second and youngest daughter. This is the mindset that is important to instill from the beginning.

My initial response was a combination of, now everything makes sense; oh, my gosh; and, wow, I need to absorb this! I also realized that everything in my life has prepared me for handling this, so I know we'll all get through it okay. While carrying her birth name as a boy, my daughter was involved in a lot of things offered to young boys at the time in our small coastal community, among them, playing various sports, skateboarding, chess club, and a local theater camp. She was always an extremely sensitive child with a softer sensibility than usual.

In retrospect, I realize that a lot of her struggles as she was growing up were directly related to her having to hide and push all these feelings deep down, unable to share what she was going through. Certainly, one of the biggest sadnesses for me was not knowing any of this at the time and not being able to help her in any way. Then, as the reality set in about her desire and, in fact, need to transition, I began to think about what this meant from the practical aspects, let alone the personal ones.

Did you feel caught off guard or blindsided?

At one level, I was taken by surprise. I had no idea she had been feeling this way since she was eight years old. I could tell this was very hard for her to share with me, fearing my reaction, I'm sure. But at the same time, I felt a light go on. It suddenly explained a lot of things, such as the unusually sensitive and softer nature she'd always had, so I never felt unsteady or ungrounded.

Was this a loss to you?

Once I realized my daughter had been dealing with this since childhood, I knew her decision to transition was a path she had to take. There was no choice for her; it was a necessity for her wholeness and sense of well-being. I realized that I wasn't losing a son because I never had one to begin with. Nor was I gaining a daughter because she had always been one; I just didn't know it. I feel to truly honor her journey, it is important that I think of her just that way, as always having been my daughter.

I think the biggest sense of loss has been felt by my daughter and her partner in their relationship, though they continue to have a deep bond as they navigate their lives and their shared child together. To the extent that they can, they look at it as a transition in the relationship, not a loss. This simply takes time and will support all of them as time goes along.

I will always feel a bond with my daughter's partner, the birth mother of my granddaughter, and regard her as another of my children, but I know that our relationship will change, too, as she becomes involved in her new life and our opportunities to be together diminish. This is sad for me, but I know we will all make an effort to be as inclusive as we can, to share in my granddaughter's life as much as we can. They live in France, so living in a country on the other side of the world doesn't make it easy anyway, but it's about everyone following their hearts, their hopes and dreams, toward whatever makes them happy, and each of us honoring that.

Many trans people have clarity regarding their gender identity and think about transitioning for a long time. By the time they make the announcement, they are way ahead of where everyone else is. Did you have any clues that she was feeling this way?

We were not able to see each other for months at a time, so if she had begun to change the way she presented herself before she told us, I wasn't aware of it. Even when I visited her the first time after she told us, she was still wearing pants and a shirt to work and making the transition to feminine clothing very gradually, mostly for special occasions.

Some parents are tempted to talk a transitioning child out of a choice they have clearly already given a lot of thought to, essentially being willing to lose a child because it is too hard for them. Were you ever tempted to do this?

After my daughter told me about her decision to transition, we spoke at length, over the course of time, about what this would mean for her personally and for her family. At the same time, I did a great deal of research to find out what it meant to be transgender and what other people's experiences of transitioning were. At no point did it occur to me that I would stop loving my child. What is this corporeal body we all have, anyway? Isn't it only an extension of the spirit within? Why would you stop loving that spirit?

Many parents are beside themselves and wonder what they did wrong. Did you ever wonder if you had done something wrong that caused this?

It is important to understand that it is no one's "fault." I never felt that it was anything I did as a parent. There was no doubt in my mind that my daughter needed to align her body to that which she has been feeling on the inside all these years.

Being transgender has been around through the ages, as long as there have been people. We still have a long way to go in certain areas of the world regarding the gay and lesbian experience, and being transgender is even less in the mainstream consciousness, though it is becoming more acknowledged. In some countries, such as France, transitional surgeries and protocols are being covered by health insurance, as there is an ever-increasing understanding that this is saving lives. The suicide rate among transgender people who are able to get the right care, treatment, and support is still high, though, let alone for those who aren't able.

Did you look at yourself differently after your daughter told you this news?

At first I felt a lot of guilt, but then my daughter said that one of her counselors told her to be sure to share with her family that it was no one's fault. Because of my relationship with her, my feeling for her as my child could never change, so I certainly felt nothing had changed as far as my being a mother.

How long did it take you to internally change to using her correct pronouns and name?

It took a least a year to completely integrate referring to her with the proper pronoun, with occasional slip-ups for a while after that.

Since we primarily talk on the phone, this may have added to the time to establish the integration. Now, about six years later, I don't think of her as anything but a young woman, so any reference to her is naturally automatic.

Did you ever experience confusion, frustration, anger, or denial when she was in transition?

I don't remember experiencing any of that. I know enough about gender dysphoria to know there is nothing a parent can do to cause gender dysphoria; a child is born this way. The hardest part for me was not knowing what my daughter had been dealing with, that she was never able to tell me or the rest of her family.

Your daughter, when she presented as male, had married a woman and was now transitioning to female. Was this confusing to you?

My feelings were not so much of confusion as they were of concern for what this meant for her, for her partner, for their relationship, for her partner's family, for our family. She had told her partner before they were married of her desire to transition, and they agreed to go ahead with the wedding. Neither one was completely aware, I think, of what this would mean in all of its dimension; how could anyone, really. Their bond was strong enough to see it through for the immediate future, wherever it took them. As a result, they have a beautiful daughter. I knew that my grandchild might face obstacles that weren't the norm, but I also knew that they both loved her so much that they would do all they could to help her adjust through it all. And children are quite resilient, after all.

What was it like to see your daughter wearing feminine clothing?

The first time I visited her after she told me, she had just begun her transitioning process. For quite a while she wore what she had always worn, pants and a shirt, but she had let her hair grow out so that it was quite long. She had added a few dresses and other feminine clothing to her wardrobe, but she was still shy to change her look too much at her workplace, wanting and needing to gain confidence in her decision to transition before becoming too obvious about it.

By the time I came back the next year, she wanted to go to women's clothing shops and look around with me. I realized this was part of our new reality, and while I took a moment to take it all in, it struck me how much this meant to her, and me, to start shopping for the kind of clothing she had always wanted to wear. I felt so honored and proud to be with her, that she would want me to be, and I remember thinking how lucky I was to experience this now with her.

Did you notice her becoming more confident or having greater self-esteem once the transitioning process began?

While I could tell there was a big weight off her shoulders after she told me, she was far from feeling self-assured and confident. As I spoke to her on the phone over the months, and then each time I saw her, I could see her blossoming and coming into her own. At a fundamental level, she looked happier than I had ever known her to be. And yes, she was beginning to have more confidence and self-esteem as the transitioning progressed.

How did you describe what your daughter was going through to your friends?

This was one of the trickier aspects, dealing with other people while she was going through the transition. On the one hand, she emphatically didn't want people who knew her and our family to know at the beginning because she felt there would be so much gossiping about it, and she wasn't living near these people to be able to discuss anything with them herself. It was much easier to evade specific questions about her, especially if they were from people who were not close to our family.

As she moved further into her transition, she was more relaxed about it and didn't mind if I shared this with people we knew. All of us were in the precarious spot of wanting people to know but not knowing how they would react.

When you talk to others about your daughter's transition now, how do you deal with their questions or concerns?

Most people are taken aback at first and don't know how to respond, so they don't follow up with many questions, to tell you the truth. Those who know my daughter and our family do have questions about the process, which I try to answer.

What are some of the least helpful things that people have said to you about your daughter's transition?

No one has said anything inappropriate or unhelpful to me, but my daughter can tell you that there have been lots of times where she felt dishonored by people who clearly would not acknowledge her now-obvious gender. Early on, she was sensitive about people who mistook her gender, and at that point they couldn't be blamed. Now she rarely has anyone mistake her gender, and when she tells them she is trans, they often are surprised. Gaining confidence in herself has helped this a lot, too.

Were you ever tempted to not tell someone about her transition?

There are people who will never understand. It's simply not in their paradigm and never will be. I could correct them when they refer to my daughter as a "he" since that was how they knew her, and then explain everything to honor her path. But it's not my job, or hers, to try to elevate their thinking, and I become exhausted doing so, especially if I'm pretty sure we'll never see them again. On the other hand, there are those who simply didn't know and I feel my daughter would want them to know, so I plunge right in and explain the whole thing.

Did you ever wish you could have more say in your daughter's transitioning process?

I did have mixed feelings about her final surgery. I know how important it was for her to have it, but from a selfish standpoint, and because the surgery she was having is so final, I do think that having to wait five years because of the long list of people requesting this specialized surgery gave her ample time to think things through. But in truth, it was I who needed ample time to think things through, as she knew what she wanted all along.

Did the process move faster than you were comfortable with?

This was never about me, and I know it would have been much easier on her if she had been able to have the surgery sooner than she did. Still, everything went smoothly and she had such good care. I believe in a sense of right timing for everything, and I think this was no exception.

Parents are usually at least forty years old when their teen or adult child comes out as trans, and they most often did not grow up with an understanding of or language around the trans experience. As a result, they struggle to find a way to relate. Did you have any prior experiences that prepared you to go through this experience?

I was fortunate to have had a number of gay and lesbian friends and acquaintances throughout my life, and in later years, I befriended a trans couple. When my daughter finally told me of her desire to transition, the communication lines were completely open. I was able to talk to one of the couples early on, and that was a big help and reassurance.

Is it surreal to look at baby pictures and think, this is who he was, and this is who she is now?

I love all the baby pictures that remind me of who she was when assigned as a boy, but I love as well the pictures of her now, as a woman, especially knowing that she is aligned with her true self.

How do you hold space for both of those realities?

Over my lifetime I have sought to live in the now, so I find it easier to tune in to the part of life that truly matters. This has also allowed me to connect with people at the heart and soul level, with less attention paid to physical appearances. Thus, I connect with my daughter at a level that has nothing to do with her appearance or gender identity. This is how I am able to hold space for both of those realities.

Societies and cultures have all sorts of opinions about the LGBTQ+ community. Did you ever want to protect your daughter from potential discrimination?

I constantly have feelings come up about wanting to protect my daughter from any potential discrimination, and it has made me even more acutely aware of discrimination across the board, be it due to color, race, or the LGBTQ+ community. I have to work at not being overwhelmed by these feelings at times, since there is so much discrimination in our world today and because I am so far away, living on the other side of the earth from my daughter.

I find that the trans person is often confident and almost fearless in how they move forward in life, assuring others that they are going to be okay. How did your daughter reassure you and show you that she was going to be okay?

I continue to be truly in awe of her courage and confidence, and yes, a kind of fearlessness she has, which anyone who is trans has to develop in order to move forward in life. But she has always seemed an old soul who was unerringly given reassurance about many things in life, not the least of which is her ability to navigate this life that she did not choose. She has learned to speak fluent French, assimilate into another culture, become certified as a pâtissière—a French pastry chef—and is helping to raise a young daughter. This gives me reason to believe she will be okay.

How do you stay centered so that you don't get lost in your daughter's journey?

Maybe it's been long enough since my daughter first told me about being transgender, but I do not remember being particularly emotional around this topic. Actually, I very much want to be there for as much of my daughter's journey as I can, especially since I feel we have some lost time to make up, time she was not able to experience as a little girl or young teen. At the same time, I don't feel any time lost in terms of her childhood, even though we thought she was a little boy.

Did you do a ceremony or ritual to honor your emotional experience of your daughter's transition, or to honor the son you gave birth to and to celebrate the daughter you have?

I thoroughly enjoy ceremony whenever I am fortunate enough to be a part of it. I think it's something we all need at some point, to feel that connection with the things that really matter in life, to connect with our ancestors, with our past and our future. While I have not felt drawn to create a special ceremony for my daughter and her transition, I have felt tremendously supported by all those around me who are connected to ceremony all the time. I feel unending gratitude for that.

What intentions, prayers, or practices helped you honor this experience?

My form of ceremony has perhaps taken a pragmatic form by simply being with my daughter and enjoying things like shopping for women's clothing with her, going to the beauty parlor and having our hair done, and brushing through her hair to smooth out a few tangles as she sat in the hospital bed after her surgery. This is ceremony to me.

These are the things I cherish that we were never able to do together as she was growing up.

Parents who are supportive of trans teens and adults ask themselves how they can best support their child. How did you support your daughter?

My questions about what she needs or how I can best support her have not changed since before her transition. Her being my child has not changed, nor has what I would do for her. The truth is, her really important needs have not changed. One of the biggest aspects of the whole concept around transitioning from one gender to another is that, ultimately, the trans person doesn't want to be considered any different from the person they always were. The only difference is the gender they want the world to see them as now. They want to be accepted and given every consideration that anyone else of that gender would get. They want to fit in seamlessly, to go on with life as if they had always expressed as female, or male in the case of transgender males.

What core strengths did you gain from going through this experience?

While my daughter's transition is still relatively new in comparison with the years she spent as male, whenever we speak over the phone or I visit her in France, I have the most extraordinary experience, as a parent and as a person, to witness the exceptional and courageous evolution of a spirit that has come into this life to break barriers, to be a pioneer, to be a wayshower, as are all transgender people in the world today. Few people have the opportunity to experience being both male and female in one lifetime. There is no one in a better position than transgender people to understand and be understanding of others about the male/female condition of humanity. They have a lot to teach us in this area of human experience.

When a child transitions, the parents have to make a huge internal transformation in how they look at, think about, feel, and relate to their child, simultaneously experiencing a loss of how they knew their child and acknowledging that this is who their child is becoming. They are in an emotional transition. What is helpful for parents to know as they process this loss and rebirth in real time?

Having had time to process the transitioning of my daughter, having felt most of what all parents feel when they experience this, I think it's important to not look at transitioning as a loss. The things that really matter, like the heart and soul of a child, are not lost. Equally, it's important to remember that their child was never really their birth gender to begin with, so how can you lose something you never really had?

We grow accustomed to how we perceive our children, so we're not prepared for when they tell us they're something different. If we feel we've lost something, it's our *idea* of that something we think we've lost. We have to get over ourselves and rejoice in our children's courageous decision to be "rebirthed," to finally let their outside align with their inside. I'm not saying this way of thinking comes easily, but it is the way to support the true birthright of our children, their wholeness of soul and spirit, health and well-being.

What would you say to a parent who is so afraid of what their child is telling them that they want to abandon or disown their child?

I am so sorry for the tragedy of parents not seeing beyond themselves and having no concept of what love for their child is, for not wanting to continue to share and experience their lives together in whatever form it takes. Support starts with parents, and if you want to contribute to destroying your own flesh and blood, then abandoning that flesh and blood is a sure way to lose them forever in a final and permanent way. While some trans people are able to survive that abandonment and find their own family tribe to buoy and support them, many do not, and they perish.

A trans person might have all the support in the world from family and friends and still not make it, being unable to adapt to a society that is cruel, narrowminded, and unforgiving in its outmoded mores, which dissociate the human spirit and soul from the physical body. Come on, people, these are human beings we are talking about here!

What wisdom do you carry from this experience that has made you an expanded version of yourself?

I'm not sure what wisdom I have gained or whether I have an expanded version of myself, but perhaps this experience underscores a clear picture to me that nothing in this life is as it seems, that our task is to let go of all our ideas of how we think things should be and embrace the quantum field that includes every possibility. But, heck, the bottom line is, I just hope I'm a good mom to both of my daughters and a good grandmother to my granddaughter. They are the future. Let's look to them!

~

Reflections on Kathy's Story

Kathy embodies an openhearted love for her daughter that every child wants to feel from a parent. She was able to reframe what some parents see as a loss to an expanded understanding of her child, a reality that had always been there. She respected her child's desire to transition and did not let fear sideline her clarity. She made herself available to her daughter and let her daughter come forward as herself. As a loving parent, she held space for her daughter to live the best expression of her own life. This is a parent's highest calling.

Kathy gives us a model for how to maintain healthy boundaries when someone we love is going through a momentous time. She shows us that the highest calling of a parent is to guide and support their child. Hers is a message of honoring and supporting the true birthright of our children, their wholeness of soul and spirit, their health and well-being. Her elegant perspective transcends the story of her daughter's journey; she gives us a template for how to see ourselves and others. She imparts her deep wisdom of what it means to be a soulful, empathetic human being.

No one knows the path that their children will take in life. Most parents want the best for their children and honor whatever expression they choose, but some parents have a prescribed idea and expectation of what their children will or should do while denying their right to their own life decisions. Some parents see their children as needing to achieve things that are the parent's agenda alone.

I have worked with many parents of trans people, and I will say that nothing prepared them for the odyssey that is their late teen or young adult child's desire to transition. The parents of a trans child must make a huge internal pivot to adjust to their child's reality, one that the child is often already clear about. Parents of trans children experience an emotional journey different from that of parents of a straight, gay, or lesbian child. Conceptualizing the fact that their child was born with a gender opposite to what the child feels inside is mind-bending for most parents.

Every trans person I have worked with felt that their identity did not match what they were assigned at birth. Usually, there is absolutely no question in their minds that they would like to, and in some cases need to, transition. They often have hesitations about how their family or community will see them, but they know the truth about themselves. Trans people embody a tremendous sense of courage, and I now understand why tribal cultures the world over acknowledged and gave a place of importance to the trans members of their communities. For millennia they were regarded as the mystics and the ones who could link earth and heaven.

Whatever your feelings are toward a trans person, most have a uniquely challenging path in life. My heart ached as Kathy expressed her sadness of not knowing early on of her child's struggle, not knowing that her child's pain was hiding in plain sight, unacknowledged until much later. It's clear that Kathy had her own process of working toward understanding and accepting what her daughter was going through. She had to dig deep inside and connect with her core values, which set the course for how she would interact with and experience her daughter's transition, her love consistently unwavering throughout the process. As the expression goes, a parent is only as happy as their saddest child.

Even with everything her daughter went through, I appreciate Kathy statement, "The truth is, her really important needs have not changed [with her transition]." Her daughter is still her child no matter what, and she loves her daughter in whatever way she chooses to go through life. Kathy's unconditional love is inspiring for any parent—or anyone—who is challenged by things they don't understand.

The trans community is in a phase of history similar to that of the gay and lesbian community in the early 1980s. During that time, many gay and lesbian people were coming out and wanting their voices to be heard, but a closed society wanted it all to go away. But once a movement starts, the surge of energy that comes from the group wanting to be seen is hard to deny. There is still a lot of misunderstanding and fear, still a lot of growth to do on all sides of the issue. Parents like Kathy and trans people like her daughter are wayshowers for all of humanity. They teach us how to hold something that can be scary and confusing while reaching deep within for eternal values such as love, trust, and respect.

Many cultures have had a huge shift toward openness and inclusion, but that doesn't mean that it's easy for parents and families to understand or accept trans people as readily as young people do. If your child or someone you know says they are curious about or interested in expressing their gender identity or sexual identity in a new way, ask them what this means to them. Their having questions about their identity or expression is a healthy sign of their growth. It doesn't mean they are transgender; it could mean that they are curious or exist somewhere along the continuum of sexual expression or are gender fluid, genderqueer, gender nonbinary, or gender nonconforming. They might just want to know more so they understand what their friends are talking about. Have them educate you in their own words, and learn the language they use. This will help you to align with how they see themselves and the world. If your child begins to appear or act in ways that are unfamiliar to you, it doesn't mean that you've lost your child, just that you are learning more about them. Please help your child find gender-affirming care so that they can receive the best support available to help them find their place in the world.

Addressing these issues is important because when they are not talked about and normalized, there exists a potential for misunderstanding on both sides. Young people who are questioning may already have a lack of self-esteem and self-worth, so by inviting them to talk, you are letting them know that you can hold this reality for them. When this open discussion is not encouraged, your child may go within, shut down, self-harm, or emotionally act out with other behaviors to give you messages about their emotional state. When feelings are brought out into the open, they can be talked about even when they challenge your status quo.

Be patient with yourself and the person who is curious or transitioning, and be patient with those around you. All of this is a brave new world for many. Parents and families who want to be supportive will not always get it right. You don't have to fully understand someone to respect them. Being trans is not a choice, although transitioning is. Have patience as you gain insight into their unique challenges and opportunities.

Our reactions to these situations often reflect where we are emotionally—whether we are healed or unhealed—than it reflects what is going on with the other person. Kathy's expanded spiritual connection helped her transcend any fears she had, and she was able to reach an elevated place of understanding. Are there aspects of this higher spiritual knowing that may help you see beyond any fears you hold so that you can reach a place of peace around something that is troubling you?

- What feelings came up for you when you read Kathy's story?
- Has your status quo ever been challenged by a friend or someone in your family?
- If so, when you went through this experience, what came up for you? What is still lingering or waiting to be examined?
- Are there parts of your life that you can reframe as Kathy did?

Kathy's charity of choice for her story contribution is Basic Rights Oregon, an organization that "works fearlessly and tirelessly to build a strong, vibrant, powerful, and progressive movement for LGBTQ equality." Learn more at www.basicrights.org.

~

Additional Resources

Amaze.org is an organization that "envisions a world that recognizes child and adolescent sexual development as natural and healthy, a world in which young people everywhere are supported and affirmed and the adults in their lives communicate openly and honestly with them about puberty, reproduction, relationships, sex and sexuality" (from the website's About Us page).

Trans-Kin: A Guide for Family and Friends of Transgender People, Eleanor Hubbard and Cameron Whitley, Boulder, CO: Bolder Press, 2012.

The Transgender Child: A Handbook for Parents and Professionals Supporting Transgender and Nonbinary Children (2nd ed.), Stephanie Brill and Rachel Pepper, Jersey City, NJ: Cleis Press, 2022.

Wonderfully and Purposefully Made: I Am Enough: A Journal All About Me, Cheryl B. Evans, Ontario, Canada: Cheryl B. Evans, 2018.

Never a Girl, Always a Boy: A Family Memoir of a Transgender Journey, Jo Ivester, Berkeley, CA: She Writes Press, 2020.

Human Rights Campaign. Learn more at www.hrc.org.

CHAPTER NINE

Practical Tools for Honoring Loss

Hope is the thing with the feathers
That perches in the soul,
And sings the tune without the words,
And never stops at all.
—EMILY DICKINSON

Happy and joyous occasions in our lives are easy to see and hold, but times of loss are hard to embrace or cherish. Going through loss is such a hard thing to experience that most of us neglect an important step in the loss recognition process: the honoring of the feelings that surround the loss. A major part of the tender path is taking the time to find a place inside to honor the loss, to create a safe container to hold this sacredness as we continue on with our lives. Being able to hold a stillness inside for the loss is akin to watching the last fifteen minutes of a sunset over the ocean. Every second the colors change, the light shifts, the clouds move, the water ripples. Our relationship to the loss is an ever-changing kaleidoscope, and the minute we think we have it figured out, it shifts again. We are a part of it, and it's a part of us.

There is a place and a purpose in our lives for rituals, honorings, and ceremony. These expressions can happen internally or outwardly, silently or loudly, individually or in a group. The main purpose is not how elaborate or perfect the honoring is, but the intention behind it. You've probably had experiences of honoring or ritual where you just went through the motions and others where you were deeply moved and the experience stayed with you for a long time. The difference is usually the intention that is put into the experience and the focus given to the process. As psychotherapist Francis Weller writes in his book *The Wild Edges of Sorrow*, "There is a reparative function to ritual. It sutures the tears in the soul that occur in the daily rounds of living. . . . Rituals are intended to take us into those places where we can engage with the difficulties in our lives in ways that are potentially transformative. They help us move from places where we feel stuck into territories of fresh living."

Ceremonial honoring actions can be deeply personal demonstrations like saying a prayer or intention, or lighting a candle. They can also be public and shared remembrances or celebrations. Each act of ceremony emphasizes the importance of that person or event in the arc of our lives. The ceremony itself marks a moment in time and signals to the subconscious that what we experienced was important, impactful, and meaningful. Through this action, we respect and honor ourselves and help to heal the pain of the loss. Participating in acts of ceremony and honoring supports and comforts us in our stretch as we move toward solace.

Transforming the energy of loss takes us from feeling empty and disconnected to feeling validated and wiser. All of the following tools for honoring loss are designed to help your deeper heart open up and gently heal. Even if you feel you aren't ready to hold your pain in an honoring way, see if you can give yourself a mercy and a grace to create a beautiful openness and curiosity within as you choose an exercise that fits you today. You will discover those unique aspects of yourself that you need to pay attention to for the benefit of your awakening. The more you stay focused during these activities, the more the gifts of wisdom from your losses will flow. Honoring tools help us in our stretch to bring in positivity, hope, and a return of joy.

Honoring exercises help to move the emotional energy that is wrapped around your loss, freeing up emotional real estate so that you feel lighter as you move through your stretch.

The message of each of the honoring exercises is to learn how to bring the totality of yourself into the moment and respect it. When we don't do this, we may feel unfinished or unfulfilled, sort of the walking wounded. When we don't make space for honoring, when we say we don't have time or don't need to, we neglect a big part of the healing process.

Say you want to feel more at peace on your journey along the tender path. Think of a feeling you'd like to bring into your life, such as, *I want to feel more at peace* or *I want to feel hopeful*. Write this down, make a mental note of it, or carry it in your heart. By doing this, you set an intention and tone for how you want to experience your honoring process and what you want to get out of it. This will make more sense once you read over of the exercises.

Read through all of the honoring tools in this chapter, then choose one that resonates with what you are feeling. Manage your expectations as you do an exercise, as they are not magical, they are intentional processes to use in the moment. Over time and with attention given to the process, you may feel a sense of transformation and movement. Experiment with different exercises to see which ones you relate to and come easily, as they will help you to see your inner life with more gentleness and clarity. You may connect to one exercise now and a few months later find meaning in another exercise.

How you choose to honor a loss is unique and special to you. It may take the form of writing a symbolic letter to your loved one or keeping a daily log of how you feel. If writing isn't your best expression of honoring, you may instead choose to create what I call a "This Really Sucks" box of feelings, or embrace your playful side with neurographic art. There is no wrong way to honor your loss. Your loss just wants and needs some kind of acknowledgment. Open yourself up and invite in creativity, curiosity, hope, and wonder to get the most out of these exercises.

Each exercise is designed to help you move stuck emotions and give you strength, hope, and courage. The first tools are calming and meditative practices, followed by writing suggestions and then action-oriented exercises. Together they comprise a tool kit to help you acknowledge, name, honor, and find the gift in your loss as you move through your stretch.

As a suggestion, you may want to bookmark this chapter so you can come back to it as a resource to help you move stuck energy and enter into a space of wholeness.

TOOLS FOR QUIET HONORING

There's a wise place inside of you that is eternally patient. It silently holds all of your hurts and pains, waiting for you to open the box, take these emotional treasures out, and examine them one by one.

Our interior world has much to tell us, but most of the time we shut ourselves off from this rich resource of knowledge and wisdom. Most people don't like to be quiet and still because they may start to connect with sorrowful, hurtful, or confusing feelings that bubble up from their loss bucket. When we find the courage to do them, quiet honoring exercises allow us to truly hear our wisdom, which has been trying to get our attention for a long time. I know that the feelings we have pushed down often seem like unwelcome intrusions, but they are just feelings, messengers that are trying to give you clues as to how you feel about an experience. Our heart pain has a lot to say.

Breath Medicine

Don't be afraid of the silence as you breathe. Let the living happen in the silence with your breath.

When we go through a grief and loss experience, especially during the shockwave, we are in a state of anxious fear and panic. The amygdala, a part of the primal limbic system, gets triggered, gearing up the body for defense. Breathing becomes shallow, which tells the central nervous system to be on alert in preparation to fight, flee, freeze, or fawn. In modern society, we experience this shallow breathing and amygdala response even when we are not in mortal danger, as the amygdala doesn't know the difference. While the loss experience we are going through is upsetting, it is probably not life-threatening, so this shallow breathing gives the body the wrong feedback. Once you understand this natural and automatic response to trauma and loss, you can use the breath to calm the central nervous system and restore equilibrium to the body.

As you read the instructions for how to do this breath medicine process, follow along with the actions. Use what I call belly breaths. Place your hands on your belly and feel it rise and fall as you breath in and out. This is part of the feedback loop that reminds us to take deeper breaths and helps stop the habit of shallow breathing, which keeps us in a state of anxious readiness.

> Place one or both hands on your belly. Breathe in through your nose to the count of six.
>
> Slowly release the breath through your mouth to the count of six, as if you're blowing out a candle.
>
> As you breathe, feel your belly rise and fall with each inhale and exhale.

We all did belly breathing naturally as babies and toddlers, and parents often rub their child's belly to help them feel calm, safe, and relaxed. These natural breaths calm down the triggered amygdala, sending the message that we are safe and don't have to prepare to defend ourselves. A message you could give yourself here is, *I am calm and safe.*

Easy meditation with breath medicine

We usually hold stress in the weaker parts of our bodies because these are the easiest places for stress to hide out. As a boy, I held stress in my gut and so had a lot of intestinal aches. As an adult, I hold stress in my shoulders. Sometimes when I am in a state of stress, I realize my shoulders are squeezed so tight that they are pulled up to my ears. When this happens, I take a few minutes and do the following exercise.

This exercise of breathing and meditation allows you to check in with your body and help those stressed parts to relax.

> Sit in a place with few distractions. Start with the breath medicine until you are breathing fully and peacefully.
>
> Close your eyes. Picture a gentle white light coming in through your crown chakra at the top of your head. As you breathe, gently and slowly pull this light energy down through your entire body. You can ask that this light energy be warm or cool, based on what your body or emotions need at the time.
>
> Take this light to the tips of your fingers, then back up your arms, down your torso, along your mid-section, tops of your legs, knees, calves, ankles, then out the soles of your feet and into the earth. By extending this light through you and out the bottoms of your feet, you are grounding yourself, helping your body restore itself and become filled with light energy.

The most important thing the breathing does is remind you to be in the flow with your body. The body knows what to do in the flow. Breathe into the areas where you carry your stress, and tell your body it's okay to unclench. You may also incorporate a mantra you can silently say to yourself, such as *I am safe and calm at this moment. I trust in the flow of life. With each breath I take, I connect myself to* (God, Source, the Universe).

You can do this simple exercise in a few minutes or stretch it out for as long as you need. You can do it anywhere, as no one else needs to know that you are taking these big belly breaths and imagining this light energy. I've even seen people do this during breaks in meetings as a way to bring needed energy back into their bodies to get them through the rest of the day. This simple process reminds the central nervous system that we are okay right now. It doesn't mean that everything is perfect and fixed in our lives, it just means that in this moment, in this chair, in my car, at this meeting, I'm okay. You may find that you hold your breath throughout the day without realizing it; this is an indication that you are stressed about something. Using this breathing technique will help to restore a natural flow to your body's system and balance your energy. Be creative, and give yourself this gentle, healing gift of the breath of life any time you want to de-stress.

This process of honoring helps us to connect and recalibrate ourselves bringing us into the now. Not the past where sadness and regret lives, not the future where anxiety and worry lives, but now. Our bodies naturally want to return to a place of harmony, and this is a gentle way of helping ourselves.

Grounding and Centering

Building on what you know about breathing and meditation, you can ground yourself in the present as another way to feel safe amid a loss. Grounding is a process whereby you reconnect with a stable and strong part of yourself, a centering back into your body. You can ground yourself when you feel out of sorts or floaty and disconnected. Some grounding techniques are drinking water, eating chocolate, using essential oils that calm and restore, and deep breathing.

The following is a grounding technique I teach to help people ground back into their bodies and not feel as dissociated or floaty. I also use it for people who have symptoms of PTSD, specifically to help with dissociation following a loss. This helps them to stop the trauma movie that runs in their heads and brings them back to the present moment. It will help you to reconnect with your authentic self, your truth, and to center yourself so you can face chaotic situations in your world.

Sit with both feet on the floor. Feel your body in this position, feel the chair hold and support you. Begin the breathing exercises you learned earlier, then recite some qualities, silently or out loud, that you know are positive and true about yourself. They don't have to be big, grand statements, just aspects that sound like the healed version of yourself. As you recite, you are exclaiming your value and worth and reconnecting with yourself.

Here are some positive statements you can use when you are thrown off course by a loss:

- I'm a good partner/spouse/friend.
- I'm a hard worker.
- I'm a good listener.
- I value my relationships.
- I try to do the right thing.
- I love my family.
- I try my best every day.
- I'm good to those around me.
- I am able to meet my needs.
- I am loved.

Some people find it difficult to think of positive things about themselves because they are so used to putting themselves down. If you have this challenge, see if you can set aside the false narrative that you are less-than, and think of some descriptions that are affirming. You could think of positive things others have said about you, and use those to get you started. If you can say even one of these, it will help you to become grounded and rooted in the present. One patient of mine would say "I'm safe in this place" when she was in my office, and this was the start of her learning this practice.

When you do this exercise, you may want to have a weighted blanket over your lap or a warm towel around your neck. You can also wrap a blanket or throw tightly around yourself, as if you're giving yourself a big hug. Be creative, as bringing your own ideas to this process will deepen the experience for you. You will come away from this time feeling centered and grounded in the present moment, back in your body and in a more solid place to make clear-headed decisions.

Pivot Point

When you feel hopeless and distressed because your world has changed as a result of a significant loss, you can shift your perspective by using objects or environments that ground you as a turning point. Look at what you have control over, then see how you can look through a different lens, even if it's just a little bit. This exercise takes more practice than the others but can result in a shift of how you see your life. This is how to pivot from feeling hopeless and being distracted by the loss to seeing a new perspective:

Think of a loss that is creating a lot of distress in your life. Now think of one thing that was a constant in your life before the loss, something or someone that has been in your life for a long time, such as your house, family, job, hobby, or pet. This is your touchstone.

Stand up. Close your eyes and visualize this person, place, or pet in front of you or off to one side. This will anchor you in the exercise.

Physically turn your body and look out in a different direction. Imagine looking out over an open space such as a field, a body of water, or a big sky. You are anchored in place with the constants in your life. You are looking out to a new place of hope and possibility, leaving lack and fear behind. You are beginning the process of creating a new narrative about your life and how you see yourself.

Standing in place, notice yourself feeling grounded in the midst of the swirling changes coming at you. Stay focused on this new direction. Trust and love yourself. Breathe.

Grab hold of or connect in your mind's eye to that constant in your life, your anchor, to steady yourself as you look out to a new horizon. You are literally turning away from the hopeless and the heavy loss feelings that no longer serve your best and highest good. Your touchstone is giving you strength. Know that you are bringing more opportunities and joy into your life.

Feeling strong and confident, set your sight on the new path forward. There is no need to look back anymore. You are moving in a new direction and no longer transfixed by the loss. You are moving from hopelessness to hopefulness.

Be at peace with this new plan. Gently let old ideas and worries fall away, as they no longer serve you on your new path. Practice with this tool until you begin to feel some internal shifts.

Now say: *I am moving on from this place and not looking back. This is my starting point of my life going forward.*

You may need to repeat this process before the part that is sad and holding on to the loss finally surrenders to your new perspective. For some, it's a one-and-done exercise. You will still have the loss in your life after you do this exercise, but you will be looking through a new, clearer lens. Check in with yourself to see what you need. You can shift the narrative by exclaiming: *This is how I want to live and feel on the inside now. I move forward with a sense of confidence and calm.*

Guided Imagery

Guided imagery is a relaxation and mediation technique that most of us have done at some point, as it's similar to a daydream but more focused. Easy to do and totally within your control, this process will help you shift your energy inside. Using guided imagery will help you visualize your goals, create clear intentions for yourself, and imagine different outcomes for a situation. I give various examples of guided imagery throughout the honoring section, but here's one I created that you can use as a starting point to create your own.

Imagine yourself standing in a field that stretches out farther than you can see. It is the same view in all directions. You feel safe standing tall in this field, the sun shining on your cheeks. This is a place of perspective, a place of options and possibilities. The field represents the limitless choices before you, even those you cannot imagine yet, and stretches farther than you can see.

As you stand in this space, begin to picture what you would like your life to look like, and more importantly, what you would like your life to feel like. What would you like to feel each day of your life as you go through your routines? All options are open, so you don't have to do or feel the same way as before. We are limited only by our imagination, so you can create anything you want in this field. What would you like to bring in to your life that is not there now? What or who can you look to for inspiration to expand your lens? Is there someone you'd like to bring into your life, a situation you'd like to transform, or a new feeling you'd like to have?

Maybe you have a secret wish for something you'd like to do or see. How you would feel if you were to experience that? In this field of unlimited possibilities, open yourself up and give yourself permission to dream, and imagine your secret wish coming true.

Now check in with yourself. How do you feel once you've given yourself this freedom to dream? Let your imagination guide you to bring new energies into your life and help you feel unstuck.

Give yourself the gift of play and wonder. You can find many examples of guided imagery and meditation on YouTube, which is an easy way to access this relaxation and calm.

Finding the Wound

*We know we are healed when something new
or different shows up.*—Anita Mandley

Creativity is the space inside of us; it is the opposite of trauma. Being creative unlocks stuck trauma and says we can dream again and that no one will take that away from us. We have to feel a sense of safety to be in a creative space, so you may need to do some of the earlier exercises to get yourself in the right energetic space. Use some of the breathing, centering, and meditation exercises to get into this calm state. This exercise is a way of opening yourself up to your creative mind.

Sit in a quiet place and begin to connect with your body. Ask yourself in a gentle voice what grief wound or emotional pain of loss is showing up. Suspend logic and open up to your creative mind, where you can soar and dream, helping yourself to heal.

Close your eyes. In your mind's eye, observe yourself from above. Scan your body with a soft gaze in an observational, nonjudgmental way. See if you can imagine or actually locate where you have physical or emotional pain right now.

Ask yourself: *Where is the wounding within me? What does my pain have to tell me? What does it need? What is the gift this pain brings to me today? What is my body saying that I cannot?* It may take a while to give your pain a voice, but just check in with yourself and see what shows up. Gently hold these broken pieces.

Feel your loving ancestors come through, surrounding you and giving you gentle support as you hold your broken pieces. Feel their love as you weave new experiences into your life's tapestry.

For this next part, locate one pain area, physical or emotional. This could be your grief wound you have identified or another area that is getting your attention. You may have multiple areas that are in physical or emotional discomfort, so focus on the loudest one right now.

Can you determine the shape of the pain? Is it round, sharp, squared off, pointy?

Can you determine a color that this pain shape holds?

Ask this pain shape-color what emotion it carries.

Ask this pain shape-color-emotion what it needs. Does it need coolness or warmth?

Gently give this area some coolness as you imagine a soft icepack, or warmth as you imagine a gentle, warming towel. The coolness or warmth molds perfectly to the shape.

As you give this area coolness or warmth, see if it begins to change shape, color, emotion, or intensity. Don't rush the process; let the coolness or warmth do the work. Let the pain shape-color-emotion gently unclench and unfold like origami. Use your breath work to help facilitate this healing. Be gentle with this part that has come forward. This is a tender, vulnerable part of you that needs extra care.

As you acknowledge and name this pain, is it lessening? Let this area speak to you, as it's giving you a message. When you acknowledge it, it will ease up.

When I take people through this exercise, they are able to immediately connect to this area and their pain lessens, at least in the moment when they are practicing this meditation. Pain is the body's messaging system. When we recognize our pain in this way, it doesn't have to work so hard to get our attention. Pain isn't the enemy; rather, it is our ally for healing. You can use this exercise as a meditation tool throughout the day. Use the power of your mind's intention to give yourself some relief.

We can learn a lot from a painful trauma experience. Trauma wounding holds a deep memory with a story to tell. Even if a trauma happened years ago, it's sometimes as fresh within the cellular body and being as if it happened yesterday. Your body holds your felt sense of your own truth. The more you reject its message and shame yourself for having trauma, the more you push this body wisdom aside and remain fascinated and distracted by the pain and the drama. Become a compassionate, warm comforter for yourself. Hold that tender, sore part of you that carries the shadow of that pain. Listen to its wisdom. What has it taught you, what was the reason this came into your life? How has this trauma made you stronger, wiser, or more careful?

Reconnect with yourself. Deep wisdom is your teacher. It is patiently waiting in a quiet place inside of you. This heart wisdom will reveal itself when you finally understand your pain and have prepared yourself for the answer.

Thank your ancestors who travel with you on your journey. Ask for their wisdom as you walk this tender path.

(This exercise was inspired by the work of integrative psychotherapist Anita Mandley.)

Loving Detachment

Many losses simply cannot be fixed, controlled, or resolved when they are truly out of your control or not yours to fix, such as an ongoing illness, a court case, someone else's addiction, or crushing debt. These are all losses of what you knew from before and feel big and overwhelming when you are in the middle of it. The process of loving detachment will help you to disengage from the weight of worry that occupies space in your mind and heart. Loving detachment is akin to holding someone or something at arm's length that you once held very close.

Use the following guided imagery to put some distance between yourself and the issue. You are creating a space of loving detachment within yourself, which is a fancy way of saying you are creating boundaries. In order for us to create loving detachment boundaries, we have to find a place of patience inside and place trust in the unknown and the unanswerable.

Sit in a quiet space and practice the breathing techniques you learned earlier.

When you are internally calm, picture yourself in a field and see the loss issue at hand a few feet away from you. You can imagine this issue as a shape, an object, a person, or whatever best represents this at the moment.

Say the following mantra to yourself: *With each breath, I'm sending love and making space between myself and my loss. I lovingly detach from this issue* (or person or outcome).

Repeat this mantra as you picture the loss moving away from you, getting smaller with each breath. It could happen a few feet at a time or in greater increments. See how far you can move it away from you, all the while beaming love.

As you breathe and say the mantra, feel a larger space opening up between you and the issue or person, creating a buffer between you and the intensity. You now no longer feel overwhelmed by this issue, as it's not as massive or formidable.

I once had a patient who put her parents on another planet. Her parents represented the loss of her innocence because of the physical abuse she experienced in the form of extreme discipline as a child. She needed to feel safe from their abuse and required this great metaphorical distance from this trauma. This exercise is not about putting the issue or person out of your life, however, as that may not be realistic. This woman still interacted with her parents and took care of them as they aged. This boundary exercise is about creating a feeling of loving detachment within as you navigate life with the reality of the loss. It doesn't change the experience, it changes your relationship to the experience.

Use this exercise when you feel overwhelmed and need a break from trying to figure it all out. Your loss experience may be bigger than you, so know that you're not in charge of making sure everyone else is safe. It's not your job to protect others or make sure their lives work out perfectly. You are responsible for yourself and any minor child in your care, not for the outcome for everyone you love.

Tools for Honoring through Writing

You are learning various ways to acknowledge and honor your feelings, and writing is a great way to bring out feelings that are buried deep or tucked away. Some people balk at the idea of writing out feelings because they don't want to remember the associated events or unlock a wave of sadness or anger. Many people are content to have these hurt and sad feelings to stay in their loss bucket, reluctantly knowing they are languishing in the dark, too hot to touch. But when we let those feelings fester in the shadows, they control us. We unknowingly give them license to show up unannounced in the form of anger, unexpected tears, or abject melancholy. When we expose our feelings to the light of day through writing, we take them from their shadow cave and give them a place of rightful honor. The feelings aren't the enemy, they are simply messengers. Writing gives our feelings a voice so they may sing our song of love, life, and loss.

Symbolic Letters

When feelings from an experience are inside of us, we know them only one way. Writing them out changes our relationship to the experience.

As you know, grief and loss land on us in different ways. Symbolic letters are meant as a personal expression just for you and a way to move this compacted energy out of you. I call these letter symbolic because they are not meant to be mailed, given, or shared. Writing these letters can help us process pain, sorrow, and confusion. When we feel lost, writing a symbolic letter can give us a greater sense of centering and being grounded. This is practical tool to honor the feelings around an impactful emotional experience of loss, such as betrayal, sadness, grief, or hurt. It gives us the space to honor what we are feeling and then transforms this energy, moving it outside of us.

Don't worry about what you write, as you're not going to tell anyone any of this, and you're not going to hurt their feelings or make them mad. These letters are not meant as a diary nor meant to be kept, and I'm sure you wouldn't want anyone else to find all of your emotional release. It is a healing exercise just for yourself.

You accomplish many things at once through writing these letters. You name your feelings so you can claim them as yours. You transfer balled-up energy that's been causing you distress and put it on paper so you can look at it more objectively. You make something that you've been carrying around within you into something you can look at and feel and experience in a new way. You create movement instead of letting a festering lump of tangled emotion sit inside of you.

Don't pre-plan what you want to say. When I write these letters, I write fast and furious, by hand with pen and paper. I'm not concerned with penmanship, as I just want to release and let go of everything I feel inside.

Dedicate a space and time for this exercise, then follow these steps to write a symbolic letter:

Set an intention for yourself to honor this time. For example, *Today I want to understand why this loss is hurting me so much.*

Pull out a sheet of paper or sit at your computer. Bring your focus to a loss situation that is currently loud in your life today, or one that happened in the past that you're having a hard time moving past, or a feeling that keeps recycling.

Think of how this situation takes up a lot of space inside of you. Notice everything that comes up when you think of the situation or feeling. Address your letter to a person, place, or situation: Dear Mom, Dear accident, Dear diagnosis.

Start writing in a stream-of-consciousness flow. Don't stop. Let everything come out, acknowledging the pain, hurt, anger, and sadness you've been carrying inside.

When you stop writing, ask yourself if you've said everything you need to say. Were you too nice? Did you protect someone else or yourself from your real feelings? Write until it's all out. Continue to write even as those hot tears stream down your face and you're yelling at the top of your lungs.

Once you've written everything, when there's nothing else you want to say to this person or situation, when there's no emotion left knocking on the door needing acknowledgment, then sit back and know you've given yourself a gift of self-love. Get up and stretch. Maybe re-read it and sit with the feelings you just revealed to yourself.

Tear up, delete, shred, or burn the letter.

Once you've cleared this all out, go for a walk, drink some water, or watch the clouds drift by. Take a deep breathe and say, *I'm proud of myself.* You've just given yourself a simple gift of healing.

You may have multiple letters inside of you regarding these feelings. Often the first letter is related to feelings that are easy to access, such as *I'm really angry with you*. The second letter is when you get to the deeper feelings, such as *You really hurt me* or *I feel betrayed by you*. The letter won't right the wrong or bring someone back into your life, but it will help to release some feelings around the loss. Most people feel a sense of relief, even if it's temporary. The biggest thing is that you change your relationship to your feelings.

Write these letters whenever something is sitting inside of you and not moving, or when you are searching for answers. Symbolic letters help us move stuck energy out of the shadows into the light of day.

Writing Prompts

Feeling prompts help us find a starting point to name our feelings. They are the start of a statement that we can build on. Sometimes answering a question or completing a statement helps to us understand how we feel. You may be surprised at the spontaneous answers that arise when you "fill in the blank."

The logical mind often wants to jump in and say the "right" thing (what we "should" feel or say), but our emotions speak in a raw truth. Whatever your answers are, know that they are simply an emotional weather report of what's going on inside of you right now. You could answer these prompts a month from now and give different responses, as your experience of your loss is always evolving.

If there's a statement that doesn't fit you, move on to the next one. As with all of these honoring exercises, this is just for you, so be gentle with yourself when you review your responses.

Sit quietly in a dedicated space with paper and a pen. Don't overthink your responses; just write down the first thing that comes to you. Be as spontaneous as you can. Respond to each one as you read it.

Think of a recent grief or loss experience in your life, then begin.

I'm feeling _____ today because of my loss.

I get frustrated about my loss because _____.

Others in my life don't realize that my loss took away my

_____.

My loss was hard for me because

_____.

I wish someone could read my mind and know that I'm feeling _____.

The loss I'm going through feels a lot like _____

_____.

Because of my loss, I now really need someone to

_____.

My feelings around grief and loss are usually triggered by

_____.

No one knows that I'm _____.

After my loss, I realize I should have

_____.

As a result of my loss, I now want to _____.

Thinking of how I felt about my life before my loss, I felt

_____.

Since my loss, I realize that I _____

_____.

My loss is teaching me _____.

I believe my life will get better when _____

_____.

Once the prompts are completed, look back over your answers. What themes or patterns related to your loss do you notice? What did you reveal to yourself? Would talking with someone else help you understand these feelings in a deeper way? Your answers will usually give an honest reflection of what is going on with you emotionally. Sometimes it's hard to hold an emotional truth. Know that these are your feelings and have great meaning for you. Each prompt is the beginning of a larger exploration within yourself or a conversation to have with someone you trust.

Take care of yourself at this time because only you know how you feel. There are many resources to help you talk through and understand your feelings in a better way. Reach out.

Daily Success Log

Find the courage to embrace this new day.

When we are going through a loss experience, we often begin to focus on what's missing, what's not working, and what doesn't feel right. This hyperfocus on the negative becomes really loud, and we begin to feel tired and defeated. We want everything to go back to how we knew it; we don't want to feel this new reality of holding the loss. It's hard to see anything good when our loss looms large.

One way to reset this perspective and develop a positive attitude is to keep a Daily Success Log, either on paper or on your phone. Simply record any activity or experience you have that is encouraging and supportive and gets you out of the void.

Any one of the following examples would give encouragement by showing that things are moving forward:

- I was able to take a shower today.
- I got out for a short walk, and it felt great.
- A friend stopped by, and we had a good conversation that wasn't all about my troubles.
- I feel more hopeful today for some reason.
- I set a boundary today, and I feel stronger for doing so.
- I'm taking my medication, and I feel better.
- My pain level has gone down today.
- I don't feel as angry today.
- I got some good news today.
- Things are moving forward toward getting back into the house after the fire.
- A check came through that I was waiting for.

When you record your successes in a notebook, you are making a conscious note of how they helped you feel better. They don't have to be big things; it could have been a big deal to take a shower today day, for example. These are examples of how to remind yourself that you have power and control, even in a situation where you feel uncertain and unsteady.

The Daily Success Log will help to move you out of the space of what's missing and to recognize all of the positive things that you have in front of you. Even as you accept that, yes, the loss happened, you can see that there are still many hopeful things that you can hold on to. This practical tool feeds your sense of resilience and accomplishment. It adds to the energy supply that you can draw from to help your healing journey.

If keeping a physical log doesn't appeal to you, then make a mental note of these successes each day. Give yourself the gift of validation that you are helping yourself heal and that everything isn't all bad.

Tools for Honoring through Movement

The unfoldment of life is uncertain, but trust in your heart that it will all work out.

Doing creative and engaging activities helps us to literally move energy that is stuck. In this section, I give you practical tools that encourage you to interact with your grief and your world in a different way. Movement can be in a physical sense, but I reference movement here in the form of energy movement in your body. Each honoring tool helps to dislodge compressed emotion so you can transform this energy into something that encourages healing.

Day of Distraction

During the grieving process, when we have our heads down and are trying to get through a tough time, the mind is working 24/7. We are trying to solve complex logistical and emotional puzzles using all of our bandwidth. We can keep up with this pace to a point, but this process is exhausting, and sometimes we need a break. If we are fortunate, we have a friend who recognizes this and will help us to take time with some much-needed distraction.

A day of distraction is when you do an activity that is totally different from the grief and loss puzzle you're trying to figure out. Whether on your own or, ideally, with a friend, you spend time doing silly activities that are not related in any way to your loss experience. This is a day away from procedures, paperwork, pokes, or scans. You may be tempted to talk with your friend about the status of what is happening and how you are feeling. Allow yourself to do this to a point, but then stop yourself and say, "I need to relax, and I want to enjoy my time with you right now. I will get back to these concerns soon enough, but for now, let's have fun."

Sometimes feelings of guilt come up during a day of distraction. Many people feel they shouldn't have any fun or relaxation after someone has died or they are undergoing medical treatments. While the loss needs to be respected and acknowledged, you also need to create a balance inside so you can go through the phases of loss and come out as whole as possible.

If you are open to the experience and seeing others for who they are in the moment, you can navigate this much more easily. You can focus on being in the NOW of the experience rather than the outcome. Take this time to give your overactive mind and worn-down body some much-needed relaxation. Just drift along and escape for a while. Afterward, you will have a sense of perspective and breathe a little gentler because you've had a respite. You need a break.

Five Things

This grounding exercise of Five Things will help bring you into the present. It is especially effective for those who experience anxiety. It is a quick and easy calming tool that you can use anywhere to bring your focus into the moment instead of worrying about the future.

Start by centering yourself with the intentional breathing you learned earlier.

Name the following items found in your surroundings:

Name five things you can see in your field of view, such as a candle or a book.

Name four things you can touch, such as the chair you are sitting in or your clothing.

Name three things you can hear, such as a bird outside or music playing.

Name two things you can smell, such as the soap from your shower or food cooking.

Name one thing you can taste, such as something you ate earlier. If you can't taste anything in the moment, name one of your favorite tastes.

Naming these things helps you to reorient to the present moment. The trauma is in the past, and the future hasn't happened. Right now you are safe. Breathe.

"This Really Sucks" Box of Feelings

Give your anger a voice because if you don't, it will either bury itself into a depression or explode in ways that you will have to clean up later.

We all have loss events or situations that don't turn out how we want them to or are out of our control. Maybe you have intense feelings toward someone else but there is no way you could tell them how you felt, or you have an ongoing situation that brings up painful feelings on a regular basis with no clear resolution in sight. With this in mind, I came up with the idea of the "This Really Sucks" box. This is where you can put all of the unexpressed feelings and unresolved, angry hurts you carry inside, or the complicated emotions you feel about a situation that is out of your control.

You are not your anger or your feelings, you just experience them. Putting your feelings into a box is a way to move stuck energy inside of you, transferring it to a place outside of you. The situation may never be resolved, but you can move this energy inside of you so you don't have to carry it anymore.

To make and use a "This Really Sucks" box of feelings, follow these simple steps:

Find a medium-size empty box, such as a shoe box. Tape it shut, transforming the box into a container. Make a slit in the top just wide enough to slip pieces of paper through.

Decorate it however you want with stickers, markers, stamps, or whatever you have at hand. I know someone who used images of a butterfly transforming from a chrysalis to represent change and growth. You have now created a "This Really Sucks" box for your feelings.

When you are triggered and some feelings bubble up, write them out on a slip of paper. You could write a curse word, a meaningful word, or words that you'd like someone else to hear but you won't or can't say. Fold up the slip of paper and put it in the box.

Add your feelings to your box as often and as much as you want to. The box will begin to fill up with all of those heavy feelings. Once you have expressed all that you needed to about the loss, it is time for all of the feelings inside the box to be transformed. Save the box until you can take it to a fire. (Fire is a symbolic way to cleanse and release.)

Prepare a small fire outside. Stand in front of the fire holding the box, which contains all of the heavy energy that you've transferred out of you. (If burning up your box doesn't fit with you, think of what you can do with the box so you can transform the energy, such as smashing or shredding it.)

As you prepare to destroy the box, bless your words, honor your feelings, and know that these feelings and thoughts no longer serve you. Know that you have received the messages from this situation and that you are ready to let these emotions go.

Place your "This Really Sucks" box into the fire with love and light. None of this is done with anger or spite; you've already explored those feelings. You are just letting go.

You can say a prayer or an intention, whatever comes to you, at this time to help you honor your work and celebrate your healing. You can simply say, *I release that which no longer serves me. I bring peace into my life, and I am filled with warmhearted love.*

As the fire burns up your box, take some deep, cleansing breaths. Gently acknowledge how hard you worked to process those feelings. Be proud of yourself that you examined how you really felt, put this into words, and acknowledged your truth.

You don't have to talk to anyone else about your box. It's not their process, and they may not understand what or why you're doing this. Having done these types of ritualistic ceremonies, I can say that it symbolically transforms the energy we carry. When we do this work, we show the wiser part of us that we understand there's a bigger picture here, a bigger perspective. We put these complicated feelings into a context so they have a place in our life's tapestry.

Stopping the Trauma Movie

Loss gives us the wisdom to know the difference between what we took for granted and what is no longer in our field.

Replaying a scary or traumatic loss over and over in the mind is a natural post-traumatic stress response. It is one way we try to make sense of what happened. Often we replay the trauma or loss scene to look for how we could have made a difference in the outcome. When we replay the movie, we are incorporating and trying to understand something that happened really fast and in slow motion at the same time.

When we are triggered by emotional landmines that remind us of the loss, the movie starts up automatically. We become paralyzed and transfixed as we watch this interior movie, staring into space and disconnecting from reality. This behavior, called "dissociation," is a normal part of processing intense trauma experiences and emotions. This trauma inside of us will continue to get activated until we heal it.

One way to take control of this reaction so that you don't dissociate every time you're triggered is to learn how to stop the trauma movie. This process takes practice, as emotional trauma is very intense and persistent. Read over the following simple steps, then put them into practice right away.

> As soon as you recognize that the trauma movie has started up, gently say to yourself, *I don't have to watch this. I know how it is going to end. It is scaring me, and I want to close it down now.*
>
> Abruptly end the movie by "cutting" it or seeing a stop sign.
>
> Immediately move on to something else. Distract yourself with the familiar.
>
> If the movie starts up again, just go through the same process, as it may take multiple times to quiet this triggered response.
>
> You may not realize the movie is happening until you've been watching it for a while. Just close it down when you recognize that it's playing.

In my experience, as you practice this technique, you will be able to stop the movie earlier and earlier. Eventually, you will feel it coming on after you've been triggered and can say to yourself, *That's a trigger. I'm going to use my coping tools and move on to something else so that I don't start the movie and dissociate.* You will learn how to circumvent the movie entirely so that it doesn't ruin your day and put you in a depressed mood. Eventually, you may be able to heal the activated wounding so that it doesn't come up at all.

To take this exercise to the next level, move the energy of the story by shifting and pivoting to a new direction (you learned pivoting in the Pivot Point exercise). Your mind and heart have the ability to create a new narrative. You can have a different perspective on the situation if you give yourself permission. See if you can imagine a new outcome or see it playing out differently. You can't change what has happened, but you can change your emotional relationship to that experience.

Practice, and be patient with yourself. Give yourself some intentional loving energy. It takes time to learn to stop the movie, but it's well worth the effort as you work through the emotional weight of such heavy trauma. If you experience PTSD traumatic memories that are hard to move past, look for a therapist who does the Eye Movement Desensitization and Reprocessing technique, or EMDR.

Neurographic Art

> *This being human is a guest house.*
> *Every morning a new arrival.*
> —*Rumi*

What is the shape of your grief? How does it look? Using neurographic art as an expression of your healing asks you to suspend logic and open yourself up to your creativity. Creating neurographic art is basically doodling with a purpose. This process was invented in 2014 by Russian psychologist Dr. Pavel Piskarev, who invites us to draw freeform lines on paper he describes as neurolines. It is through this simple process that we can have a sense of release and, surprisingly, a level of control and integration. You will read more references to this honoring tool in Willow's story, which follows chapter ten.

Here is an illustration of a simple drawing I did to give you an example:

Start with a blank piece of paper. On one side, write an intention of what you'd like to bring into your life or something you're working through, such as love or fear.

Turn the paper over. From the edge of the paper moving inward, start drawing in a free, continuous line, making big circles and winding loops. Don't think about it, just loosely scribble. It will only take a few minutes at most to fill the page with big interconnecting loopy squiggles and circles. Don't worry if your drawing doesn't look like mine. This is your playtime, it's not about perfection.

This next step is a big part of the process. Round out the corners of the sharp edges formed by where the line intersects itself. Do this by creating little triangles that soften the intersections. This step creates more flow in your drawing. A deep, subconscious process happens within you as you soften and calm the sharpness in your drawing. In feng shui, rounding out corners is referenced as promoting and balancing chi energy. You may find that your body responds automatically to this process and your breathing softens.

Color in the drawing and add creative touches to untwist tangled feelings inside of you.

Spend time letting your mind flow with the drawing. It's a simple process that doesn't take a lot of time or money and is a way to take care of yourself in a creative way. This expression is a break for the mind, as you are doing an activity that doesn't require a lot of thought. Activites such as coloring, knitting, pulling weeds, and chopping wood are ways that we can give our logical minds a much-needed rest.

Neurographic art is more easily understood by watching it. To learn more about this technique, search "neurographic art" on YouTube, where you'll find lots of examples. You can also Google it and see the various videos that come up.

Still, Small Spaces

When we set aside a special place in our home to honor someone who has passed, we engage in a deeply personal way to recognize that person's place in our lives. In some cultures, people create altars with candles, incense, flowers, fruit, and pictures of the deceased. Other cultures set a place for the person at the table.

There are many ways to create a still, small space. It doesn't have to be grand; it can be a simple space that is still, respectful, and honoring. I like to set a out a picture of the person I'm remembering on a side table, then light a candle and say a prayer, recalling this person's importance to me. As I do this, I feel their love and send them love. This is a way that I can connect to their energy and honor our shared experiences. It helps me to acknowledge and grieve. I feel that I'm "doing" something to honor them instead of doing nothing. Another way to do this is to wear or hold an item that was theirs or an object they gave to you.

Holidays are never the same after a loved one has passed, but there are ways to create new traditions that have just as much meaning. On the holidays following their death, consider setting a place for your loved one with their framed picture. Everyone there misses that person, so this is a visual way to acknowledge that you all miss them and that you are including them on this day. You each will feel the loss, so go ahead and name this experience, as it is heavy on everyone's heart anyway. With that big lump in your throat, say, "I miss them." In doing so, you will bring a sigh of relief to the heart's pain by naming what everyone is already deeply feeling. Invite your ancestors to be with you, feel their love give you a warm heart hug, and know that they are with you in spirit.

There's a belief that the soul takes three days from the day a person dies to fully cross over. I often light candles for three days with this in mind. Lighting candles, remembering who they were, what you learned from them, how your life was enriched—these are ways that you can consciously connect to your feelings of grief as you honor their place in your life. You may want to honor the person simply by remembering their smile, your love for them, or fun times. You don't need to create an altar or light candles, as that's certainly not everyone's style. Any of these ways of honoring can also be used to acknowledge the loss of a pet.

You can also honor someone who is living but who you are estranged from. I helped a family work through many painful emotions they had about their adult son, who had made some very poor choices as an older adolescent and young adult. The parents told me they would get triggered by the Christmas ornaments their son had made long ago. Every year at Christmas, when they picked up an ornament he had made to put on the tree, they had deeply conflicted, heartbreaking feelings. They still wanted to feel the love for their son, but they felt badly betrayed by him as well.

We worked through a process that helped them to honor their estranged child. They picked an ornament that meant the most to them, then held it as they remembered that special moment in time and embraced that precious feeling. They lit a blessed candle, held each other's hands, and said some prayers. Once they felt filled up with this connection and the support from each other, they put the ornament on the tree and honored the little boy who had made it so long ago. They thought of his bright smile and all the wonderful parts of that moment in time. They were able to separate out the little boy for whom they had open, loving hearts and their adult son, who had hurt them and from whom they felt separated. This ceremony gave them a feeling of solace and marked time instead of letting everything their son did in the present get tangled together with the past. They were able to transform the energy around the ornaments, which meant so much to them, and their son's adult behavioral choices. It was a way for them to connect with each other and the moment on a different level, and created a free flow of their love. This helped them integrate all of these different events into their life's tapestry.

~

We honor ourselves by creating sacred space to honor our loss. Ceremony marks time in our life's tapestry and declares that something big happened. We respect this experience by paying homage to our feelings. We give ourselves the gift of acknowledgment and self-awareness by using the practical tools of honoring as we lighten the emotional load in our loss bucket. No longer are we in the dark about our feelings, as now we can hold our pain in a new way, with a sense of strength and belonging in our stretch as we move toward solace. We enter into a new relationship with grief and loss on the tender path.

H old

O n

P ain

E nds

GARY'S STORY: AN UNEXPECTED JOB LOSS

Gary is the football star who married the pretty girl. Over the last twenty-five years, the couple created a loving family and raised three children together. Gary is humble, but he is proud of his accomplishments. He can talk to you about quantum mechanics and then tell a funny joke on himself. He climbed the corporate ladder his entire working career, the loyal soldier fighting the good fight. Honest as the day is long, he tried to do everything right, but despite his best efforts, he was let go from an executive position at a Fortune 500 company. Gary's self-discipline, drive, and unwavering commitment to himself and his family empowered his resilience through this tremendous loss.

Gary had been in a promising high-level position for a while, engaged in developing products and opportunities for the company. He never anticipated that he would lose his job, and he had to look deep within for a sense of strength and hope. These are his reflections on how the job loss impacted his view of himself, his world, and his career trajectory. He thoughtfully reveals how he came out the other side with a sense of enriched inner life fulfillment and wisdom from the experience.

What was it like to be let go from your position when you were in the meeting with Human Resources?

The event that triggered the dismissal was quite dramatic and surreal, like something from a movie. I had performed a set of tasks that had been approved in the previous weeks but were no longer deemed necessary. In a draconian moment, the CEO cleared the conference room except for my manager, himself, and me. He reprimanded us and excused us from the rest of the session. I was in pure disbelief.

What feelings did you have immediately following that event?

I received a call from the head of HR later that same day. I simply asked for time and kept a professional and positive tone throughout the call. Looking back, my having been a football center at the goal line on fourth down, with thirty thousand people watching, had paid off by my ability to keep myself together, as there is a certain amount of grit that comes from intense competition and focus. Overnight, I had no idea what my fate would be, but I figured I was gone and hoped for six months of severance instead of the policy's standard three. I didn't get much sleep, but I found solace in replaying in my mind a near-death experience (NDE) that had happened to me at the age of seven. I figured if I could come back from the dead, then this piece of corporate malfunction would somehow work out, too.

The company gave me the three months' extra severance. I needed literally every day of that six months to get back on my professional feet. As the last severance check hit, exactly six months after dismissal, I received two offers within two hours. I had not received a single offer in the five months and twenty-nine days prior to that.

Did you see this loss coming?

I was so focused and tunnel-visioned on my work that the idea of a loss was not in my vision, and hence the magnitude of shock when it did occur. It wasn't even that failure was not an option; that phrase wasn't any part of my drive to succeed. I had blind faith in my capabilities, the opportunities, and financial reward. To borrow a phrase from Bruce Springsteen, "Blind faith in . . . anything will get you killed."

The following are Gary's perspectives when he was still working at the job and then after he was let go.

When you were working at this job, did you ever feel that you had "golden handcuffs" on and that you couldn't leave if you wanted to?

The position provided an amazing upside of wealth in the form of per-formance-based company stock. If my tenure had lasted there five years or longer instead of the two and a half, becoming a millionaire was quite possible. The company was private-equity based, which is a fast-paced environment with heightened and aggressive risk/ reward scenarios. So, yes, there were significant financial reasons to try to survive this "hurry-up offense" of capitalism.

Did you ignore warning signs about the upcoming job loss because of that trapped feeling?

Interestingly, the warnings signs were not purely mental. The team I was managing and the work I was doing were the best of my life. Global travel was a practical element of success; at one point, I had to take the longest intercontinental flight out of the United States, at nearly eighteen hours, and had to work twelve hours on the flight to be ready for three days of meetings at the destination.

That pressure to perform, the jet lag, and the success at stake are all hallmarks of the revered "international road warrior" status, the perks and the physical and mental strain it took to proudly earn the coveted 1 million+ miles of points over my career. That period of my life included spending two weeks in China and two weeks in the United States, on average, for sixteen months, when I was with a different company. In retrospect, this caused severe long-term jet lag effects with mental and physical consequences. I reached out, got help, and put things in perspective—or so I thought.

Over time, I forgot about those things—as one is wont to do when forgetting pain—and got into the cycle again in my next job. The constant stress, travel, and deadlines started to manifest as bouts of anxiety and panic attacks, additionally fueled by jet lag. That was the warning sign, but not of the job loss. I figured that there was no way the situation was going to beat me or have me and my family miss out on the financial rewards.

How did you stay motivated to work at this company?

At that time in my life, I needed the financial security, and especially the cash flow, to take care of the typical expenses related to being an American father with three children going through college. The position was a great opportunity to capitalize on the professional work and extremely long hours from earlier in my career. If I simply worked as hard and as smart as I should, I would be over the hump financially, just like the brochure for the American Dream and MBA programs promise.

Over the course of your career, did you ever feel defeated and worn out, wanting to run away and follow a personal dream?

I did feel exhausted and strung out at many instances during the high-work-cycle parts of my career. I never felt like running away, but I battled, and still battle, to create enough time to invest the energy to make an independent run at business, or at least a meaningful and profitable side hustle.

Were you working so hard for yourself or because of your commitments and obligations?

I rationalized the capitalist, white-collar, high-potential status trap. There was plenty of rationalization along the way down that road. The occupation absolutely swamped my time schedule, and any leftover time I had was for the family. If I were to step aside and find a different career path, that would have been seen as a loss. I was worried about what others would think.

Did you feel that you were missing out on other parts of life because of your need to earn a certain amount of income?

I missed out on a normal balance of family time due to domestic and international business travel. I needed the income to support my family's activities, which I would, ironically, sometimes miss due to the travel. Sadly, I regularly missed birthdays, anniversaries, and holidays like Halloween.

Could you have verbalized this, or would that have challenged your early-life programming as a man?

I never even thought to push back. It's always been, "If you work very hard, good things will come from it." Positive reinforcement from sports and academic achievement during my youth ingrained the work ethic. My experience in college was particularly difficult, balancing an engineering degree and playing D-1 level football to pay for it. It was absolutely mentally and physically exhausting, but I would not trade it for anything. That experience preloaded and hardwired my mentality for the professional world after graduation.

How did you answer the question, why me?

The reaction to why me changed over time after I was let go. At the instant of shock, I quickly realized that the situation was caused by an X factor I could not control or see coming, like an unintentional victim of a sniper: unfair, undeserved, and unjust. After rewinding the film of that corporate incident over and over from the grassy knoll of my career, I realized that hard work and expertise cannot guarantee survival. In fact, I eventually needed to be a different person to survive and thrive after the event. I needed help from my belief system in a healthier and more meaningful way.

How did you tell others in your inner circle what happened?

On the professional side, I was lucky to have an outplacement program that was supported by an excellent adviser for executives who have been let go. Also included in the program was a tool kit of templates to get moving on some obvious and not-so-obvious tasks to get back out in the market. So, after a recommended week of reflection, I set to work on the tactical, professional side, working with the material and his advice. Therefore, the announcement through my family, circle of friends, and professional colleagues went pretty quickly. This work provided practical distraction from the fears that came naturally after being let go.

How did you manage your self-perception and cultural programming (the traditional binary role of man as provider), going from a man who supports others to one who now needed support?

On the emotional relationship side, the largest change was the flip between my wife and me, from being the supporter to being the supported. She started working full time, for insurance coverage, at a local employer for special-needs individuals. While we were blessed with that opportunity, it created a daily stress to the relationship because we were both in a state of anxiety.

On the logistical side, I live ten minutes from a small town that had an office for rent for only a hundred dollars per month. With that office came a closer acquaintance with a couple who were, and are, great friends of ours. They worked remotely from the building, and they and the office provided me a place to go do the work of finding work. This also allowed me to show some vulnerability in a safe place as I worked through the process of the job search, reporting back wins and losses, interviews, rejections, and the like. These friends were also sounding boards for interview presentations, which was key, as I could not constantly use my wife and my family for these dry runs.

What were the darker thoughts that dominated at this time?

There were fears I told myself about my abilities, worth, and finding a new space to work. I was afraid that the all-in work ethic had not succeeded this time. Setting up the day-to-day work environment to keep me focused was, in retrospect, key to surviving the fears and manifesting the next steps.

The essential habit my wife and I developed to work through this period was a daily morning prayer time with the book *Jesus Calling*, which has daily Bible-based reflective points of prayer. We lit the same candle for months, until I received an offer. A picture of that lit candle now holds a prominent position in our living room as a reminder of the struggle and eventual success of those times. We still have these morning sessions, and that helps us stay grounded as we move forward together for the next challenges of life.

Did you sense a growing urgency the longer you went without a job and income, or did you trust the process and yourself?

Oh, yeah, it was a nail biter, financially. We got help from our angels on the whole timing of the recovery. My wife was heroic in her switch to a demanding full-time job. During that time, she was involved in a workplace accident and suffered a concussion, leading to a workman's comp case. That was the darkest of times for us throughout the entire experience! I am forever grateful to her. Add to that the graduation of one of our children from college and the need to purchase a car to start their career, and it was incredibly stressful, financially.

How did you reinvent yourself for the short term and patch the financial hole while keeping an eye toward finding a position that would be fulfilling and rewarding?

I started donating plasma twice a week. It paid between four hundred and six hundred dollars per month, which helped. While that was initially quite a humbling experience, it allowed me to read up and research for an hour during each visit while I created true passive income (ha!).

As you were looking for another job, what personal coping skills did you invent to find yourself again?

A whiteboard and an office away from home were the primary concrete coping elements that I worked with. The centerpoint of what I do well and what people generally see value in is imagining new products and new markets, and launching them. I had to create a safe place to recreate and continue that dynamic, and that clean space of a whiteboard to map out the approaches to my job search, redevelopment, and proposals was essential to this. The stand-alone office, separate from my home, was also instrumental in creating the "my new job is finding my next path and job" environment, as it created normalcy.

What did you turn to, such as meditation or faith, to bring in hope and trust and to decrease or minimize the fears?

Lighting a candle, a morning prayer with my wife, and reading a *Jesus Calling* passage every day. Also, at one of my sessions, my therapist said that meditation is a great tool. It took me a while, through discovery and practice, to truly understand that simple phrase. Meditation isn't everything, but a lot of things are made easier and more accessible through it. My regular use of the Headspace app was, and is, a huge factor in creating the background for the day, in creating hope and trust and pushing back on fear and uncertainty.

A job search means you need to have your head in the game. What helped you to focus, center yourself, create opportunities, and move forward?

My therapy sessions were the most impactful influence and force for this period. I was blessed with this thoughtful guidance and the multidimensional spiritual connectivity. I was extremely fortunate to have worked with my therapist for several years prior to this professional catastrophe, and that saved me from a deep depression that could have resulted.

A key event in my therapy was hearing the message that you can't just envision the next step and pray with specific words for meaning and the path forward. The breakthrough involved actioning a suggestion that the spirits in our lives, our angels, are most supportive for change when we communicate to them what we want to feel *emotionally* in the state we want in the future. This is what I wrote to that end, what I wanted to feel in the future, in the next place in my career: "Looking over the lake I live near, feeling accomplished and sound, using my God-given skills, and being in peace, joy, and abundance. Feeling healthy, vibrant, loving, and joyful creating a space, an environment, and love for a growing family. Feeling professionally abundant and giving and inspiring through work and speech, a total personage. Love and security."

The exercise of writing down what I envisioned I would feel like in my desired next position, a simple paragraph envisioning my work and environmental feelings around me, seemed at that time just an exercise in wishing. However, I believe that reflecting and praying on that paragraph, forgetting it and then going back to it at times, was instrumental in my passage through this time and finding work happiness again. The Universe, my therapist said, is following the direction of our emotions and feelings. I can say that is absolutely true.

I was also blessed with a protégé from the outplacement firm who had also been through the same professional devastation and could relate directly to my professional pain. This, I believe, was no accident in the grand scheme.

For both of the above, I had to put the work in to get the positive results back. That work was not always easy, did not automatically provide a natural dopamine kick just because I did it, and had many twists and turns of painful self-discovery along the way. You really have to tear yourself down sometimes to get to a core that can be strengthened and is more sustainable than what you went into the disaster with.

How did this experience change your priorities and self-identity?

I worked through a couple of books recommended by my therapist that helped form and reiterate these ideals. At the beginning of every day of my new job, I re-read some elements that I had gathered from those books. Saying them at the beginning of each workday helps complete the cycle of trauma, self-discovery, and a more fulfilling road ahead, professionally.

Some of these ideals are to be successful with my sense of potential, to leverage all of my skills and escape the corporate world, to be the best parent I can be, to enjoy a meaningful life with a wonderful sense of home, to be a good mate to my wife, and to be spiritually fulfilled. Others are determination, grit, humility, spirituality, and hard work.

Do you have a different perspective on the combination of financial rewards, security, inner life fulfillment, and work-life balance now?

Yes! Inner life fulfillment was probably one of the weakest areas of my psyche until this experience, and getting the help to recognize it. So, in some sense, it was not an element in the dynamic of this job loss. The element in that equation, regarding the outer-life fulfillment and the trappings of being a successful provider, was drive.

The massive trauma of losing this job had me look hard into who I would be identity-wise. Therapy and a mix of tools, thought processes, and methodologies have helped me change the view of that treadmill, what a warrior is, and the actual meaning of mentality.

My orientation to and moving myself through vectors of work has been a large change in my psyche and life. Work has become more personal, an expression of myself as opposed to the definition of myself, and that energy alignment has made me much happier. It has taken a long time, a lot of help, and something I can call "working reflection" to understand the massive weave of big and small fundamental filaments that make inner life fulfillment, outer life fulfillment, monetary security, emotional security—and work—have some sort of pleasing pattern and strength in the weave.

You are a man who works hard at everything he does. Do you have a new perspective on what you are working for now?

I would distribute the energy described throughout my loss journey with more balance across career, family, and my own interests. Working for security and balance, now and going forward, is my goal now, along with actually enjoying the day, both inwardly and outwardly. Regular meditation and a mix of mental, spiritual, and reflective techniques have helped me to transform myself along these lines. I use a mix of Headspace, information from the book *The Secret*, rosary-based prayer, vision practice, and focus.

What is your new narrative?

My new narrative is that I am taking a different approach, one that is more aligned to a purpose-driven life. After I started to rebuild my psyche and refresh my drive, I found a prayer with a different angle on success and approach to motivation. Some of the key words I took away from it, the ones that made their imprint, were generosity, kindness, and seize life—all heartfelt expressions of optimizing life.

The other key element in my new narrative is the focus on, demonstration of, and praying for the ideals of gratefulness and abundance. My therapist taught me the exercise and expression of these ideals by designating a special bowl for these intentions. I write an intention on a small piece of paper, then fold it and place it in the bowl. I have been doing this, along with a short meditation over the intention, for the last three years. I am immersed with gratefulness in this moment as I reflect that all of the intentions have manifested and appeared in our family's lives. It's just incredible and indescribable how this focus has helped weave spirits and action to manifestation.

If you were unfortunate enough to experience this type of loss again, would you be better prepared for it because of what you experienced?

Yes, I feel better prepared for future losses. That preparedness includes financial planning and action. I've also been blessed with tools and, more importantly, coaches in my life that have instructed me on how to use them. I also developed the spiritual muscle of what I call a core strength of prayer and realized, again, that other dimensions are real and work in this world. Envision the feelings of a positive future, and they will manifest themselves with your work.

Did you have any experiences earlier in your life that helped prepare you for this loss?

I was blessed, so to speak, with an NDE as a seven-year-old child; I drowned at the bottom of a pool. I was in another dimension, in front of an oaken door with a heart-shaped opening in the middle of it. I was informed that I could not come back to this space and that I needed to help someone on earth who was having great trouble. It took years for the other details of this event to reveal themselves to me. I know and have experienced a part of the other side. It provided a context of how expansive reality is, the reality that we can and can't see. While I had a great sense of loss of my identity and pride through being let go, I had this NDE experience to provide context, which provided comfort.

I also had the amazing experience of a past-life regression with my therapist that gave me insight into where my spirit had been before, its habits and learnings and unresolved issues. It became clear to me that in order to succeed and overcome the career crater, I needed to leverage the gift of this experience for a literal soul-searching perspective. I needed to address my shortcomings in a spiritual and practical sense in order to keep my path clear and recover from the job loss. Balance was the lesson I needed to learn in this life.

What advice would you give someone who senses something is off at their workplace and that their job may be at risk?

My advice would be to prepare by getting the blinders off and getting a larger perspective. It is the most difficult thing sometimes to truly see ourselves as others see us. To that end, start getting deeper levels of feedback loops within your current company. Great primers for this are the fundamentals in the books *The First 90 Days* and *The 7 Habits of Highly Effective People*. The first book does an excellent job of teaching how to create virtuous feedback loops that will keep you connected to the political climate, key players, and decisions within your company. The seven habits are tried-and-true ways to immediately create a calibrated approach to your day-to-day interactions. Both books put together make a great platform for lowering the blindspots that can manifest themselves into being shown the door, and for having a great strategy for either recovery in your current situation or getting traction at your next career venue.

What suggestions do you have for those who are walking the painful part of having just lost their job and are trying to figure out a way to move forward?

My strong advice to anyone in this situation is to be the class act in the room. Not just superficially, but from the core. You can be knocked down but not be defeated. You are more than the situation, more than the construct of work at that time and place. You will be going to a frightening place mentally, emotionally, and professionally, but in the moment you can shine with your personal strength; be personable, serious, but positively moving forward. That bought me time.

What advice do you have for someone whose identity is wrapped up in their job and, having lost that job, now feels worthless and without purpose?

It is a difficult thing to even partially deprogram from the treadmill warrior mentality. I've been blessed with a terrific therapist who has helped keep my life and my marriage intact through turbulent seas. When thinking through this question, I look back on that therapy process and think that it had two effects: changing what I do and changing who I am. Transformation occurred before, during, and after this process through a lot of work that changed what I did emotionally and spiritually in myself. I came away from therapy understanding that if I work from my inner being first, and align my energy genuinely with the outside world, it is a much stronger place to be.

What dos and don'ts do you have for others going through a similar loss experience?

Do network beyond your first-pass circle of professional colleagues. One of the helpful pieces of advice from the outplacement material was to go deep into your circle of friends and family and reach out to them for help. The key here is that you must give to get. From a professional side, that means forwarding material of interest for their career goals and helping them with their next steps, genuinely providing valuable items of knowledge. I went all the way back to my college football team on LinkedIn. Do not be embarrassed; you'll be surprised at the similar stories of loss and getting back into the game from sometimes long-lost friends.

Volunteer, and get involved in local and national professional organizations. Again, give to get; it's just good corporate karma and keeps you professionally sharp and functioning. Network through Meetups and Eventbrites for local and national events (but see my "don'ts"). The majority of these are free and are not to be confused with job search groups.

Become a member of Toastmasters International. If you are uncomfortable in ad hoc conversations with new people or want to have another regimen that impacts how you project your presence, this is a great organization. It allows you to be genuine, authentic, and prepared for the key conversations you need for your livelihood.

My highest recommendation for literally transforming loss into a net gain after a job earthquake event is to set milestones for fitness, weight, and learning new skills. The new skill does not necessarily have to align with what you have done in your past.

Here are a couple of don'ts: Don't self-medicate. This is self-explanatory. Don't network through local job search groups or Meetups created specifically for job searches.

What wisdom do you carry from this experience, just for yourself, that has made you a better man?

While reflecting over the weeks as I wrote my thoughts down to these questions, I had an interesting discovery as I cleaned out my business backpack to get ready for my first international business trip as COVID restrictions opened up. I rediscovered a valentine from my wife that I always carry on trips, and a slip of paper with the following I had written on it: "Don't get mad. Don't get even. Do better, much better. Rise above. Become so engulfed in your success that you forget it ever happened." Now, three-and-a-half years after the job loss event, I am living that last line every day with a wonderful company and work environment, and am enjoying success. I am finally armed with the think-through of an inward and outward success balance.

～

Reflections on Gary's Story

Our job often holds our sense of self and identity, and when it goes away, many are faced with the question of who they are now. In this story, we learned of Gary's emotional reaction to the abrupt shock of losing what he thought was his perfect job. As he recounted the story of that day, we could feel the dread of what had just happened. For a man who was always goal-driven, this loss was a blow. Immediately, his world changed and he was faced with an unexpected loss.

We learned how Gary had to dig deep and devise a plan using all of the discipline and tactical skills he had to forge a new path. Even though he struggled and felt defeated at times, he found strength from his faith and from deep within himself. He had to work hard throughout the job search process not to spiral into a depressive state and spin in fear.

Gary tells us how new and different parts of himself needed to show up in order to survive and then thrive after the job loss. He had to reinvent his idea of himself and his identity, as this loss challenged his status quo. Centering himself in his prayerful intention and staying on task helped him to ground himself in this new reality and manifest a job that was even better than the last.

Many of us have experienced a loss like Gary's, by either voluntarily leaving a job or being downsized, leaving us with a bruised ego. When I was a young man, I was laid off from a job on a Thursday. I was really lost, as the week prior, I had had to let my entire staff go. The next day I went to the grocery store and felt self-conscious and defeated. I felt like everyone was looking at me and thinking, What's he doing here? Of course, they weren't, but that's how I interpreted it because I should have been at my job. *What just happened? How did I get here?* The world and my place in it had changed overnight. Now I realize I was in a state of shock and mourning after this loss. In my midthirties I wasn't as wise as Gary; I hadn't learned how to grieve and honor my job loss. I just thought I needed to move on and get another job!

Many people subconsciously wrap big parts of their identity around their jobs. This is reinforced by our culture, as the first question we are asked when we meet someone new is often, "What do you do for a living?" This is a reasonable get-to-know-you question, but it promotes the idea that we are what we do. In my experience, men wrap their identities around their jobs far more than women do. When the job goes away for whatever reason and there's nothing lined up, many people feel adrift and without purpose. With the backdrop of a loss, they tell themselves stories about how bad they are, how they messed up, or put themselves down in other ways. They get lost in supporting a false narrative that confirms they are not worthy.

Gary went into that emotional place but was able to pull himself out of it, staving off depression and thoughtfully developing a plan for his next steps. He entered into his stretch by challenging himself, creating an organized process, and doing some kind of outreach and connection each day. He kept his head in the game by developing a tactical approach as a way to focus himself.

It would be easy to stay in a state of shock and just stare into space, feeling hurt and victimized by the company that just let you go. This frozen grief paralyzes people into inaction, and they end up kicking themselves later for wasting so much time in the wallowing. It's tempting to drift into a pity party and spin in the worry instead of turning fears into actionable energy. We get caught up in the shock instead of naming this experience as a loss, honoring the loss and its impact, regrouping, and then developing a plan to move forward. We can find a sense of purpose and power when we get out of our own way, when we declare that this loss just happened and this is how we feel. When we name it, we can claim it.

Picture yourself taking a loss out of your bucket.
Hold it, name it, honor it, and heal it.

Gary's story is one of focused intention, gratitude, humility, faith, and perseverance. His solace today is demonstrated in the pride he holds in how hard he worked to create a new life of balance for himself and his family. There are gifts in loss, but we must heal our pain to see the hidden sparkle inside that is revealed in the polishing.

To paraphrase Gary's words: Get centered. Get outside yourself. Provide energy to others.

～

- What was stirred up in you as you read about Gary's journey after his job loss and how he went about reinventing himself?
- Have you or someone you know lost a job?
- If so, what new perspective do you have after reading Gary's story?
- How can Gary's story inspire you to look at your life in a new way today?

～

Gary's charity of choice for his story contribution is the Green Lake Area Animal Shelter, which enhances the lives of animals and people through education, adoption, and compassion. Learn more at www.glaas.org.

~

Additional Resources

The First 90 Days: Proven Strategies for Getting Up to Speed Faster and Smarter, updated and expanded, Michael Watkins, Boston, MA: Harvard Business Review Press, 2013.

The 7 Habits of Highly Effective People, 30th anniversary ed., Steven Covey, Manhattan, New York: Simon & Schuster, 2020.

Jesus Calling: Enjoying Peace in His Presence, Sarah Young, Nashville, TN: Thomas Nelson, 2004.

Headspace: Mindful Meditation (app), Mindful meditation and relaxing music to help manage sleep, stress, and anxiety.

CHAPTER TEN

Helping Others through Loss

*Caregiving has no second agendas or hidden motives.
The care is given from love for the joy of giving without
expectation, no strings attached.*
—GARY ZUKAV

We never know when a significant loss will strike someone we know, whether it's a coworker, friend, family member, or partner. When a loss happens, we all have the capacity to be of great service to others. The simple acts of listening and holding space can express compassion and support, yet it is one of the most frequently overlooked ways we can help others. There is often no need for words, actions, or attempts to "fix" the pain of loss; rather, we can simply be present with another, sharing in this human experience.

There will be times, however, when gentle acts of care are just what is needed. From ensuring the dignity of a friend who is no longer able to open a jar to bringing a warm meal to a bereaved friend, small, thoughtful acts offer far more than the outward action alone. These acts of compassion, of being present, speak to our heart wisdom and are felt more than the specific act we did for the person. The more we can create a blanket of softness and understanding around someone who has experienced a devastating loss, the more gentle their tender path toward healing may be. They gain strength from our support.

We all experience trauma or loss differently. Not one of us goes through such an event exactly the same way. There are themes, patterns, and parallels of experience, but not a single path for how we process a loss event. You read in chapter eight how to set boundaries for yourself when you are going through a loss, and here you will discover how to set boundaries for yourself as you care for someone else. By honoring how we and others go through a loss experience, we give ourselves and them a great gift of agency, acknowledgment, and grace.

Setting Boundaries

Before we can effectively help others through their loss, setting clear and solid boundaries for ourselves is important, as boundaries protect us from taking on their pain. Setting boundaries means creating internal and external "bright lines" that we don't cross. This is not our loss experience, we are outside looking in at someone else's experience, so we need to create these boundaries for ourselves before we can effectively help them.

Briefly, an internal boundary is a promise or commitment to ourselves of how we are going to take care of ourselves or someone else. For example, we might say to ourselves that we are going to the gym, we are not going to eat pizza every day, or we are going to call our mom every two days. An external boundary is a statement to someone else about something we want or need. These are clear statements made without anger and without pushing them onto the other person. Yes, I would like to have tacos for dinner. No, I don't like it when you demean me and put me down. (You can find an extensive description of the many boundary types in my book *Healing Your Lost Inner Child*.) As much as you may want to jump in right away and help someone who is experiencing a loss, it's important to check in with yourself to see how you best can give them time, resources, and your energy without losing yourself in the process.

Perhaps you are in a position of feeling great empathy for another's situation and want to help them in any way. As you give them assistance, it is crucial to watch for signs of "compassion fatigue," which builds over time. This happens when, from a place of caring, you repeatedly do too much to help, giving your all and getting lost in their journey. Showing compassion for others does not mean depleting yourself to the point where there's nothing left over. When we have not checked in with ourselves to see how much we can give another, overextending ourselves is not hard to do. Caring is like a well inside of you. When you keep pulling resources out of the well for everyone else, you're left with nothing to take care of yourself. It's a selfless act, but it can also be incredibly exhausting and draining when it's repeated over time.

If you are giving care to someone else right now, take a moment to look at the internal boundaries you have set for yourself. For example, you have decided that you can spend an hour with your friend today, going to the grocery and pharmacy. Once you have this clarity, reinforce the boundary and manage expectations by stating to the person that you have about an hour to give today. This clear boundary statement defines your time for both of you so that your entire day is not swallowed up with their errands and chores, and they will not expect more of your time.

Resentments tend to show up within us when we have not honored our own boundaries. A person who is infirm or incapacitated may not have the best boundaries, so they can't always define this for us. They may keep asking for help, not seeing that they demand or ask too much of others, and not realizing they are wearing their helpers down. They just want their needs met, and they are probably frustrated with their own loss of control. Setting boundaries and asking others to help you give care will create balance and help keep you from doing too much and becoming exhausted and resentful.

You may find yourself in a unique situation where you are caring for the caregiver. For example, your friend's spouse is dying, and you're helping your friend as they struggle with anticipatory loss and caring for their loved one. This complex caregiving scenario has many moving parts and can quickly become emotionally confusing. Be consistent and steady at this time, and work through your own emotional reactions so you will have the strength to be there for your friend. Just being your loving self will provide a welcome distraction.

Your love and care for someone else doesn't mean that you sacrifice yourself and all of your time, money, and patience so they don't feel any pain. It means that you honor yourself as you honor them. Strong boundaries are not selfish; they show that you love and respect yourself by helping to prevent compassion fatigue.

Enmeshment

Enmeshment happens when there is a lack of strong boundaries. This is usually seen between family members who are overly involved in each other's situations, where each person involved doesn't know where they end and the other person begins. We are at risk of enmeshment when we start to feel what someone else feels and then take on their struggle as if it's our own. You read about my enmeshment with my mom in my story, "Loss of Innocence." As an adolescent, I couldn't define this lack of boundary and felt overwhelmed with the sense of responsibility to fix my mom's problems. I didn't understand how I was giving all of my power away trying to help her.

Enmeshment can begin innocently enough, such as when a friend's parent dies, our spouse was in an accident, or our adult child has a setback at work. When we love someone, it's hard not to overidentify or overempathize with their loss and "carry" their feelings. When we have enmeshed, fuzzy boundaries, we imagine how they feel and begin to feel the same way.

"Bystander enmeshment" happens when we jump into the middle of someone else's drama instead of maintaining a healthy distance. The overinvested bystander perceives that they are showing their love, care, and concern for the other, but this behavior often has the energy of worry or fear: *I'm so worried about you* or *I can't stop thinking about you*. The healthy reaction to a bystander event is to be emotionally available and set good boundaries as the other person goes through their loss. Do what you can for them, but know your limits.

Enmeshed feelings can quickly become confusing. For example, we are concerned about someone so we give advice expecting a certain outcome, then get mad at the person for not following our advice. We care and want them to be okay, so we give this unsolicited advice because we feel out of control and scared or spinning in uncertainty. We want them to feel better so we don't have to feel this fear. The person who is going through the situation needs support and empathy, not someone who adds a burden to their situation. It's one thing to care for another, but when we get into the deep end of the pool with them, we weigh down their healing journey more than we help them. We don't need to jump into the deep end with them to be of service to them. Some people feel that not jumping into the deep end is uncaring, but to be fully available, we have to be solid within ourselves and not lost in their story. This is what respect looks like.

If you become enmeshed with someone else's loss and begin to overidentify with their pain, step back and ask yourself how you can best be of support to them right now. What is yours and what is theirs? In general, people in grief and loss need us to sit and be a witness to their pain rather than mirror the same emotional intensity back to them. A person in distress is looking for a strong shoulder to lean on, not someone who is crying as loudly as they are. Someone who is looking into treatments and options, for example, doesn't need their decisions second-guessed. If you do offer alternatives and options, simply put them at their doorstep, without expectations. When we are not attached to their situation or outcome, when we are clear about where we end and they begin, then we can give the best support. A good measure for this is to ask yourself how you feel fter you help someone. Do you feel that you made an effort and are still in balance, or do you feel drained and disappointed? If you feel drained, you're probably doing too much, are overly invested in an outcome, and are putting expectations on yourself and your friend.

A loving action toward someone in a grief or loss cycle is to ask them how you can best help or be of service. Do they need to talk about things? Do they need you to help them find a solution? Do they need you to just sit and be, to just hang out with them? Do they need a hug? Asking them what they need works much better than arbitrarily deciding what is best for them. When you ask, you set a boundary within yourself and with them, a line that you're not going to cross.

It's important to recognize that not everyone is cut out to be a caregiver and that some people become frightened when a loved one or friend gets sick or experiences a loss. They don't know how to separate their own fears from what another is going through. If you have this reaction, it may be useful to spend some time doing some of the honoring exercises in chapter ten to see where this fear is coming from. If you have an urge to deny or run away from someone else's loss experience, there may be someone else better suited to attend to their needs at the moment.

If you are on the receiving end of caregiving that does not meet your needs, know that those giving care try their best with the tools they have. You learned in chapter eight how to speak your truth and ask for what you need, so use those tools to help you express your needs and set healthy boundaries.

The hallmarks of a healthy caregiver are compassion, boundaries, strength, humility, and patience. Healthy caregivers know their limits, have good communication skills, know when they are in over their head and need assistance, have great patience, practice good boundaries, and anticipate the needs of the one they are caring for.

Worry

If you think that worrying about another is helpful, know that it is not as altruistic as you think. Your concern and love for them is one thing, but carrying the energy of fear for them is another. When you spin in worry and fear for someone, you send a laser beam of fear and worry out to that person even though your intention is to protect and care for them. When you are preoccupied with fear, that is what you project from your heart chakra. Instead of sending them the light and love you want to deliver, you send them heavy, dense fear.

If you feel love for someone else, send them love and an intention that the outcome is for their best and highest good.

An alternative to worry is to beam a soft and gentle intention that declares your hope that the outcome to their situation is for their best and highest good. The difference is that you turn over this control and trust to them instead of prescribing an outcome. You don't load up their situation with an expectation. You declare internally your desire that your loved one achieves what is best for them right now, what they can best hold. This shows respect for their experience and takes your ego out of the equation and is an example of respectful boundary setting. This action took me a while to learn because it asks us to suspend control and blindly trust. When we are in a state of worry, our minds give us the illusion that we are in control. The mind likes activity, so worry makes us think we are busy caring for the other person, that we are right there with them. Of course we don't want our loved one to be sick or in pain, but we can't walk the path for them. The other person most needs us to help them be strong, hopeful, and encouraged, and for us to trust in the best outcome for them—the exact opposite of fear.

Loss of Independence

The loss of one's independence through age, accident, disease, or illness is an extremely difficult loss to accept. What one has been able to do their whole lives is taken away, slowly or suddenly, and the inability to do for oneself is not only frustrating but also traumatic. Older or differently abled people often don't ask for help because they believe they can, or should, still be able to do those things that were once effortless. Their natural inclination is to try to do the familiar activities of daily living to see if their bodies will respond, and they become self-conscious and frustrated when they are not able to. They then begin to tell themselves how weak they are, how useless or inadequate.

Remember this the next time you are with someone who is struggling with a new challenge. They feel vulnerable and exposed, even if that's not how they appear on the outside. They may put up a strong exterior so as not to show weakness, but inside they may feel disheartened and frustrated with themselves. It may be hard for them to see that when they try to do things on their own, and sometimes because of their stubbornness, they actually create more work for you. See if you can find a way to gently point this out so that they can begin to work with you in your caregiving. Ask them to carry their phone or a call button with them even when at home, as this will help you and them. They may see this as an intrusion and an affront to their sense of independence, so craft the message in a way that lets them see how doing these actions will help you out.

> *Caregiving often calls us to lean into love we didn't know possible.* —*Tia Walker*

When someone who is not able reaches out for help, this admission to themselves, and to you, probably took a lot of courage. Find a way to help them, especially if they rarely ask for help. If you see that they are struggling, offer to help or find other resources, and give them the option to say no. This reinforces their sense of power and control. The wise part of them will be thankful for the support, but the ego part may grumble that they can do it on their own. People give up a certain amount of independence when they ask for help. If we do things for them without their asking, they will either be appreciative or think that we are overstepping our bounds. When we overstep, we are not respecting their boundaries, their sovereignty.

What we want for those who have lost this independence is that they have the best options for their lives today. What they want is to make their own decisions. They work hard to find ways to have the same lifestyle they had before and to do things they once took for granted. They still want to feel like themselves, even though their situation has changed. They will adjust and stretch with their loss in their own time. A prognosis for a disease, for example, may not be anything they want, and their feelings and reactions to it may be more than you can handle. Check in and be honest with yourself, as you may not be able to physically help those you love. Explore the resources in your community to help you help your friend.

After a Death

After a loss experience through the death of a loved one, people are often bombarded by the typical platitudes the bereaved so often hear. There are many ways you can offer support during this time without resorting to unhelpful comments. Saying you are sorry for their loss is well-intended, but you could also ask what they need, ask if they want to talk about their loved one, or ask them about a favorite memory. If you're at a loss for words, ask them to tell you about the best of the person who has died and how they felt when they were with them. This way, you honor and hold a loving place for them to celebrate the life of their loved one. Many people get tongue-tied and are afraid to say the wrong thing. Just know that your friend is comforted with you being by their side at this time and that acknowledging their loss is better than saying nothing.

You may also want to say that you will check in with them in a few weeks to see what they need. This is preferable to telling them to reach out if they need anything; the grieving rarely do. This chapter offers many examples of outreach for the bereaved you can use when someone you love is in pain.

Opening Up

Talking about their loss is one way people process a loss event, but many avoid it or don't want to talk about it because it's painful. In order for people to open up about their loss, we have to create an environment that says it's safe for them to talk about it. We have to give them clues that we are okay with listening to them talk about their sadness. We give them the invitation and the choice because if they don't want to or are not ready to talk, then our asking questions may feel abrupt and highly invasive. Let them know you are there for them and can hold space while they talk about their sadness. If they signal that they do want to talk, then invite them to do so by asking open-ended questions. Open-ended questions ask for complete answers, not yes-or-no answers. How did you feel when you saw your mom's functioning decrease over time? What are some things about your dad's death that are hard for you to move past? How do you feel to have lost both parents? This gives them the platform to share when they are ready and willing. This is what is creating a safe container means.

Asking open-ended questions instead of making statements is a respectful way to enter into a conversation. When we project onto others our own biases or feelings about their loss, we may shut them down without realizing it. Avoid saying things like, *You must be devastated by this*, or, *I bet you are torn up because of this*, or, *I can't believe that happened to your family*. When we say those things, we prescribe how they should feel and project onto them our own bias. We say this is how we feel, and put words in their mouth. If they don't feel that way, these expressions may make them think they are doing something wrong, leading them to feel ashamed or that they are bad in some way. That is crossing a boundary.

You don't need to talk someone out of a feeling. Your kindness is to gently hold the feelings they express.

Know that you don't have to have the perfect answer for your loved one's pain. There is nothing you can say that will bring back the loss and make it all better. Just sit with them, reflect back what you hear, and continue to ask open-ended questions. Hold their pain as they move through their stretch. They will give you signals when they can't talk about it anymore.

Anger

Many people go through a loss experience with a great deal of anger. They may act out to try to gain control and remind themselves they still have personal power. Expressions of anger are their fear coming forth, how they defend themselves against something they don't want to know or hear. They surround themselves in the thick cotton of denial burnished with anger.

If you are caring for or are around someone like this, see if you can look past their fear and anger with compassion. See their denial or avoidance as their way of going through this experience, yelling to the world how angry they are. They are in an internal battle and a great deal of fear as they try to hold this new, unsettling information. They are wrestling with control, and they want this loss experience to be on their own terms instead of anyone else saying they have to accept it and move on.

It's hard to be a caregiver to someone who refuses care. Be patient. Their rejection may be their anger (fear) talking.

The more you try to get them to be positive, the more they will resist. Talk with them about their anger, and empathize with them. Help them know that their feelings are normal, and avoid the urge to talk them out of a feeling. At these moments, stay strong so they can feel their anger. Anger is movement of emotion. Anger pushed down into the loss bucket will fester into depression, and depression is much harder to transform and heal than anger. I'd rather someone be angry about their situation than depressed, as anger is much easier to work with and heal. That being said, it's not okay for them to blame, shame, or project their anger onto you with personal attacks. If they start to project their anger onto you, use your boundary statements to put up emotional guardrails.

Once they've gotten to the point where they can no longer ignore their reality—when they face and wrestle with the monster and reach their personal threshold—their anger will transform, and they will suddenly become weepy and emotionally needy. They surrender to this unwelcome visitor. This is especially hard for strong-minded, independent people, and once they have surrendered, they can appear defeated, like they have lost a battle. Their reality becomes loud, as a part of them has woken up and realized that their loss experience is really happening. They hold this inconvenient, thorny truth and can no longer play games with it. They are truly being in their life instead of busily doing their life, perhaps for the first time. After the shock, they surrender and merge into the stretch. See if you can help them find strength again in their stretch. They will be learning how to set internal boundaries to deal with their new situation. Through your encouragement, they may understand that all is not lost and that there is hope in the darkness. Hopefully, they will learn that their actions of anger, surrender, and claiming is all part of their tender path.

Practical Communication

Be a witness to someone else's pain so they can receive this healing for themselves. Reflect back to them their own greatness.

After a death in the family, the bereaved are often bombarded with sympathy, offers of help, and requests for details of what happened, all of which can, counterintuitively, add to their stress. You can help them manage this influx by suggesting that the family designate a specific family member or friend to give updates or other information. This person then becomes the point person for people to call, taking pressure off the family and allowing them to take care of themselves and heal.

For complex or ongoing medical issues, you can help the family by offering to set up a website where you or a trusted family member can post updates and progress on the patient.

This creates a central hub for information and streamlines the communication away from the patient and family. It also creates a consistent message and clearly defines what is going on to minimize any confusion. Doing this for the family will take the stress off them.

A patient of mine is going through chemo and radiation, and she was trying to arrange all of the drop-offs and pickups for her treatments. I suggested that she ask her friends who have already offered help to manage this schedule among themselves. Whatever the situation is around your desire to help, see how you can ease the burden by putting boundaries around the mechanics of the situation. Those who are not going through loss have greater clarity and can help organize things better than those who are lost in the process of grief.

Your Partner's Valley of Grief

It was through you that I learned I could be strong.

If your partner is going through a grief and loss cycle, there are many things that may help you navigate what they are going through. In the case of your partner's parent dying, they may be deeply lost in their grief, and you may see parts of them come forward that you've never seen before. These feelings are new for your partner, even if their other parent had previously passed away. Your role is to be as steady, kind, patient, and forgiving as you can. You may also have your own feelings of loss, so take care of yourself at this time as well. You are both on this journey together but with different perspectives. Your role is to create, in the best way you can, a sacred space for your partner, a soft place to land, so you can come home to each other to recharge and replenish the wounded heart.

Think of your role as the gentle, patient, attentive witness and unobtrusive supporter. You are there for them, witnessing their pain and holding space for them. One of the ways you can support your partner at this time is to anticipate some needs, such as having their favorite things to eat, doing chores that they would normally do, and anything else you know brings them comfort. Ask how you can best support them. Do they need conversation, a hug, problem-solving, or for you to just let them be? You probably know your partner's love language. Think of what would speak to them now, that would show them you are there for them in a patient, loving way. Then do those things.

For some couples, the extreme stress and loudness of grief shatters the equilibrium of the relationship. Whatever the emotional state of the relationship was prior to the loss, the loss will expose every crack and fracture. The relationship will be tested, especially in the shockwave. Sometimes, though, the couple becomes closer, as the loss has disrupted the status quo and introduced new routines and feelings. There is a lot happening, and even though there are new opportunities for healing, it's important to take one emotion at a time and honor the grieving process first. Be gentle with each other, as you are being stretched in new ways than ever before. There will be a time and place for all of those long-standing issues to be healed.

*A key thing to remember at these moments
is that the loudness of grief is deafening.*

As you talk with your partner about their feelings, re-member that they are lost behind thick cotton clouds of grief. When they stare into space, they are not trying to ignore you or refusing to follow through on tasks; they are just consumed by the shockwave of grief. To the observer, the grieving person may seem like they are a million miles away, while the griev-ing person thinks they are doing a pretty good job of managing their life and taking care of the basics. They may be comforting themselves by being absorbed in grief and isolating. They may be holding on by a thread, so the kindest of gestures from you will have the most meaning.

Lashing Out In Pain

Work on balancing and addressing your own needs when you are in the midst of taking care of your partner's needs.

As you are learning, a part of grief work involves tapping into anger, and sometimes this spills out onto others. As you watch your grieving partner lash out in pain, you see their spiraling, their numbness, their checking out. This is when you need to have a good set of internal boundaries, to not take their lashing out personally, and to try to reach through their pain to give them comfort. At the same time, you need to have contextual boundaries by checking in with yourself as to what's okay and what is not. Just because they are in pain doesn't mean you can't express yourself. You can still maintain the guardrails of your relationship; just know that your partner and your relationship are being stretched and stressed at this time. You are not telling your partner how to grieve, you're saying that this is what you can do for them and asking them to help you help them.

The grieving partner may not always be rational and may overindulge to deal with the pain. In a moment of calm, ask your grieving partner if it will be okay for you to give them feedback if you see them start to overindulge. For example, ask if it will be okay to ask for the car keys or the credit card. This is a safety check for you to give when your partner slides and takes something too far, when there could be long-term consequences. Give your partner this feedback in a sober moment when they can best hear you, not when they are acting out.

Loss often exposes unresolved wounding in the person or the relationship, bringing it to the surface.

If both you and your partner are grieving over the loss, then both of you are lost in your own grief and experiencing it differently. You are both in the deep end of the pool and can't reach the edge. You may have never jointly lost something significant before, so you don't have the right tools to help yourself or be available in the relationship. Comforting one another is hard in these cases, which is why you may not have any more to give to the relationship or each other. You are doing okay if you can just get up and shower, as you are skimming the surface of life in a state of misery. You may need individual and couples counseling to help you navigate through this new experience. A third party can help normalize what is happening and determine effective coping strategies to help you ride the storm together.

Here are some things to remember about your grieving partner:

They may be lost in their grief and unable to participate, even in activities that are enjoyable.

They may need to sit in their grief and not be talked out of a feeling. Ask if they need to talk about what they feel or if they just need quiet.

They may seem distant or upset with you, but this is the pain of their grief spilling over. Ask for clarification: Is this about me or about the loss?

They may want to make rash or impulsive decisions. See if you can help them put this off until they are grounded in their thoughts and feelings.

They may say they feel alone even though they are surrounded by loving family and friends.

Observe their overindulgence to determine whether you need to gently give them feedback.

Your partner's mind is preoccupied, so you may need to remind them of things several times. They hear you, but they are having a hard time tracking everything right now.

They may make big or grand statements that sound definite and final. Just take this in, and at a later, calmer time, ask them to clarify those things for you. See if they still want to do whatever they were talking about before.

Chances are, your grieving partner needs you to just be yourself. Right now, your being the person they have always known is one of the most reassuring actions you can do for them. Be with your partner, be present and emotionally available. Practice loving detachment, where you don't get lost in their grief but can hold space for them. They need to feel your love now.

Vicarious Loss

Even my burnout has burned edges.

Vicarious loss happens when we are in proximity to someone else's trauma or loss but do not experience it directly. We can be impacted by it, but there is space between us and the loss. For most of us, our natural empathy kicks in and we have compassion for the ones experiencing the trauma loss. Simply living our lives exposes us to vicarious trauma, so check in with yourself to see if you are carrying around a worry, fear, or pain from a terrifying or scary event.

We can experience vicarious loss from many types of events. Some examples are when someone you know has a car accident, a friend or loved one has a chronic illness or terminal disease, there is a(nother) mass shooting, there is a COVID outbreak in your town, a friend is getting a divorce, a friend's parent died, or there is a natural disaster in another state or country. Most of us are naturally empathic, so we energetically absorb these traumas at some level. We begin to identify with the situation and imagine what it must be like to be in it. Witnessing any trauma can alter our mood and how we feel about the world in general, skewing our perspective to the negative.

All of humanity has experienced losses connected to the COVID pandemic, including direct loss, bystander loss, and vicarious loss. There is a collective trauma from COVID, as it is the monster in the dark, the unseen, silent miasma floating in the air. The pandemic is a confusing collective loss experience, as there are people who don't see it as real, people who see it as the flu, people who are terrified by its existence, and everything in between. As humans, we look to other humans to help us determine how to react or respond to an event. Having so many different reactions creates a feeling of unease, as then we have to rely on our own conclusions rather than on what others think. This confusion around the pandemic has made all of us check in with ourselves to see what makes sense to us, but very few of us are epidemiologists. I believe that all of us will eventually know someone who has had it, died from it, or get it ourselves. The question becomes what to do with the losses resulting from the ongoing pandemic and the inconvenient truth that it is affecting everyone, whether we like it or not.

The losses due to mass shootings are similar to the losses from COVID. In the United States, shootings are happening so often now that our loss bucket is full, and many of us are shutting down from these overwhelming waves of grief. These tragedies are still shocking, but unfortunately, they are no longer surprising. We have learned how to normalize atrocities by packaging them into sad soundbites, then tucking them away as we shake our heads in disbelief—until the next one happens.

Losses are violations of what we perceive as stable and steady, taking us into a land uncharted and unknown.

The response to this overabundance of loss in our world today is to either lash out in anger or shut down from feeling overwhelmed. We don't know what to do or think, as people whom we would normally look to are spinning in as much uncertainty and overburden as the rest of us are. At a deep, primitive level, this creates great distress throughout humanity, even though civilizations have been through massive loss cycles many times before.

I believe the answer is in our perspective and our ability to set a boundary to hold or witness all of this loss without becoming absorbed by the fear and panic. Stay steady within yourself, and take the precautions that make sense to you while not getting lost in the fear, which can cause you to lose perspective on your life as a whole. Remember your values and your truth. Use your faith or intentional energy to transmute any fear you pick up from others into something neutral. Use the honoring tools to help process your emotions. Staying steady is about not finding an answer for how to solve these issues, it is what you do with all the emotion you feel in response to them.

You can decide how you want to experience this time in history, whether from a place of fear or a place of clarity through your own beliefs and truth. It's good to periodically take a break from the news, which is intentionally designed to deliver a steady dose of fear into our lives each day. Ask yourself how watching or listening to the news adds to your life. Be gentle with yourself, and know that you don't need to have your finger on the pulse of 24/7 "breaking news" all of the time. A news fast may clear some excess fear from your system.

First responders, public safety personnel, and anyone in the medical field becomes filled up from so much vicarious toxic trauma on a daily basis. Part of the reason many go into these professions is to help others, but in order to do so, they have to take care of themselves. If you witness vicarious trauma on a regular basis, check in with yourself to see how much of the fear and sorrow you carry directly relates to your life and how much belongs to others. Even though emergency-care providers are trained to compartmentalize and look past traumatic scenes, at some time in their careers there will be at least one call or patient that will stay with them, which is normal. First responders have come to me needing to talk about a call they responded to that was similar to many other calls in their career, but the memory of that one call got to them and keeps recycling inside. This is a natural reaction, as people can take in only so much of this vicarious trauma before it builds up to a toxic level. And any one of us can become triggered by something that is unresolved from our past that we are not consciously aware of.

We all have the capacity to compartmentalize, and in some cases, we need this skill. But even someone who is professionally trained to put these things in a box can reach their limit.

Emotional reactions to vicarious trauma need to be honored and released. Sometimes a debriefing happens around the kitchen table or in a break room. But too often, egos push this need aside and the wounded heroes just get on with their day, laughing at dark humor and inappropriate jokes and pouring that hard call into the (collective) loss bucket. If an event revisits you in the wee hours of the night, reach out to a trusted friend or therapist and work through this difficult experience. There are many ways to care for others in the world than by carrying pain, worry, and fear for them. Try something different, and send them a blessing that they receive a healing that is for their best and highest good. Or maybe create a "This Sucks Box" to hold all of these distressing events. Getting them out of you so you don't have to carry this tortured pain.

What are some vicarious trauma losses that you carry around? Give yourself the gift of releasing them. With loving detachment, know that those affected are on their own journeys. Try some of the many different ways to honor loss found in chapter nine to clear these sad trauma stories from your energy field. You can be a hero in many ways, but that doesn't need to include holding on to someone else's trauma and thinking you're being strong for them.

An Adult Child's Poor Choices

*One day I realized I had to set down the stone
I was carrying for everyone else in my life.*

A common and sad enmeshed, fuzzy boundary is when parents internalize, or take on the blame and responsibility for, their adult child's poor choices. Through their love for their child, they take on the feelings they think their child "should" have following poor choices, especially when those choices affect other people. This is especially true for parents of older teens or adult children who are addicted to drugs. For any number of reasons, the child who is the addict doesn't feel the same sense of responsibility that their parents have. The parents see their child as an extension of themselves and think that the adult child should, for example, feel bad for doing drugs, not taking care of themselves, or breaking the law.

In many cases, the parents don't see their adult child as being resourceful or remorseful, so the parents carry and are filled with remorse and a great sense of responsibility. They react the way that most people would, and they don't understand why their child doesn't recognize the effects of their choices or feel shame or remorse. The parents have an exceptionally hard time separating from these internalized feelings and establishing clear boundaries.

If you are internalizing your adult child's or someone else's choices, stop and ask yourself, What is mine to carry? What part of this do I need to own? When you have this definition around the situation, it is easier to set clear boundaries. It's hard to be a caregiver to someone who doesn't want to take care of themselves. Your raised your child to have independence and agency. They are essentially acting on this and making choices, or the addiction is their master and they are lost in dependency. These are not the choices you hoped for them, but they are their choices. Hold this uncomfortable truth, then reassure yourself and ask yourself if you have done everything you could have. You can throw all the money in the world at trying to fix a problem for someone else, but if they aren't ready to heal, get sober, or take responsibility for their choices, you are just wasting your resources. Calm yourself, and project blessings to your adult child using loving detachment as you give yourself some much-needed love as well. Know that underneath all of the swirling, chaotic haze of drugs and alcohol beats the heart of the child you love.

⌒

You have learned how you can available to another during their loss by setting compassionate boundaries. You now know that you can be present for someone else, have clarity about what you can and cannot do, and still be a good friend and loving partner. Another's loss can bring up unresolved, unhealed parts of us that have been long buried. The message is to check in with yourself and take care of your needs first, then you can be of the most help for someone else. You can have a good sense of your healed and wounded parts so you can show up and help someone else with clear purpose. By doing this, you decrease the possibility of your wounded parts being projected onto another, and the most healed parts of you can be available to assist another on their tender path. The highest expression of kindness and compassion comes from respecting yourself and others when loss inevitably shows up in your life.

I'm able to take care of others by taking care of myself.
My expression of love flows through me effortlessly,
and I am rewarded a thousandfold through
my unconditional giving.

WILLOW'S STORY: ART AND COMFORT FOR THE DYING

The meaning of life is to find your gift.
The purpose of life is to give it away.
—PABLO PICASSO

Willow is a kind and gentle soul who walks the earth lightly. Those who have experienced her inspirational art classes, her kindness, and her tremendous sense of humor are lucky indeed. Willow works as an art teacher at a cancer resource center, which is part of a larger hospital system focused on cancer treatment. She brings her broad artistic talent and deep intuition to work with those who experience a terminal cancer diagnosis. Not only does she help patients express themselves through art, she also sits with their pain and offers the sick or dying a safe person to lean into. Through her compassion, she gives us a broader way of how we can go through a health challenge so that we aren't completely oppressed by it. She shows us that through art we can express what words cannot convey; art is the messenger of the soul. With her gentle wisdom, she is able to be physically present, emotionally grounded, and available to those who are facing death. Effortlessly, she is a beacon of light, hope, strength, joy, and love. This is Willow's story of how she is fully present for those who are sick or dying.

~

What is your view of how people face a chronic or terminal disease?

I'd like to first explain the core of who I am so you understand how I approach my work. I have a strong empathetic and sympathetic foundation, which I believe is a phenomenal foundation to have for this line of work. It allows me to bring patience, grace, thoughtfulness, and care to my interactions with people during some of their hardest challenges. I am sensitive to people, and they resonate with me in some way because when I am there for them, I bring my entire self to the encounter. I give them the space to do the same.

Even before working at the cancer center, I embraced death as a part of life. Many people do not. They close themselves off and shut down their emotions, and their experience can become a lonely journey. In the course of my time at the cancer center, I lost my mom, which transformed my suffering into my purpose in life. Instead of turning away and avoiding my feelings, I express them through art, journaling, and reflection. I share that with my patients, creating a safe and healing space where we can grieve with an open heart instead of closing off to the world and ourselves. I find out who they are and where they are, and guide them to where they can go as a person, not just as a "person with cancer."

In your opinion, how are some people able to go through a terminal disease experience with grace and ease, while others go through it with confusion, frustration, and anger?

Cancer invades every part of you and surrounds you in everything you do. It decolorizes your world. In my experience, it is how people access the world around them, how they experience the world, that gives them the ability to handle situations. Are they proactive or reactive? They need to find the core of who they are to work with their strengths and weaknesses.

The cancer center is a safe haven for those coming in; they can share stories that are similar to someone else's and find out they are not alone. They are each experiencing cancer in one way or another, so they don't have to explain to others where they are today. Others are on their own journey, and they understand the path new patients are on, even if it is different from their own. They welcome new people as fellow travelers.

When you are diagnosed with cancer, you are *told* so much about yourself. There are so many people—doctors, nurses, dietitians—telling you *what* you are (your diagnosis) and *how* you are (your prognosis) that it is easy to lose *who* you are in the process.

This is where being proactive can be a way to manage all the inflow of information and help you to *be* you in the middle of it all. There is a person behind that chart, a person behind that surgical scar, a person behind that end of treatment.

What are some helpful activities, motivations, and interactions for those who are dying?

Allow the bad days to happen. Celebrate the small joys. Become more mindful. Cultivate a sense of humor. Be able to laugh at yourself and others. Be who you are in whatever time you have left. Release expectations. Do what is important to you. Know your worth and value. Cancer can make you feel worthless.

Have a plan for treatment, for hospice, for dying. It helps give you back some control in a situation where you don't have much. Don't ever go to bed, slam the door, or hang up the phone angry. Share with others how you are feeling. Leave your mark on the world. Whatever you are holding on to—resentment, grudges, anger—let it out. Hold tight to your connections with people. Let go of the small stuff.

Tap into healing activities: expressive art, yoga, meditation, journaling. Cultivate gratitude and mindfulness. Take walks or sit in nature. Spend time with friends. Appreciate the small things that make you happy. Embrace spirituality: worship, sing, dance. Connect with a higher power.

Unhelpful behavior from others: Pushing you to do something you aren't ready for. Attempting to tell you how you are feeling. Giving you lists of "shoulds" instead of options. Comparing your process, journey, and grief with someone else's.

Jane Hirshfield describes the relationship between suffering, grief, and art: "We make art, I believe, partly because our lives are ungraspable, uncarryable, impossible to navigate without it. Even our joys are vanishing things, subject to transience. How, then, could there be any beauty without some awareness of loss, of suffering? The surprising thing is that the opposite is true, that suffering leads us to beauty the way that thirst leads us to water" (from an interview with Mark Matousek, April 10, 2015).

How do you find the energy to work with those who are dying?

They are so full of life. Life doesn't stop with cancer. Cancer magnifies living out loud. Finding hope and strength in each of my patients has made me more resilient. I don't turn away from sadness. I lean into it with an open heart and fill that space with compassion. I am able to be there and hold space for them.

> *When we don't push the pain of grief away, when we welcome and engage it, we live and love more fully.*
> —Francis Weller

What is the source of your strength to do this work?

I take refuge in nature, grounding myself with the earth, to reconnect with myself. I place myself near a creek with the sound of water flowing. I listen, and I am present to the silence of the forest, where I find solitude. I embrace negative space in the branches of an oak whose leaves have fallen. I get lost in the shadows; focus becomes effortless. And oh, my, the regeneration. Nature restores my spirit.

I think deeply and am an openly emotional person. I know I am making a difference. I listen, and I am present to each encounter I have. I thoughtfully consider who will be present for the experience and how to allow each person to participate authentically. I am always striving to be a safe space for growth, expression, acceptance, and comfort.

I have lived a life with huge struggles. Like others, I have many life experiences of loss, confusion, and pain. I recognize that in others and sit in it with them with grace. I bring that essence to the space. I show up authentically to care for each participant.

What do you say to yourself after a tough day?

I take time to self-evaluate after a class or a one-on-one with patients, and through reflection I note the positive and negative interactions. I don't internalize and beat myself up if it didn't go well. I don't look at it as a failed experience. I sit with my takeaway and wonder how I can elevate the experience next time, for everyone. Then I return to nature, use self-care to reflect and recover, and fill my cup again to bring my whole self to my next encounter.

How do you navigate your feelings when you become connected with a patient and then they die?

I celebrate the present of their presence and do not focus on the loss they are going through. I keep past patients present by surrounding the art room with pieces of their art, giving their artist energy to the new patients who come into the space. These patients do not know where the art has come from, but they absorb the positive emotions, hope, and strength of those angels who now inspire a new wave of cancer patients.

There is no "correct" way or single timeline to grieve. Everyone grieves at their own pace in their own way. I am able to help navigate emotions and feelings patients are drowning in, submerged in grief. Grief will last as long as it lasts. I hold space for patients and family members for as long as they need.

A mix of emotions creates a weight that we all carry at some point. I felt relief after my mom's long illness, but then I felt a trickle of guilt for feeling that: *The weight has lifted; am I feeling gratitude and joy? Oh, no, can't be. My mom just died.* We grieve because we loved. There isn't a day when my mom isn't in my heart. I hear her laugh, and I am left with a smile.

What kind of support do the family and friends of patients need that they don't always know how to ask for?

I have found that what they need most is someone to listen to them and guide them. I always reach out to caregivers and family members to let them know the services and resources available at the cancer center. I check in with family members periodically. I make myself available and am a compassionate listener for them. Each participant has different needs for services and support.

How do you gauge whether someone accepts their terminal disease and faces their reality or is resistant, shut down, or avoidant?

I listen to them and observe. It's pretty clear to identify when I see their energy and hear their words. I gauge their reactions and tune in to their life energy. My imaginary superpower is not absorbing their energy but channeling it into my artist brush, colored pencil, or gel pen and helping them to focus this energy in a creative release. I feel most powerful when I am helping others.

What actions do family members and friends take after their terminally ill loved one has died?

I always let the family know how much I value their loved one. I have seen many different ways of how people process their loss: hold a celebration of life, share the loved one's art supplies with their friends, have a sharing circle to tell impactful memories of the person, and have a ceremony to mark the first anniversary. Hurtful actions are refusing to accept the person is gone and not going through the person's belongings to avoid pain.

How do you gauge whether a person is in denial or accepts the fact that they are dying?

Their energy and words. They will come to me when they are ready. I've journaled with a dying person; it was a gift to be given to her daughter after her death. We did this in the days before her death; we laughed, we cried. She spoke about her daughter, and I wrote the words and feelings, which she had never spoken of until she was dying. What a powerful gift that was for both of them.

What do the dying need as they approach their transition?

Talk to them in a normal way. Don't change how you relate to them. Give them space to come to you as they need to. Be someone who can listen and not take offense at whatever comes out of their mouth. Don't fix things. Don't judge. Be a sponge to help them release their feelings. Be honest with them. Don't be afraid to touch them. Offer a hug or hold their hand. Spend time with them. Help them see the positives.

After working for years in this field, watching others experience a terminal diagnosis and death, how has your view of yourself and life changed?

I acknowledge that every person's life and death experience is different, and I accept them where they are in a particular moment of the journey. I always treat them as the same person they were before their diagnosis. They have cancer, they are not cancer. I hold their hand and let them know they are not alone.

I make myself available and am present. This allows me to live my life more authentically because I see the struggles. It allows me to balance out the challenges that come. I am super grateful for the many blessings in my life. Life is not a guarantee.

After you learn of a loss, how do you get back to Willow?

I am open and in a raw and vulnerable state. I allow myself permission to be wrecked every day. I have created a safe space for everyone I encounter at the cancer center. It is my realm of power, my energy zone, where patients can open up and know they are not alone. With them by my side, I follow my heart with courage, grace, patience, and hope. I breathe. I light a candle that flickers for those we have lost. Inhale. Exhale.

What do you do with the heavy grief you see and feel from others?

I feel like the wave of grief comes and goes, and I have been riding that wave for sixteen years. I quietly and calmly ride my board. No panic. Hold on until the next wave comes. I take them as they come, undulating with the power that is just below the surface. I close my eyes because the ocean, the beach, these are my comfort. The sound of the water lapping up against me. The gulls diving and rising around me. The sand beneath my toes, when I am near enough the shore to feel it. As if I am being led to wonder, not worry. I am the calm in the storm. The water always bringing me back, although I have never left. I have found peace within that withstands any storm.

What strengths have you gained from working in this career, this sacred space?

I am a much better public speaker, communicator, and listener. I have gained confidence in my skills and know what my strengths are: grace in challenge, patience in uncertainty, and compassion for all. My planning skills have sharpened. I can think globally with an individual takeaway. Take a negative and make it positive, or at least neutral. Show people how to acknowledge the good. Balance. I focus on my purpose for each class and the needs of the participants. I have learned to guide those on the journey with cancer with a purposeful plan to be a guiding light, leading with hope.

⌒

Reflections on Willow's Story

Willow's work of consistently holding space for others as they experience cancer is possible because of her care for herself. She has wisely learned many self-care and meditative practices to help herself so that she does not absorb or get lost in their pain. She channels her emotional processing through her artist's brush. She's able to do this because she has clarity within herself as to what her role is and what it is not. In other words, she practices gold-star boundary setting with herself and others. She is the safe place in the storm, permitting the heavy energy from others to flow through and out of her; she doesn't hold on to it. She shows us how to let go of misperceptions and emotional woundings that no longer serve and to focus on what's important in life. She gives us practical tools of honoring, such as drawing or painting our feelings or combining journaling with art. Through her work, she helps the shadow side of pain become manifest and golden.

She describes how to make space for holding a truth that is hard to hear if we are given a diagnosis or prognosis that scares us. With no agenda, she guides the infirmed to a gentle interior place through art to help them gain insight and wisdom. Through her respect for her participants, she reminds us that we all have agency and control even when our lives are in turmoil. Her perspective offers a quiet confidence for when news about health feels overwhelming. She illustrates that there can be a different way to go through this kind of experience. Even though it is devastating news, we don't have to color each day with a grim brushstroke.

There is a silent strength that comes through her words, a deep well of compassion that sings through her being.

Willow shows up authentically as she effortlessly holds space for the participants in her classes to be in whatever state they are in that day. She instructs others how to give their subconscious and shadow selves a voice, a purpose, a meaning. She makes this work look easy, but being with someone as they near the end of life, being respectfully present and allowing them to be, is one of the hardest roles in the medical community. She gives us practical advice that applies to anyone who is holding space for someone going through a life transition or loss process. There is a profound simplicity to her work that transcends words. She reminds us of the grace within each of us that we may give to ourselves and share with others.

Willow's work provides a great template showing us how a master at her craft creates a gentle place for those who are making their transition. She's an inspiration for caregivers, death doulas, and anyone who works with hospice or in palliative care.

- Did Willow's story bring up some feelings for you?
- What insights do you have about your feelings around dying?
- Have you ever sat with someone who was dying?
- If so, what was this like for you?
- What part of Willow's story is inspiring to you?
- Will any of Willow's techniques help you today?

Take a break from your reading and let Willow's words and perspectives sink in. Give yourself permission to hold space for yourself and for these new ideas of how you can be when you are with someone who is going through their last days.

⌒

Willow's charity of choice for her story contribution is Earth Paint. This nonprofit organization "recycles old latex paint into a high-quality, sustainable product that works for any job, inside or outside." Learn more at www.earthpaint.org.

⌒

Additional Resources

Accompanying the Dying: Practical, Heart-Centered Wisdom for End-of-Life Doulas and Health Care Advocates, Deanna Cochran, Maui, HI: Sacred Life Publishers, 2019.

Being Mortal: Illness, Medicine and What Matters in the End, Atul Gawande, New York NY: Metropolitan Books, 2017.

Toolkit for Caregivers: Tips, Skills, and Wisdom to Maximize Your Time Together, Deidre Edwards, self-published, 2019.

Healing Trauma with Guided Drawing: A Sensorimotor Art Therapy Approach to Bilateral Body Mapping, Cornelia Elbrecht, Berkeley, CA: North Atlantic Books, 2018.

Neurographic Art Step by Step: A Quick and Simple Tutorial on How to Make Your First Neurographic Art Image, S. J. Seferi, self-published, 2022.

CHAPTER ELEVEN

Growing Hopeful

Hope is like the sun, which, as we journey towards it, casts a shadow
of our burdens behind us.
—SAMUEL SMILES

You have come far along on your tender path, growing through
your grieving. The losses that once scared you, you now gently
hold. With a piqued curiosity, you see this part of you that
carries the wounded loss with a soft gaze. You are now able
to name your loss experiences to make them real and, with
compassion, envelope them in a way that eluded you before.
You're doing the necessary important work of the tender path:
naming, acknowledging, claiming, and healing your loss.

You are now holding up the feelings that were once buried
at the bottom of your loss bucket, writing and speaking about
them, owning the experience. You see loss from an elevated
place even when it brings up sorrow or sadness. You no longer
push away these feelings, and in the place of fear, you now
carry hard-won wisdom. The understanding you have toward

loss now helps you transcend what was once a limited view of this pain. With a newfound confidence, you bring your pain into the light of day, declaring that yes, this happened, this is how I feel, and this is how I'm transforming this stuck energy. The pain is still throbbing, the death still sad, but you now have a better idea of how to interact with and hold these feelings. You now realize that there is no need to compare your journey to anyone else's, as this is your own walk with grief. You are curating your own expression.

THE TENDER PATH

Through honoring my grief, I have come home to me. Who I thought I was yesterday has transformed into a new expression. No longer am I constricted by outdated ideas of myself, for today I am expanding into my wholeness with my traumas and triumphs by my side.

You are now able to hold your loss with new respect, even as you walk your tender path of the shockwave, the stretch, and the solace. Each phase along the tender path teaches us something about ourselves in relation to the loss, and each phase takes as long as it's going to take. You now know what happens on each part of the path, so you are more able to identify where you are in your process. Each phase embodies its own signature feeling and purpose.

Universally, we have all felt the trauma of an abrupt shock that sucks the air from our lungs, faced the agonizing reality that something unbelievable just happened. As the dust settles, we look over the landscape and begin to get our bearings, acclimating to this disquieting truth as we enter into the long stretch. We are stretched like a rubber band in new directions as we hold this problematic loss and wonder what in the heck we are supposed to do with it now. We know we have to face it, yet at the same time, we want to discard it through resistance, rejection, and ignoring. We do not want this bogeyman. This internal tug-of-war, conscious and subconscious, continues until slowly, patiently, we begin to reluctantly accept that this is who we are now.

Over the arc of time, as we name the loss and discover all of its prickly edges, we find an internal context in our tapestry for this error, misstep, or trauma. Shaking our heads in disbelief but no longer in denial, we meld and fold our still-smarting loss into a place of semi-solace. With quiet resignation, we give ourselves permission to bring in a partial acceptance of this new reality. We adopt a sense of solace with many unknowns, like taking in an orphan, but hidden gifts await us. Solace becomes the bittersweet feeling that wraps around our grief, a confirmation that we have achieved a sage discernment with our loss. We now have a new relationship to something we once thought unimaginable. We have agency with our loss, even though it was never wanted. Loss now has a place and a purpose in our tapestry, even though it's unfixable or unforgivable. We may never get used to it, never like it, but it has a belonging in our narrative nonetheless.

Along the way, you have learned how to weave your loss into your life's tapestry so that it is in context and has meaning, giving you a bigger sense of your life's journey. You can now keep it all in perspective and not overidentify with it, whether it's a death, a medical issue, a relationship or job loss, or any other significant loss. You're learning how to give your lost inner child a voice that offers clues to your wounding and points out the pain that shaped your narrative. You see now how the effects of the accumulated losses from childhood still show up in impulsive, reactive ways. These patterns can heal now because you realize that your inner child holds many keys to that healing, revealing long-dormant wisdom. You no longer want to erase these woundings from your life, as now you see how they support what came before and what comes after. Now you recognize their meaning in the arc of your life. The memories of your loved ones and those special times that are long gone come upon you like unseen angels. They sit with you in your melancholy as you mourn their touch, their sweetness. Those feelings and memories are bittersweet, as you miss the vibrance and joy of their life force, you miss the special times together.

Now you have a window into the tender path and understand what it's like to go through the experience of the unbearable loss of a child, a spouse, a parent, or a friend and the deep pain that brings. You've learned all the other ways loss shows up, such as losing physical functioning, losing a job, and vicarious trauma, and that people can and do come out the other side. You have read how we stretch and mourn for ourselves, sad for the fact that a loved one is gone or a situation is no longer, as we absently look for those times that are no more. Each situation varies from the last, but the constant is that there was some kind of loss from what we knew before. Nothing can replace the specialness of what was lost, and any indulgent response is a poor attempt to replicate such a treasure.

This is what loss teaches us, the recognition and respect for that which is in front of us right now, that this person is the most important one to us or that this event is the most important time in the world. Loss teaches us to truly treasure what we offhandedly take for granted because one day it will be gone. No one likes the harshness and finality of death or unrecoverable loss, but it invites us to hold this impermanence and, over time, polishes our lens so that we can recognize and connect with how important life is. This is why older generations hold on to us so tightly when they greet us or say goodbye. They get it. They understand the impermanence interwoven with the preciousness. After decades of seeing birth and death with the passing of time, they fully realize the treasure that has been in front of all of us the entire time. They are trying to say to us, wake up! life is short! as they demonstrate the secret hidden in plain sight. It is the gift of life and the joy of living even in the midst of inevitable loss.

You have read many rich and deep stories of how my contributors and I have gone through various losses in our lives and come out the other side with an expanded view of ourselves. Each soulful story reflects aspects of love, life, loss, death, rebirth, resilience, and hope. Each story contributor showed us how they found hope even in their darkest moments, even when things looked barren and hopeless. We saw the raw grit, determination, and resilience they didn't know they had until the shock of loss thrust them into the spotlight, demanding they deal with their new reality. They generously shared how they uniquely honored their loss, how through their self-care they more gently walked their grief path.

Perhaps you related to some of the stories and now feel inspired. You have unstuck and brought forth some unacknowledged losses in your loss bucket that have been waiting for recognition and honoring. As you read the stories, perhaps you were writing your own imagining how your story would be revealed. An eternal truth about loss is that it's always turning like a diamond, always bringing up a new facet and inviting us to see its blinding brightness. No matter how hard you try, you won't be able to forget about your loss. It has its place in your tapestry that, at first, is loud, glaring, and harsh. Your pain may feel inconsolable, unforgiving, and a part of the pain may never go away.

Honor the feelings that you have now, as they are real. As you heal, you may develop new a relationship with your wounding. You get used to the idea that the loss happened, and know that using all your new tools lessens the pain. You may never like it, you may always want it to go away, and you may always feel sad when those memories of loss come up. But there's a perspective shift that comes through when you have done your grief work, when you have walked the tender path. Perspective, love, and compassion for yourself is the fuel for your healing. Time doesn't heal the pain, we do, as we honor and cradle the memory, shaping it into a salve for our soul.

THE GIFTS OF LOSS

The tender path is patiently waiting for us to walk when we are ready to receive its gifts.

The gift of loss comes forward when we name loss and embark on our journey with grief. Our grieving begins with the naming of loss; not when the loss happens, but when we surrender to this uncomfortable truth. Gifts that we receive from a loss are not always readily apparent and sometimes take years to come into our awareness. The loss itself isn't the gift; that is, we aren't glad that someone died or that we were betrayed or lost a job. As you have learned, a loss is a catalyst that begins our grief journey, and through this grieving, the gifts or treasures slowly manifest if we pay attention. But first, we have to be open to the possibility that there could even be a gift from a loss.

If we are shriveled up in pain and push away any healing or perspective, it will be very hard to see any gifts. Sometimes people feel guilty that they could receive any sort of gift from a loss. But the gifts come after much hard work and we have been in our stretch, entering a state of solace. From this place of calmer emotion and perspective, we can begin to access a pearl of wisdom, a knowing from the loss experience. In this more healed place, we can observe and realize what we learned from the experience and how the loss opened up new doorways for us to explore. When we connect the dots and things fall into place, this is where *aha!* moments are found that help us know our tender path a little better. The loss opened this doorway; we have to choose to go through it to find the treasure on the other side.

The following are examples of how an outcome from a loss can be perceived and felt as a gift:

A new job turns out to be more fulfilling than the one we lost.

We expand and learn more about ourselves following the death of a spouse because we have to show up differently in life now.

We speak more honestly, with a potentially deeper connection, following a betrayal in a relationship.

We improve our health and pay attention to physical issues following a health scare instead of avoiding making changes.

We feel stronger after creating loving detachment boundaries and can protect ourselves following a loss of trust in a relationship.

We become our authentic selves and claim sovereignty with boundaries after having experienced a sexual, physical, or emotional violation.

We feel more connected and available to someone else with a heartfelt conversation after an estrangement.

Bankruptcy, DUI, or legal issues force us to be accountable.

We speak a truth that may be hard to hear as an invitation to have an authentically available relationship.

Each of these examples demonstrates ways that gifts can show up in our lives following a loss. Usually, the gifts appear slowly over time rather than in a grand, demonstrative way. Often there is a bittersweet quality to them, as we clearly remember the pain we had to feel and heal to get to the treasure. This is why I refer to these gifts as pearls of hard-won wisdom. Each example represents the proceeds from difficult experiences and challenging conversations, and none of them come easily.

What are the gifts you have realized from your loss? If you feel a tinge of sadness or guilt that you even have a gift from your loss, hold this emotion. Know that you are healing and that any goodness that enters your life following a loss will help you expand and grow. You've earned this grace.

As you read the stories in the book, you probably saw where each contributor eventually found the gift in their loss. They were able to find the treasure, but in some cases it took years for the gift to appear. In the moment of pain, saying that there are gifts within a loss is incomprehensible. When we walk the tender path, go through the fire, and come out the other side, we are transformed. We raise up the gifts from the ashes of this transformation and hold them in our hearts.

Over the course of our lifetime, the gifts, the treasures of our losses, are enduringly available to us, but we are usually so distracted by the pain that we can't recognize the gifts. We diminish and reject the idea that out of something so painful could come a treasure. Yet, it is through the pain that we can feel the joy. Through the darkness, we can see the light. If every day was filled with happiness, sunshine, and roses, we would not know of pain and therefore would not regard our soft contentment as a solace. Grief and loss aren't demanding; they patiently wait in the wings until we are ready to receive their gifts.

GROWTH THROUGH HONORING

*I honor myself on my tender path
by asking for what I need.*

You have new words and tools of honoring to use so that you can provide compassion to yourself and others who are confused and in sorrowful pain. You know how to ask for help and to clearly communicate to others what you need instead of taking what they think is best for you. You know how to sit with your feelings and gently resist attempts by others to cheer you up by trying to talk you out of a feeling. You know how to hold your truth. Your clear boundaries give you the guardrails for all of your relationships so that you don't lose yourself in another's journey, and you're able to recognize that which you most need. You can be present for yourself and another, with a clear sight of your path.

Now you can approach your life emboldened with quiet confidence. You know the difference between escaping into your pain with indulgences and honoring your pain with balanced, restorative choices. You know how to recognize if you're cycling in a grief loop. You now know that while replaying the movie of a loss and its accompanying sadness feels comfortable, it ultimately means you are stuck, resisting the pain and ultimately the healing. You feel more whole by restoring and reconnecting with yourself and by honoring loss through rituals and respectful celebration of life. You can use your quiet tools, writing tools, and movement tools to honor your loss, helping to move the energy inside of you so you can better understand yourself. You know that keeping the honoring tools as a resource will help you to more easily process your feelings around a loss when you need to give it a voice.

Kindness, compassion, love, trust, and respect are companions along the sacred path of grief and loss. Each experience of triumph and trauma, different from the last, is woven into our tapestry. The divine miracle of death and rebirth is omnipresent in the cycle of life. The supernatural wisdom within each loss, even if it is similar to one before, feels like a brand new experience, a new knowing. Each vibrates excitedly with its own signature, in its own meaning and language, and invites us to hold its heaviness and weight until it becomes light, soft, and healed. What we now recognize as a loss doesn't define our lives; it is how we respond to loss that creates meaning in our lives.

Time doesn't heal the pain, we do, as we honor and cradle the memory, shaping it into a salve for our soul.

In your quiet moments and meditations and when you are feeling empowered, pull out your loss bucket. Discover with curiosity what is there, languishing in the dark. You are braver now with your new tools, so if your fear monster comes up, know you have methods to help you hold this thorny wounding. Reach deep, hold this loss, cry for it, scream out as you grab it, bring it close, hold it dear. It's not your enemy, it's your friend, a beautiful part of you. Now you can declare to others, This is my loss, this is how I feel!

The moments when we most need tenderness and kindness are those times we are least able to ask for or access it. Be gentle as you walk your sacred path. Be gentle even when you're frustrated because the pain doesn't seem any better. The pain may feel the same, but you probably know more about this wounding than you did before. You can hold it in a softer way instead of gripping it tightly. Know you are stronger than you think as you walk through your fire and come out the other side, perfect in your imperfection, whole in hopefulness, with newfound wisdom, contently fulfilled in self-love. Pull up a soft blanket of kindness, and hold your new tools with the hope that your consistent self-compassion will ease your pain, will give you some distance so you can hold your loss like a bird in the palm of your hand. Know that you are loved even when you are in the most pain.

You have taken an amazing journey as you have walked your tender path. You are now equipped with expanded knowledge, tools of honoring, and words to describe and name parts of your journey that before may have felt like a blur. You can now sagely witness the raw truth bound in the sadness of loss, knowing that it will not be the end of you. You have embarked on the beginning of a new relationship to grief and loss. This is your wisdom portal opening up for you to hold these eternal truths in strength as you gently walk the tender path.

NEXT STEPS

Loss is the gift that we didn't know
we needed in order to become whole.

When you're ready, look back at those sections or chapters that were hard for you to read and take in. There's probably a message for you in that uncomfortable truth. Those sections that were hard for you may indicate that there's something there that you are resisting and really need. Don't force yourself, just breathe and hold space as you stretch into this feeling. Read those words again, and let them wash over you. Hold on to them just a bit longer before you push them down and away. Our feelings rarely if ever kill us, they are just sometimes painful. Stretch into your work and give yourself the permission to look deeper, because now you have the tools to help yourself in this exploration. You are stronger than you realize.

Thank you for reading this book. Hopefully, it has provided you with some strength and served as a companion to help you observe and hold your grief and loss. Some of the stories may have been hard for you to read, as they brought up long-dormant memories and shone a bright light on sorrowful things. Perhaps you were able to open yourself to new insights into your own grief process and learned new tools of coping and honoring to ease your burden.

I appreciate your hanging in there and staying with this work. I want you to know that I was right there with you along the way. All of the emotions I asked you to examine, I was also holding. I had to gently observe and examine all of my grief and loss experiences, emotions, and memories so I could write this book for you. In this holding, in this sacred space, I was stretched beyond where I thought I could go, beyond what I thought I could feel, sorrowfully crying deeper than I had before. I thought I had examined all of this, that I was over it, but grief as my teacher asked me to go deeper, that there was more to feel. It was in this crucible of examination that I became more healed, surrendering to the loss and receiving its wisdom. I have been able to more fully heal by giving the sorrow in my heart a voice so it could sing its wise song for all to hear. It is a perennial path, this work. I hope you experience the same lightness and relief.

> *Grief and love are sisters, woven together from the beginning. Their kinship reminds us that there is no love that does not contain loss and no loss that is not a reminder of the love we carry for what we once held close.*
> *–Francis Weller,* The Wild Edge of Sorrow: Rituals of Renewal and the Sacred Work of Grief

Blessings on your journey.

⌒

Use this book as a resource. Use tabs or bookmarks, or dog-ear the sections that you know you will want to come back to. Think of your friends and the sections that may be valuable for them to read, then offer the book with loving kindness. You now know how to be present for someone else who is walking their journey with grief, and you can recognize what you have to offer to help ease their pain.

Check out the Resources section at the back of this book for more materials, as there are many amazing books that will help you go deeper into your work. Many of the references there were given as suggestions by my story contributors and link to their specific journeys. Each resource is part of the puzzle, as no one book will have all of the answers. They illuminate only a part of the journey, not the entire distance.

SPARK

By Robert Jackman

My loss stings a prickly pain
Reluctantly I'm thrust on a new path
in an untraveled barren land
Rejecting offers of comfort, twisting myself in disbelief
that this could be happening
Alone in my sorrow
Go away as I curl into my despair
Stumbling, this path feels anything but tender
Unfolding in a void of space and time, the flash of a spark
Rummaging in the darkness, I find an opening in the portal
Reaching out, I am lifted up
I give my sorrow a voice so I can sing my own song,
make my own path
Bestowing and accepting soft compassion
My song connects to my heart wisdom
Anticipation, this is the way through and out
I grow in my grieving
Hopeful

Resources

Mental Health Hotline: 988

If you are having a mental health crisis, please call 988 right now (available only in the United States).

Accompanying the Dying: Practical, Heart-Centered Wisdom for End-of-Life Doulas and Health Care Advocates, Deanna Cochran, Maui, HI: Sacred Life Publishers, 2019.

Becoming Supernatural: How Common People are Doing the Uncommon, Joe Dispenza, London: Hay House UK, 2019.

Being Mortal: Illness, Medicine and What Matters in the End, Atul Gawande, New York NY: Metropolitan Books, 2017.

Beyond Tears: Living After Losing a Child (revised), stories as told to Ellen Mitchell, New York, NY: St. Martin's Griffin, 2009.

Broken Open: How Difficult Times Can Help Us Grow, Elizabeth Lesser, New York, NY: Villard Books, 2005.

Confessions of a Funeral Director: How the Business of Death Saved My Life, Caleb Wilde, San Francisco, CA: HarperOne, 2017.

Grief Day by Day: Simple Practices and Daily Guidance for Living with Loss, Jan Warner, San Antonio, TX: Althea Press, 2018.

Healing after Loss: Daily Meditations for Working through Grief, Martha Whitmore Hickman, New York, NY: Avon Books, 1994.

Healing Trauma with Guided Drawing: A Sensorimotor Art Therapy Approach to Bilateral Body Mapping, Cornelia Elbrecht, Berkeley, CA: North Atlantic Books, 2018.

Healing Your Lost Inner Child: How to Stop Impulsive Reactions, Set Healthy Boundaries and Embrace an Authentic Life, Robert Jackman, St. Charles, IL: Practical Wisdom Press, 2020.

Healing Your Lost Inner Child Companion Workbook: Inspired Exercises to Heal Your Codependent Relationships, Robert Jackman, St. Charles, IL: Practical Wisdom Press, 2020.

Healing Your Wounded Relationship: How to Break Free of Codependent Patterns and Restore Your Loving Partnership, Robert Jackman, St. Charles, IL: Practical Wisdom Press, 2021.

I Wasn't Ready to Say Goodbye: Surviving, Coping and Healing after the Sudden Death of a Loved One, Brook Noel and Pamela Blair, Naperville, IL: 2008.

Jesus Calling: Enjoying Peace in His Presence, Sarah Young, Nashville, TN: Thomas Nelson, 2004.

Life after Suicide: Finding Courage, Comfort and Community after Unthinkable Loss, Jennifer Ashton, New York, NY: William Morrow, 2019.

Mataora: The Living Face: Contemporary Maori Art, Witi, Sandy Adsett, and Cliff Whiting (eds.), New Zealand: D. Bateman Publishing, 1996.

More Beautiful than Before: How Suffering Transforms Us, Steve Leder, Carlsbad, CA: Hay House, 2017.

Neurographic Art Step by Step: A Quick and Simple Tutorial on How to Make Your First Neurographic Art Image, S. J. Seferi, self-published, 2022.

Never a Girl, Always a Boy: A Family Memoir of a Transgender Journey, Jo Ivester, Berkeley, CA: She Writes Press, 2020.

On Death and Dying: What the Dying Have to Teach Doctors, Nurses, Clergy & Their Own Families, 50th anniversary ed., Elisabeth Kübler-Ross, New York, NY: Scribner, 2014.

Peaks and Valleys: Integrative Approaches for Recovering from Loss, Sherry O'Brian, AR: Ozark Mountain Publishing, Inc., 2014.

Second Firsts: Live, Laugh, and Love Again, Christina Rasmussen, Carlsbad, CA: Hay House, 2013.

Shattered: Surviving the Loss of a Child, Gary Roe, Wellborn, TX: Healing Sources Publishing, 2017.

Surviving and Thriving with an Invisible Chronic Illness: How to Stay Sane and Live One Step Ahead of Your Symptoms, Illana Jacqueline, Oakland, CA: New Harbinger Publications, 2018.

The 7 Habits of Highly Effective People, 30th anniversary ed., Steven Covey, Manhattan, New York: Simon & Schuster, 2020.

The First 90 Days: Proven Strategies for Getting Up to Speed Faster and Smarter, updated and expanded, Michael Watkins, Boston, MA: Harvard Business Review Press, 2013.

The Five Invitations: Discovering What Death Can Teach Us About Living Fully, Frank Ostaseski, New York, NY: Flatiron Books, 2017.

The Game of Life and How To Play It, Florence Scovel Shinn and Joel Fotinos, New York, NY: St. Martin's Essentials, 2020.

The Invisible Kingdom: Reimagining Chronic Illness, Meghan O'Rourke, New York, NY: Riverhead Books, 2022.

The Transgender Child: A Handbook for Parents and Professionals Supporting Transgender and Nonbinary Children (2nd ed.), Stephanie Brill and Rachel Pepper, Jersey City, NJ: Cleis Press, 2022.

The Wild Edge of Sorrow: Rituals of Renewal and the Sacred Work of Grief, Francis Weller, Berkeley, CA: North Atlantic Books, 2015.

Toolkit for Caregivers: Tips, Skills, and Wisdom to Maximize Your Time Together, Deidre Edwards, self-published, 2019.

Trans-Kin: A Guide for Family and Friends of Transgender People, Eleanor Hubbard and Cameron Whitley, Boulder, CO: Bolder Press, 2012.

What Doesn't Kill You: A Life with Chronic Illness—Lessons From a Body In Revolt, Tessa Miller, New York: Henry Holt and Company, 2022.

Wonderfully and Purposefully Made: I Am Enough: A Journal All About Me, Cheryl B. Evans, Ontario, Canada: Cheryl B. Evans, 2018.

Your Grief, Your Way: A Year of Practical Guidance and Comfort after Loss, Shelby Forsythia, New York, NY: Zeitgeist, 2020.

Websites

Adult Children of Alcoholics and Dysfunctional Families: www.adultchildren.org

Planned Parenthood: www.plannedparenthood.org

Support After Abortion: www.supportafterabortion.com

Unplanned Pregnancy: www.unplannedpregnancy.com

About the Author

 ROBERT JACKMAN, a board-certified psychotherapist with the National Board of Certified Counselors, has been helping people along their healing path for over twenty years in private practice. He has taught master's-level classes at National Louis University in the Chicago area and led outpatient groups in clinics and hospitals. He has been a guest speaker on national radio programs and numerous podcasts, panels, and telesummits, focusing on the topics of codependency, boundary setting, couples communication, inner child work, grief and loss, mindfulness, and the role of spirituality in healing, and has participated in numerous weekend retreats for Victories for Men.

Robert is also a Reiki master and uses energy psychology in his practice and in his personal development. He considers himself a codependent in recovery and is always working on setting boundaries, nurturing his relationships, and connecting with the authentic self. He and his partner of more than three decades live in the far western suburbs of Chicago and on the Oregon coast. He enjoys metaphysics, photography, kayaking, rockhounding, and spending time with family and friends.

For more information about Robert and his books, including *Healing Your Lost Inner Child, the Companion Workbook,* and *Healing Your Wounded Relationship,* visit www.theartofpracticalwisdom. com.

Made in United States
Orlando, FL
19 May 2023

33266088R00235